Baseball's Forgotten Black Heroes

Bill Leibforth

outskirts
press

DEDICATION

First and foremost, to my wife, Susan, who believed I could do this project and gave me constant encouragement, advise, helped review, edit and type it. Without her, there would be no book.

To all the baseball fans that know that baseball is America's favorite sport. Whether playing, coaching, watching, listening, reading, arguing about or just discussing.

"He who rejects change is the architect of decay"

Harold Wilson
(Former British Prime Minister)

Table of Contents

Prologue

Several years ago I was watching my favorite Chicago baseball team play on April 15th, the day baseball remembers Jackie Robinson by having all players honor him by wearing his number "42". As I watched the game, I was thinking how very hard it must have been for Jackie and the other first black players to remain nonviolent (and still play baseball) with the verbal, mental, and physical abuse they encountered. Jackie's and the others player's courage was shown in risking their lives to pursue their dreams of playing Major League Baseball.

Later after contemplating the question myself, I asked several friends what they knew about the first black players. Most people know Jackie as the first major-league black player for the Brooklyn Dodgers, and some knew Larry Doby as the first black American League player for the Cleveland Indians, but little else about who the other 16 teams' first players were.

Baseball history added a new chapter on April 15, 1947 when a black baseball player named Jack Roosevelt Robinson opened the game playing first base for the Brooklyn Dodgers.

BASEBALL WOULD NEVER BE THE SAME

With the eyes of 14 million black Americans watching and hoping for the best, Jackie was brilliant. While Jackie opened the door to baseball integration, its success was also dependent on the character and talent of the black players who followed him. As skilled as any major-league player must be, many of the black players, like their white counterparts, were just average ballplayers. Few possessed the all-around skills of a Willie Mays; yet, each played and overcame the great difficulties of integration. They came to the big leagues from Negro leagues, sharecropper fields, steel mills, high school, baseball fields, and the military. They came from all parts of America, the Caribbean, Panama, Cuba, and Puerto Rico.

THIS STORY IS ABOUT THOSE MEN

Specifically, who were they and are some are still living? How did they perform, and how were they treated? Do we remember Willard Brown or Dan Bankhead, who were the fourth and fifth black players in the major leagues, and one is in the Hall of Fame?

I hope that this book will bring some recognition to all of these black heroes and pioneers who faced similar racial problems and hatred that came from cities, teammates, media, and fans that Jackie and Larry faced.

I will be covering the first players for all of the 16 teams existing in 1947, plus some additional black players, scouts, and writers who played a role in the integration of baseball.

In 1947, there were 16 major-league baseball teams; yet, it took until 1959 (over 12 years after Jackie first played and 3 years after Jackie retired) before all 16 were integrated.

In 1947 much of America kept whites and blacks apart. The armed forces still were separated. It would be seven years until the U.S. Supreme Court decided that racial segregation was unconstitutional and eight years before Rosa Parks refused to sit in the back of the bus. The Civil Rights Act of 1964 and Voting Right Act of 1965 were still just dreams.

The black players who followed Robinson shattered the stereotype—once widespread among many team owners, sportswriters, and white fans—that there weren't many African Americans "qualified" to play at the major league level.

Between 1947 and 1959 black players won 9 out of 13 Rookie of the Year awards, and 9 out of 13 Most Valuable Player awards in the National League, which was much more integrated than the American League was at that time. The first black MVP in the American League was Elston Howard in 1963 and the first black rookie of the year was Tony Olivia in 1964.

From 1947 until 1959 there were 116 black players on Major League teams. There were 56 players in the American League and 110 players in the National League. Cleveland accounted for 32% (18) of the American League players during this period. The NY Giants and St. Louis Cardinals had 17 players each. At the low end, Boston had 2 players while the NY Yankees and Detroit Tigers had 3 each.

Black players encountered racial barriers, both on and off the field: teammates refusing to shake hands, fans shouting out insults, whites-only signs, and many other painful struggles just to play baseball. Today's athletes and major-league players have no idea what they had to endure.

It was not until 1959 that the last of the 16 major league teams were integrated.

Who were the black Latin/American players who followed Jackie Robinson and Larry Doby in integrating major-league baseball?

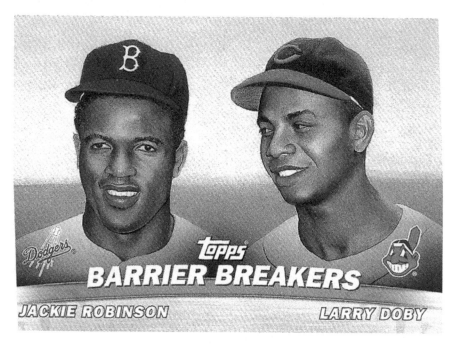

Players by Team
(bold denotes they were first black on their team)

Last Name	First Name	Team	League	Date
Jethroe	**Sam**	Boston Braves	NL	4/18/50
Márquez	Luis	Boston Braves	NL	4/18/51
Green	**"Pumpsie"**	Boston Red Sox	AL	7/21/59
Wilson	Earl	Boston Red Sox	AL	7/28/59
Robinson	**Jackie**	Brooklyn Dodgers	NL	4/15/47
Bankhead	Dan	Brooklyn Dodgers	NL	8/26/47
Campanella	Roy	Brooklyn Dodgers	NL	4/20/48

Newcombe	Don	Brooklyn Dodgers	NL	5/20/49
Banks	**Ernie**	Chicago Cubs	NL	9/17/53
Baker	Gene	Chicago Cubs	NL	9/20/53
Miñoso	**"Minnie"**	Chicago White Sox	AL	5/1/51
Hairston	Sam	Chicago White Sox	AL	7/21/51
Boyd	Bob	Chicago White Sox	AL	9/8/51
Escalera	**Nino**	Cincinnati Reds	NL	4/17/54
Harmon	**Chuck**	Cincinnati Reds	NL	4/17/54
Doby	**Larry**	Cleveland Indians	AL	7/5/47
Paige	"Satchel"	Cleveland Indians	AL	7/9/48
Miñoso	"Minnie"	Cleveland Indians	AL	4/19/49
Easter	"Luke"	Cleveland Indians	AL	8/11/49
Simpson	Harry	Cleveland Indians	AL	4/21/51
Jones	Sam	Cleveland Indians	AL	9/22/51
Virgil Sr.	**Ozzie**	Detroit Tigers	AL	6/6/58
Doby	Larry	Detroit Tigers	AL	4/5/59
Proctor	Jim	Detroit Tigers	AL	9/14/59
Wood	Jake	Detroit Tigers	AL	4/11/61
Irvin	**"Monte"**	NY Giants	NL	7/8/49
Thompson	**Hank**	NY Giants	NL	7/8/49
Noble	Ray	NY Giants	NL	4/18/51
Wilson	Artie	NY Giants	NL	4/18/51
Mays	Willie	NY Giants	NL	5/25/51
Howard	**Elston**	NY Yankees	AL	4/14/55
Trice	**Bob**	Philadelphia A's	AL	9/13/53
Kennedy	**John**	Philadelphia Phillies	NL	4/22/57
Mason	Hank	Philadelphia Phillies	NL	9/12/58
Bernier	**Carlos**	Pittsburgh Pirates	NL	4/22/53
Roberts	**"Curt"**	Pittsburgh Pirates	NL	4/13/54
Alston	**Tom**	St. Louis Cardinals	NL	4/13/54
Greason	Bill	St. Louis Cardinals	NL	5/31/54

Lawrence	Brooks	St. Louis Cardinals	NL	6/24/54
Thompson	**Hank**	St. Louis Browns	AL	7/17/47
Brown	Willard	St. Louis Browns	AL	7/19/47
Paige	"Satchel"	St. Louis Browns	AL	7/18/51
Paula	**Carlos**	Washington Senators	AL	9/6/54

Note: MLB recognizes Curt Roberts as first black to play for **Pirates**, but Carlos Bernier is also included as he played before Roberts and was a Black Latino.

Minnie Minoso is recognized as First Black **White Sox** Player, but since he is Cuban some argue Sam Hairston was first, I included both.

MLB recognizes Ossie Virgil Sr as First Black **Tiger** player, but since he was Dominican some argue Larry Doby is first, I included both.

Most baseball historians agree that Moses Fleetwood Walker was the first black to play professional MLB baseball in 1884 with Toledo of the American Association League, while John "Bud" Fowler is acknowledged as the first black professional player.

Charles Grant, an African American, did try out with the Baltimore Orioles of the new American League in 1901 as the manager John McGraw tried to pass Charles off as an American Indian named Tokohama. McGraw's scheme began unraveling when the team traveled to Chicago, where Grant had played for the previous few years. To celebrate Grant's return, his African American friends staged a public ceremony. Chicago White Sox President Charles Comiskey soon objected to "Tokohama" and confirmed that he was actually Grant.

Grant maintained his disguise, claiming that his father was white and that his mother was Cherokee and living in Lawrence, Kansas. McGraw initially persisted, but later claimed that "Tokohama" was inexperienced, especially on defense, and left him off his Opening Day roster. Grant returned to the Columbia Giants and never played in the major leagues.

Moses Fleetwood Walker

Moses Fleetwood Walker (October 7, 1856–May 11, 1924) was an American professional baseball catcher who is credited with being the **first black man to play in major-league baseball**. A native of Mount Pleasant, Ohio, and a star athlete at Oberlin College as well as the University of Michigan, Walker played for semi-professional and minor-league baseball clubs before joining the Toledo Blue Stockings of the American Association (AA) for the 1884 season.

Research suggests William Edward White was the first African American baseball player in MLB, but unlike White who passed as a white man, Walker was open about his black heritage and often faced racial bigotry prevalent in the late nineteenth century. His brother, Weldy, became the second black athlete to play later in the same year, also for the Toledo ball club.

In mid-1883, Walker left his studies at Michigan and was signed to his first professional baseball contract by William Voltz, manager of the minor-league Toledo Blue Stockings, a Northwestern League team. Though Walker recorded decent numbers, including a .251 batting average he became revered for his play behind the plate and his durability during an era where catchers wore little to no protective equipment or gloves. He played in 60 of Toledo's 84 games during their championship season.

Walker's entrance into professional baseball caused immediate friction in the league. Before he had the opportunity to appear in a game, the executive committee of the Northwestern League debated a motion proposed by the representative of the Peoria, Illinois club that would prohibit all colored ballplayers from entering the league. After intense arguments, the motion was dropped, allowing Walker to play.

On August 10, 1883, in an exhibition game against the Chicago White Stockings, Chicago's manager, Cap Anson, refused to play if Walker was in the lineup. In response, Charlie Morton, the manager, warned Anson of the risk of forfeiting gate receipts and also started Walker in right field. Anson is alleged to have said, "We'll play this here game, but won't play never no more with NxxxxxS in the lineup."

The Blue Stockings' successful season in the Northwestern League prompted the team to transfer to the American Association, a major-league organization.

In 1884, Walker's first appearance as a major-league ballplayer was an away game against the Louisville Eclipse on **May 1, 1884.** Walker went hitless in three at-bats and committed four errors in a 5–1 loss. Walker's year was plagued with injuries, limiting him to just 42 games in a 104-game season. For the season he had a .263 batting average, which was in the top three in the league, but Toledo finished eighth in the pennant race. Walker played just one season, 42 games total, for Toledo before injuries prompted his release.

Walker played in the minor leagues until 1889 and was the last African American to participate on the major-league level before Jackie Robinson broke baseball's color line in 1947.

Unfortunately for Walker, his post-baseball career would take a turn for the worst that would deeply affect the latter stages of his life.

In April of 1891, in an act of self-defense, he stabbed and killed a man by the name of Patrick Murray. A jury acquitted Walker of second-degree murder, but the horrors of the trial would have an irreversible affect on his view of race relations in the United States.

In 1908, Walker published a book titled *Our Home Colony: A Treatise on the Past, Present, and Future of the Negro Race in America*. In it, Walker argued that whites and blacks could never peacefully co-exist in the United States, espousing views that alienated him from much of American society.

As an advocate of Black Nationalism, Walker also jointly edited a newspaper, *The Equator*, along with his brother.

He died in 1924 at the age of 67.

John "Bud" Fowler

First Black Professional Baseball Player

John "Bud" Fowler (Born March 16, 1858 as John Jackson, died February 16, 1913) was one of the true pioneers of American baseball and one sadly overlooked by the National Baseball Hall of Fame. **He is the first acknowledged African American professional player dating back in 1878.** He was the first to play on integrated teams. He preferred white clubs because they fielded the best players and offered the stiffest competition through much of his career.

Fowler was the first African American in organized baseball and also the first African American to captain an integrated club. He was also one of the first significant black promoters, forming the heralded Page Fence Giants and other clubs and leagues. Wherever there was an effort to form a black league during the nineteenth century, Fowler could be found in the mix. White field managers and business managers throughout the country sought Fowler's advice on fellow black players, at times hiring a man sight unseen for their roster on his say-so. Moreover, Fowler was the one who organized the first successful black barnstorming clubs, a subsequent staple of the industry.

An unnamed International League player gave a revealing interview to *The Sporting News*, "Fowler [and Frank Grant] used to play second base with the lower part of their legs encased in wooden guards. He knew that about every player that came down to second base on a steal had it in for him and would, if possible, throw the spikes into him...[Also] about half the pitchers try their best to hit these colored players when [they're] at the bat." Furthermore, league umpire Billy Hoover admitted to calling close plays against clubs that fielded black players.

Fowler first played for an all-white professional team based out of New Castle, Pennsylvania, in 1872, when he was 14 years old. He is documented as playing for another professional team on July 21, 1877, when he was 19. On April 24, 1878, he pitched a game for the Picked Nine, who defeated the Boston Red Caps, champions of the National League in 1877. He pitched some more for the Chelsea team, then finished the 1878 season with the Worcester club. Largely supporting himself as a barber, Fowler continued to play for baseball teams in New England and Canada for the next 4 years.

Fowler played for Malden in the Eastern Massachusetts League in 1879. In 1881, he joined the Guelph (Ontario) Maple Leafs. The relationship didn't last long as his teammates objected to his presence. According to the *Guelph Herald*, "Some of the Maple Leafs are ill-natured enough to object to the colored pitcher." He then played a few games for the Petrolia Imperials, another Ontario nine.

In 1882, Bud pitched for the New Orleans Pickwicks, a black team sponsored by a local social club. Later in the season, he was player-manager for the Richmond (Virginia) Black Swans.

In 1883, Fowler played for a team in Niles, Ohio; in 1884, he played for Stillwater, Minnesota, in the Northwestern League; Keokuk Indians. In 1883, Fowler played for a team in Niles, Ohio; in 1884, he played for Stillwater, Minnesota, in the Northwestern League.

Keokuk, Iowa, had not had a professional baseball team since 1875. However, in 1885, local businessman R. W. "Nick" Curtis was the chief force behind starting a new team and hired "Bud" Fowler for it. Johnny Peters, the manager of the then-disbanded Stillwater, Minnesota, team, helped Fowler get connected with the new team in Keokuk.

Fowler became the most popular player on the Keokuk team. The local newspaper, the *Keokuk Gate City and Constitution*, said of him, "a good ball player, a hard worker, a genius on the ball field, intelligent, gentlemanly in his conduct and deserving of the good opinion entertained for him by baseball admirers here."

The Western League folded that season due to financial reasons, leaving Keokuk without a league. Fowler was released and moved to play with a team in Pueblo, Colorado. In 1886, he played for a team in Topeka, Kansas. That team won the pennant behind Fowler's .309 average. He also led the league in triples. Eventually, Fowler moved to Binghamton, New York, and played on a team there. Racial tensions arose, and his teammates refused to continue playing with him.

Fowler arrived in Binghamton early in 1887 and secured a barbering position. He joined the club in the spring and ultimately appeared in 34 games and hit an outstanding .350.

The year 1887 proved to be pivotal in the exclusion of African-Americans from Organized Baseball. The International League formally banned any additional signings of African-American players on July 14, two weeks after Fowler's release. Specifically, a vote taken by club owners directed the league secretary to "approve of no more contracts with colored men." Officials were reacting to white players' grumblings and derogatory comments by the press suggesting that the International League change its classification to "colored league."

In 1888, he played for a team in Terre Haute, Indiana.

In 1892, Fowler played in Kearney Nebraska, for the Nebraska State League.

In 1895, he and "Home Run" Johnson formed the Page Fence Giants in Adrian, Michigan. From 1894–1904, Fowler played and/or managed the Page Fence Giants, Cuban Giants, the Smoky City Giants, the All-American Black Tourists, and the Kansas City Stars.

John Jackson/Fowler, nearly 55 years old, died on February 26, 1913, at his sister's home of pernicious anemia, a rare red blood cell disorder associated with the inability to absorb vitamin B-12. He was buried at Oak View Cemetery in Frankfort. In 1987, the Society for American Baseball Research purchased a headstone and placed it on his unmarked grave. It reads, "John W. Jackson: `Bud Fowler,' Black Baseball Pioneer."

CHAPTER 1

Brooklyn Dodgers

The Dodgers were the first team to bring a black baseball player to the modern day major leagues. This was made possible through the commitment of the new owner (George McLaughlin) and president/general manager (Branch Rickey). The Dodgers brought up the first black player (Jackie Robinson), the fifth (Dan Bankhead), the sixth (Roy Campanella), and the ninth (Don Newcombe).

Combined, these four players accounted for two Rookies of the Year, five Most Valuable Players, one "Cy" Young winner, two Hall of Famers, over 18 All-Star appearances and six World Series with one championship.

The Dodgers would continue to bring more black players into their team in the '50s, including Junior Gilliam and Joe Black.

In 1943, Branch Rickey started creating a plan to bring black ballplayers (American and Latin) to major-league baseball. The first need was more scouting of the Negro leagues. Rickey convinced the Dodger owner, George V. McLaughlin, to fund the expansion of the scouting system to find the right black players to integrate major-league baseball. Branch Rickey started working on these plans a full 3 years before he knew who that player would be.

At lunch one day, he decided to discuss his plan with Walter "Red" Barber, the radio announcer for the Dodgers. Rickey believed he needed Red on his side. Rickey told Barber, "Rickey said, "I am going to bring a Negro player to the Brooklyn Dodgers. Barber sat straight and silent.

Leaving the lunch that day, Barber felt the discussion becoming heavier and harder. He told himself he could not do it. Barber recalled in his autobiography that he had grown up in a very segregated world and his first reaction was to quit. After discussing with his wife he concluded he could and would stay as the Dodgers announcer.

"The player we need is playing somewhere," Rickey told every scout who came through his office. Where would they find him? He talked to everybody he knew in baseball, old ballplayers, ministers, teachers, and old friends, and asked all these people to look for black players.

Branch Rickey read dispatches from the hundreds of sandlots and fields where blacks played. He had stacks of reports with names like Campanella, Newcombe, Gibson, Doby, Paige, Robinson and others.

Rickey asked his secretary to contact Clyde Sukeforth. Sukeforth was a scout who could go out for coffee and return with a second baseman. Like Rickey, he was an old major-league catcher with Cincinnati and Brooklyn, which, to Rickey, meant he could see the entire field. Clyde could look at a ballplayer on the field and make a decisive judgment on him. He could go beyond running and hitting and measure the character of the player. On a matter of extreme importance, Sukeforth would have the last look, and other scouts would hold their breath until he reported to Mr. Rickey, as Clyde always called him. The two never relied on each other as much as they did during this time.

Rickey said years later of Robinson, "I think we knew about his playing ability. I wanted to begin to know him as a person. He is out of UCLA, an excellent university, and was a commissioned officer in the army. Sukeforth had the capability to talk to such a man and report to us."

As soon as Rickey read the report on Robinson, he wanted information on the court-martial. Sukeforth reported back that it was because Robinson refused to sit in the back of a bus in Fort Hood, Texas.

"He has spirit," Rickey said with great enthusiasm when he learned the details. "I want you to see him play shortstop. He is with the Kansas City Monarchs, and they are playing at Comiskey Park this weekend. I want to know about his arm as he is definitely a prospect."

Rickey was obsessed and made many phone calls trying to find out more about Jackie. Each time the person on the other end told him that they believed Robinson could play in the major leagues. "I want you to talk to him and see if he will come to Brooklyn with you", said Rickey to Clyde. "If he can't, tell him I would be glad to come and see him."

Clyde Sukeforth's business trip to Chicago by train was so much more that a search for a ballplayer. He took a train to Chicago and arrived at Comiskey Park on the night of August 24, 1945. He bought a box seat and a program for a Negro-league game between the Lincoln Giants and Kansas City Monarchs. He heard someone call Robinson's name, and Sukeforth leaned over the railing and called to Jackie.

Sukeforth said he represented Branch Rickey, who was starting a black team. Robinson had soured on Kansas City, so he listened attentively, but not with any great expectations. Sukeforth asked Robinson to show him his throwing arm, which he did hesitantly as he had hurt his shoulder a few days before. He also wondered why Rickey wanted to know about his arm. Sukeforth told Jackie that Rickey wanted him to come to Brooklyn, but if he couldn't, Mr. Rickey would come and meet with him.

Standing in the lights of a major-league field, rented for the night by blacks, wearing the uniforms of a team of blacks he knew, Robinson felt a bolt of excitement. Whatever this was about, Sukeforth made it pleasant. Robinson believed he was being told the truth and would go and meet with Branch Rickey.

Rickey was especially interested in making sure his eventual signee could withstand the inevitable racial abuse that would be directed at him. In a famous 3-hour exchange on August 28, 1945, Rickey asked Robinson if he could face the racial animus without taking the bait and reacting angrily—a concern given Robinson's prior arguments with law enforcement officials in the military. Robinson was aghast: "Are you looking for a Negro who is afraid to fight back?" Rickey replied that he needed a Negro player "with guts enough *not* to fight back."

After meeting with Jackie, Rickey called for a meeting of all his top scouts to discuss which player they should bring up to play for the Dodgers. These men were known wherever anyone played baseball. George Sisler, Mickey McConnell, Wid Matthews, Eddie McCarrick, Tom Greewade, Buzzie Bavasi, and, of course, Clyde Sukeforth. The meeting was about three black prospects, Pitcher Don Newcombe, Catcher Roy Campanella, and Jackie Robinson. All would be brought up through the Dodger minor-league system to the major leagues.

The first would be historic. The others would follow.

Scouts Andy High and Wid Matthews pushed as forcefully as they could for Newcombe. Not only did he have a strong right arm, but also he was a very good hitter. The other scouts were divided, but did stress that the Dodgers should continue to sign black players beyond these three.

The Dodgers chose Jackie Robinson to be the first player to play major-league baseball after some minor-league experience. Rickey agreed to sign him to a contract for $600 a month, equal to $8,156 today.

The Rest Is History

In 1945, Branch Rickey signed two black players (Jackie Robinson and "Johnny" Wright) to minor-league contracts. One went on to a Hall of Fame career, while the other never played an inning in major-league baseball except spring training.

John "Johnny" Wright (born November 28, 1916 in New Orleans, Louisiana died on May 4, 1990) was a Negro-league pitcher who played briefly in the International League of baseball's minor leagues in 1946, and was on the roster of the Montreal Royals at the same time as Jackie Robinson, making him a plausible candidate to have broken the baseball color barrier.

Being the second black player signed after Jackie Robinson, Johnny Wright never found success at the major league level.

April 12, 2013, by Ryan Whirty

NEW ORLEANS—Jackie Robinson has rightly assumed a place as one of the most significant figures in American sports, and the movie "42' is a further tribute to his legacy.

But within weeks of Robinson becoming the first African American player in modern baseball history to sign in organized baseball in the fall of 1945, lanky New Orleans native John Wright became the second Negro player to enter major league baseball. A right-hander with a solid array of pitches who had a decade of success in the Negro leagues, Wright also signed with the Brooklyn Dodgers, with both Robinson and Wright set to report to spring training in Florida for the 1946 season.

"The baseball world again vibrated as the announcement flashed across the nation," wrote Hall of Fame sportswriter Wendell Smith in the *Pittsburgh Courier*.

Wright flamed out in organized ball, however, and by the beginning of the 1947 season, as Robinson was stepping onto the diamond at Ebbets Field, Wright was back in the Negro leagues, hurling for the Homestead Grays, with any hopes of becoming a big leaguer dashed. And while Robinson had become a household name, Wright was largely lost to history, a footnote in Branch Rickey's crusade to integrate the game.

Aside from the obvious question of what happened to Wright, in the intervening years, historians have also debated why exactly the Dodgers signed him. Did the trailblazing organization view him as a legitimate prospect, or was Wright simply viewed as a companion for Robinson, who was clearly Rickey's chosen one to make history?

Many of the African American sportswriters of the day who had followed Wright's career in black baseball asserted at the time that the right-hander did, in fact, have the goods.

"When the New Orleans-bred hurler is ready, though, you're going to hear from him," Cleveland *Call and Post* correspondent Bill Mardo wrote from Dodgers' spring training camp in Daytona Beach in 1946. "Actually, Wright stands a far better chance than Robinson to make the jump into big league baseball."

So, a more credible theory, and one espoused by many people who played with Wright, is that he was overwhelmed at suddenly being plunged into an integrated world, where he was on equal footing with white players on the field, but had to face bigotry head-on away the field and in the stands.

At 27, Wright was a year younger than Robinson but had significantly more baseball experience, which prompted some to predict that he would handle the challenge of integrating baseball better than Robinson. Influential black sports writer "Sam" Lacy of the *Baltimore Afro-American* wrote: "Wright doesn't boast the college background that is Jackie's, but he possesses something equally valuable—a level head and the knack of seeing things objectively. He is a realist in a role which demands divorce from sentimentality."

Whatever the reasons, Wright did not perform on the field, beginning with a disastrous showing in a Dodgers-Montreal Royals exhibition game midway through spring training. He did manage to win a spot on the Triple-A Montreal roster, but he apparently made an immediate bad impression on Royals' manager, Clay Hopper, a Mississippian who wasn't a fan of integration. In addition, from the very beginning, the media and the popular spotlight focused squarely on Robinson, perhaps triggering Wright's slide into the shadows of history.

In late May, the Dodgers sent Wright to Class C Trois-Rivières of the Canadian-American League, where he was joined by Roy Partlow, another African American pitcher who had been signed by Branch Rickey. By then, the Dodgers had also signed Don Newcombe and Roy Campanella for their minor-league teams further dimming Wright's prospects.

Another opportunity never came. Although Wright pitched well with Trois-Rivières and helped the team win a league title, the 1946 campaign proved to be his only season in organized baseball. He returned to the Grays in 1947, where he again shined on the mound, just as he had before being inked by the Dodgers. By then, Wright's legacy—or obscurity—was cemented. Wrote Smith in 1969: "Robinson and Wright were pioneers. Jackie went on to become one of the game's great players. Wright never attained his potential and quietly faded into oblivion."

Perhaps the perceptive Rickey recognized Wright's flaws from the beginning, making his public statements about Wright's talent and opportunity just PR smoke obfuscating the fact that he was there to ease the transition for Robinson. At any rate, Rickey clearly recognized the flaws at some point, and Wright was out of organized baseball as quickly as Robinson became ascendant.

Apparently believing that it was still crucial for Robinson to have a black teammate, the Dodgers immediately replaced Wright with veteran hurler Roy Partlow, who had previously been playing with the Negro League Philadelphia Stars. Partlow was in his mid-30s at the time and had a reputation as a hard-thrower with a fiery temperament on and off the field. He hardly seemed like the ideal candidate to participate in the Dodgers' integration experiment.

Partlow was demoted after posting a 2–0, 5.59 record for the Montreal Royals. He then went 10–1 with a 3.22 ERA for the Trois-Rivières Royals in the Can-Am League, hitting .404 there as well. His demotion from Montreal appears to be unrelated to his performance, but more to his incompatibility with Robinson.

Three Rivers (or "Trois-Rivières," as it is known locally) is a French-Canadian town located approximately 70 miles from Montreal. The city had hosted a professional team during the 1941 and 1942 seasons, but the advent of World War II caused the Canadian-American League to suspend operations for the next 3 years. Baseball returned to the area in 1946, which also marked Three Rivers' first campaign as a Dodgers' affiliate. Now, quite unexpectedly, the town was host to two of the minor leagues' five black players.

While Three Rivers (and Quebec as a whole) was a racially tolerant area, neither Wright nor Partlow responded positively to their respective demotions. After all, they were established Negro-league stars who now found themselves toiling in a remote outpost three levels removed from the major leagues. Paltrow, meanwhile, did not take kindly to being demoted and briefly disappeared. This caused an enraged reaction by some in the black press, who felt that the slightest misstep by a black athlete could result in the collapse of the entire integration experiment.

"It looks as though Partlow has turned out to be an eccentric 'prima donna' and a problem child of no small means," wrote Wendell Smith of the *Pittsburgh Courier*.

Partlow reeled off nine straight wins upon arriving in Three Rivers and finished the season with a 10–1 record and nine complete games over 11 starts. An accomplished hitter, he also received some playing time in the outfield and compiled a .404 average.

The team went on to face the Pittsfield (Mass.) Indians in the championship. In the fifth and final game, Partlow came through with a clutch pinch hit and scored the winning run in a 9–6, come from behind victory. His offensive heroics made a winner of Wright, who had also earned a victory in game four.

Despite the triumphant way in which the 1946 season had ended, neither Wright nor Partlow pitched within white professional baseball ever again. Wright was released by the Dodgers in January of 1947 and went on to pitch several more years in the Negro leagues. Partlow, meanwhile, went to spring training with Montreal in 1947. He didn't make the team and played in the minor leagues through 1950.

While the achievements of Partlow and Wright pale in significance to those of players like Robinson, Campanella, and Newcombe, their stories deserve to be rescued from the dustbin of baseball history.

Both men played the game admirably well under very trying circumstances, and for this alone; they deserve to be recognized as true minor-league pioneers.

-----------------End of Article-----------------

It is now the summer of 1946, and Jackie Robinson is playing for the Montreal Royals a Dodger Minor League team. He hits .349 and steals 40 bases. Most believe his talent will bring him to the major leagues next year. Major-league teams decided he must be stopped and met in Chicago and issued a report on Robinson which read:

RACE QUESTON:

The appeal of baseball is not limited to any racial group. The Negro takes great interest in baseball and is, and always has been the most loyal supporters of professional baseball.

The American people are primarily concerned with the excellence of the performance in sports rather than the color, race or creed of the performers. The history of American sports has been enriched by the performance of great Negro athletes who have attained the mystical All-American team in football, won world championships in boxing and helped carry Americans to victory in track and field in the Olympic Games. Fifty-four professional Negro baseball players served with the Armed Forces in this war. One player was killed and several wounded in combat.

Baseball will jeopardize its leadership in professional sports if it fails to give full appreciation to the fact that those Negro players and Negro fans are part and parcel of the game. Certain groups in this country, including political and social-minded drumbeaters, are conducting pressure campaigns in an attempt to force major clubs to sign Negro players.

Members of these groups are not primarily interested in professional baseball. They are not campaigning to find a better opportunity for thousands of Negro boys who want to play baseball. They are not even primarily interested in improving the lot of Negro players who are already employed. They know little about baseball and nothing about the business end of its operation. They single out professional baseball for attack because it offers a good publicity medium.

The thousands of Negro boys of ability who aspire to careers in professional baseball should have a better opportunity. Every American boy, without regard to his race, color, or creed, should have a fair chance in baseball. Jobs for a half dozen good Negro players now employed in the Negro leagues are relatively unimportant. The signing of a few Negro players for the major leagues would be a gesture, but it would contribute nothing toward a solution of the real problem. Let's look at the facts.

A major-league baseball player must have something besides great natural ability. He must possess the technique, the coordination, the competitive attitude, and the discipline, which are usually acquired only after years of training in the minor league. The minor-league experience of players on major-league teams averages 7 years. This is the reason there are not more players who meet major-league standards in the big Negro leagues.

The report quoted "Sam" Lacy of the *Baltimore Afro-American* as saying that Negroes were "simply not good enough to make the Major Leagues at this time."

The owners were liars. They also have Lacy saying, "I am reluctant to say that we haven't a single man in the ranks of colored baseball who could step into the major leagues and disport himself as a Major Leaguer". Sam, who spent all his life trying to get a black into baseball, never said such a thing. The owners knew this.

If the major leagues and minor leagues of professional baseball raid these Negro leagues and take the best players, the Negro leagues will eventually fold up, and investments of these owners will be wiped out, and a lot of professional Negro players will lose their jobs. The Negroes who own and operate these clubs do not want to lose their outstanding players.

The Negro leagues rent their parks in many major cities from organized baseball. All of this substantial revenue would be gone. The NY Yankees net nearly $100,000 from rentals and concessions from the Negro leagues. The owners would want the Negro clubs to continue for the benefit of all. They do not and cannot properly sign players under contracts to Negro clubs. This is not racial discrimination. It is simply respecting contracts.

There are many factors to this problem and many difficulties, which will have to be solved before a satisfactory solution can be worked out. The individual actions of any one club may exert tremendous pressure for the whole structure of professional baseball.

This was the end of the report.

The vote was 15–1 in favor with only Branch Rickey voting no. He walked out of the meeting in cold anger. He realized he had no copy of the report. He called for one and was told all copies had been destroyed.

Rickey went to Lexington, KY, to meet with baseball's new commissioner, Albert B. Chandler. Rickey explained his problem that he couldn't move ahead based on the vote unless Mr. Chandler approved. Commissioner Chandler asked one question: "Can this man play in the major leagues?"

Rickey replied: "Yes, he can and is ready now." "Great ," Chandler said: "Bring him on.'

Brooklyn Dodgers
Jackie Robinson (HOF)
April 15, 1947

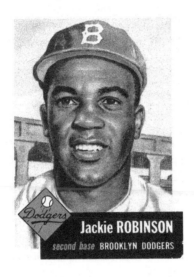

FIRST BLACK PLAYER in modern day major-league baseball

Jack Roosevelt Robinson (January 31, 1919–October 24, 1972) became the first African American to play in major-league baseball (MLB) in the modern era. Robinson broke the baseball color line when the Brooklyn Dodgers started him at first base on April 15, 1947. When the Dodgers signed Robinson, they heralded the end of racial segregation in professional baseball that had forced black baseball players to play in only the Negro leagues since the 1880s.

After graduating from Pasadena Junior College in spring 1939, where he was voted the Most Valuable Junior College baseball player in Southern California in 1938 while batting .417 with 43 runs scored and stealing 25 bases in just 24 games, Robinson enrolled at UCLA, where he played four sports: baseball, basketball, football, and track.

13

He was one of four black players on the Bruins' 1939 football team; the others were Woody Strode, Kenny Washington, and Ray Bartlett. Washington, Strode, and Robinson made up three of the team's four backfield players. At a time when only a few black students played mainstream college football, this made UCLA college football's most integrated team. They went undefeated with four ties at 6–0–4.

In track and field, Robinson won the 1940 NCAA championship in the long jump at 24 ft. 10¼ in.

As UCLA's shortstop in 1940, statistics indicate that baseball was the sport with which he had the most trouble. Robinson posted a .097 batting average the one year he played baseball for the Bruins. Nevertheless, due to his slick fielding and keen base running, fans found Robinson in the starting lineup the majority of the season. In his first game at UCLA, he went 4-for-4 and stole home twice. Due to financial hardship he dropped out of UCLA in his senior year.

In 1942, Robinson was drafted and assigned to a segregated army cavalry unit in Fort Riley, Kansas. Having the requisite qualifications, Robinson and several other black soldiers applied for admission to an Officer Candidate School (OCS) then located at Fort Riley. Although the army's initial July 1941 guidelines for OCS had been drafted as race neutral, few black applicants were admitted into OCS. As a result, the applications of Robinson and his colleagues were delayed for several months. After protests by heavyweight boxing champion Joe Louis (then stationed at Fort Riley) and the help of Truman Gibson (then an assistant civilian aide to the secretary of war), the men were accepted into OCS. The experience led to a personal friendship between Robinson and Louis. Upon finishing OCS, Robinson was commissioned as a second lieutenant in January 1943.

An event on July 6, 1944 derailed Robinson's military career. While awaiting results of hospital tests on the ankle he had injured in junior college, Robinson boarded an Army bus with a fellow officer's wife; although the Army had commissioned its own unsegregated bus line, the bus driver ordered Robinson to move to the back of the bus. Robinson refused. The driver backed down but, after reaching the end of the line, summoned the military police that took Robinson into custody. When Robinson later confronted the investigating duty officer about racist questioning by the officer and his assistant, the officer recommended Robinson be court martialed. After Robinson's commander in the 761st, Paul L. Bates, refused to authorize the legal action Robinson was summarily transferred to the 758th Battalion, where the commander quickly consented to charge Robinson with multiple offenses, including, among other charges, public drunkenness, even though Robinson did not drink.

By the time of the court-martial in August 1944, the charges against Robinson had been reduced to two counts of insubordination during questioning. Robinson was acquitted by an all-white panel of nine officers.

After his discharge in 1944, Robinson briefly returned to his old football club, the Los Angeles Bulldogs. Robinson then accepted an offer from his old friend and pastor, Rev. Karl Downs, to be the athletic director at Sam Huston College in Austin, Texas then part of the Southwestern Athletic Conference. The job included coaching the school's basketball team for the 1944–'45 seasons. As it was a young program, few students tried out for the basketball team, and Robinson even resorted to inserting himself into the lineup for exhibition games.

In early 1945, while Robinson was at Sam Huston College, the Kansas City Monarchs sent him a written offer to play professional baseball in the Negro leagues. Robinson accepted a contract for $400 per month. Although he played well for the Monarchs, Robinson was frustrated with the experience. He had grown used to a structured playing environment in college, and the Negro leagues' disorganization and embrace of gambling interests appalled him. The hectic travel schedule also placed a burden on his relationship with his wife with whom he could now communicate only by letter. Robinson played 47 games at shortstop for the Monarchs, hitting .387 with five home runs, and registering 13 stolen bases. He also appeared in the 1945 Negro League All-Star Game, going hitless in five at-bats.

During the 1945 season, Robinson pursued potential major-league interests. The Boston Red Sox held a tryout at Fenway Park for Robinson and other black players on April 16. The tryout, however, was a farce chiefly designed to lessen the desegregationist sensibilities of powerful Boston City Councilman Isadore Muchnick. Even with the stands limited to management, Robinson was subjected to racial labels. Robinson left the tryout.

Other teams, however, had more serious interest in signing a black ballplayer. In the early 1940s, Branch Rickey, club president and general manager of the Brooklyn Dodgers, began to scout the Negro leagues for a possible addition to the Dodgers' roster. Rickey selected Robinson from a list of promising black players and interviewed him for a possible assignment to Brooklyn's International League farm club, the Montreal Royals.

Among those Rickey discussed prospects with was Wendell Smith, a writer for the black weekly *Pittsburgh Courier*, who, according to Cleveland Indians owner and team president Bill Veeck, "Wendell influenced Rickey to take Jack Robinson, for which he's never completely gotten credit."

After obtaining a commitment from Robinson to "turn the other cheek" to racial antagonism, Rickey agreed to sign him to a contract for $600 a month in 1945. Rickey did not offer compensation to the Monarchs, instead, believing all Negro-league players were free agents due to the contracts' not containing a reserve clause.

On October 23, it was publicly announced that Robinson would be assigned to the Royals for the 1946 season. On the same day, with representatives of the Royals and Dodgers present, Robinson formally signed his contract with the Royals. In what was later referred to as "The Noble Experiment" Robinson was the first black baseball player in the International League since the 1880s. He was not necessarily the best player in the Negro leagues, and black talents Satchel Paige and Josh Gibson were very upset when Robinson was selected. Larry Doby, who broke the color line in the American League the same year as Robinson, said, "One of the things that was disappointing and disheartening to a lot of the black players at the time was that Jack was not the best player. The best was Josh Gibson. I think that's one of the reasons why Josh died so early—he was heartbroken." Rickey's offer allowed Robinson to leave behind the Monarchs and their grueling bus rides.

In 1946, Robinson arrived at Daytona Beach, Florida, for spring training with the Montreal Royals of the Class AAA International League (the designation of "AAA" for the highest level of minor-league baseball was first used in the 1946 season). Clay Hopper, the manager of the Royals, asked Rickey to assign Robinson to any other Dodger affiliate, but Rickey refused. Robinson's presence was controversial in racially charged Florida. He was not allowed to stay with his teammates at the team hotel, and lodged, instead, at the home of a local black politician. Since the Dodgers organization did not own a spring training facility (the Dodger-controlled spring training compound in Vero Beach known as "Dodgertown" did not open until spring 1948), scheduling was subject to the whim of area localities, several of which turned down any event involving Robinson or "Johnny" Wright, another black player whom Rickey had signed to the Dodgers organization in January. In Sanford Florida, the police chief threatened to cancel games if Robinson and Wright did not cease training activities there; as a result, Robinson was sent back to Daytona Beach. In Jacksonville, the stadium was padlocked shut without warning on game day, by order of the city's Parks and Public Property director. In DeLand, a scheduled day game was postponed, supposedly because of issues with the stadium's electrical lighting.

After much lobbying of local officials by Rickey himself, the Royals were allowed to host a game involving Robinson in Daytona Beach. Robinson made his Royals debut at Daytona Beach's City Island Ballpark on March 17, 1946, in an exhibition game against the team's parent club, the Dodgers. **Robinson, thus, became the first black player to openly play for a minor-league team against a major-league team** since the de facto baseball color line had been implemented in the 1880s.

Later in spring training, after some less-than-stellar performances, Robinson was shifted from shortstop to second base, allowing him to make shorter throws to first base. His performance soon rebounded.

In 1946, Jackie proceeded to lead the AAA league in batting with a .349 average while stealing 49 bases and was named the league's Most Valuable Player.

The following year, 6 days before the start of the 1947 season, the Dodgers called Robinson up to the major leagues. With Eddie Stanky entrenched at second base for the Dodgers, Robinson played his initial major-league season as a first baseman. On April 15, 1947, Robinson made his major-league debut at the relatively advanced age of 28 at Ebbets Field before a crowd of 26,623 spectators, more than 14,000 of who were black. Although he failed to get a base hit, he walked and scored a run in the Dodgers' 5–3 victory.

Robinson became the first player since 1880 to openly break the major league baseball color line. Black fans began flocking to see the Dodgers when they came to town, abandoning their Negro-league teams. Robinson's promotion met a generally positive, although mixed, reception among newspapers and white major-league players. However, racial tension existed in the Dodger clubhouse. Some Dodger players insinuated they would sit out rather than play alongside Robinson. The brewing mutiny ended when Dodgers' management took a stand for Robinson. Manager Leo Durocher informed the team, "I do not care if the guy is yellow or black, or if he has stripes like a zebra. I'm the manager of this team, and I say he plays. What's more, I say he can make us all rich. And if any of you cannot use the money, I will see that you are all traded."

Just before the opening of the 1947 season, Leo Durocher was suspended for the entire 1947 season for conduct detrimental to baseball. Branch Rickey asked two coaches (Clyde Sukeforth and Ray Blades) and former New York manager Joe McCarthy to take over as a temporary replacement.

All individuals refused the offer.

On the eve of the 1947 season Burt Shotton received a telegram from Rickey. "Be in Brooklyn in the morning. Call nobody, see no one." Burt had managed the Phillies from 1928-1933 and he managed in the Cardinals minor league system, working for Branch Rickey, from 1941-1945. In 1946 he had begun scouting for the Dodgers.

Rickey pleaded with Shotton to take over the Dodgers for the season. Then 62, and convinced that his on-field career was over, Shotton reluctantly took the reins on April 18, still in street clothes. (Shotton was one of the last baseball managers to wear everyday apparel rather than the club uniform. Unlike Connie Mack, however, he did usually add his team's cap and jacket.)

He inherited what historian Jules Tygiel called Baseball's Great Experiment—the Dodgers' breaking of the infamous color line by bringing up Jackie Robinson from their Triple-A Montreal Royals farm club at the start of the 1947 season to end over 60 years of racial segregation in baseball. Jackie was facing withering insults from opposing players, and Durocher had only recently quashed a petition by Dodger players protesting Robinson's presence.

Shotton's calm demeanor, however, provided the quiet leadership the Dodgers needed. They won the National League pennant by five games and took the New York Yankees to seven games in the 1947 World Series.

Robinson finished the 1947 season having played in 151 games for the Dodgers, with a batting average of .297, an on-base percentage of .383, and a .427 slugging percentage. He had 175 hits (scoring 125 runs), including 31 doubles, 5 triples, and 12 home runs, driving in 48 runs for the year. Robinson led the league in sacrifice hits, with 28, and in stolen bases, with 29. His cumulative performance earned him the **inaugural major-league baseball Rookie of the Year Award** (separate National and American League Rookie of the Year honors were not awarded until 1949).

Opposing teams often derided Robinson. Some, notably the St. Louis Cardinals, threatened to strike if Robinson played, but also to spread the walkout across the entire National League. The existence of the plot was leaked by the Cardinals' team physician, Robert Hyland, to a friend, the *New York Herald Tribune*'s Rutherford "Rud" Rennie. The reporter, concerned about protecting Hyland's anonymity and job, in turn, leaked it to his *Tribune* colleague and editor, Stanley Woodward.

The Woodward article made national headlines. After the threat was exposed, National League President Ford Frick and Baseball Commissioner "Happy" Chandler let it be known that any striking players would be suspended. "You will find that the friends that you think you have in the press box will not support you, that you will be outcasts," threatened Chandler. "I do not care if half the league strikes. Those who do it will encounter quick retribution. All will be suspended, and I don't care if it wrecks the National League for five years. This is the United States of America, and one citizen has as much right to play as another." Woodward's article received the E. P. Dutton Award in 1947 for Best Sports Reporting.

Robinson, nonetheless, became the target of rough physical play by opponents (particularly the Cardinals). At one time, he received a seven-inch gash in his leg from Enos Slaughter of the Cardinals.

On April 22, 1947, during a game between the Dodgers and the Philadelphia Phillies, Phillies players and manager Ben Chapman called Robinson a "n*****" from their dugout and yelled that he should "go back to the cotton fields." Rickey later recalled that Chapman did more than anybody to unite the Dodgers. When Chapman put out that string of unconscionable abuse, he solidified and united thirty men on the Dodgers. Robinson did, however, receive encouragement from several major-league players. Robinson named Lee "Jeep" Handley, who played for the Phillies, as the first opposing player to wish him well.

Dodger's teammate Pee Wee Reese once came to Robinson's defense with the famous line, "You can hate a man for many reasons. Color is not one of them." In 1948, Reese put his arm around Robinson in response to fans that shouted racial slurs at Robinson before a game in Cincinnati. A statue by sculptor William Behrends, unveiled at Key Span Park on November 1, 2005, commemorates this event by representing Reese with his arm around Robinson. Jewish baseball star Hank Greenberg, who had to deal with racial epithets during his career, also encouraged Robinson. Following an incident where Greenberg collided with Robinson at first base, he "whispered a few words into Robinson's ear," which Robinson later characterized as "words of encouragement." Greenberg had advised him to overcome his critics by defeating them in games. Robinson also talked frequently with Larry Doby, who endured his own hardships since becoming the first black player in the American League with the Cleveland Indians, as the two spoke to one another via telephone throughout the season.

With Durocher's suspension over, Shotton retired again, this time to a front office post as "managerial consultant" in the Dodgers' vast farm system. But the 1948 Dodgers did not respond to Durocher's return; they even (briefly, on May 24) fell into the NL cellar. Durocher was still under siege by the Catholic Youth Organization because of his extramarital relationship with, and then quick marriage to, actress Laraine Day.

With the New York Giants also floundering, owner Horace Stoneham decided to replace his manager, Mel Ott, with Shotton. He called Rickey to ask permission to speak with Shotton about the Giants' job and was stunned when Rickey offered him the opportunity to hire Durocher instead. On July 16, 1948, Durocher moved from Brooklyn to Upper Manhattan to take over the Giants. The following day, Shotton was back in the Dodger dugout—still in street clothes. On that day, Brooklyn was 37–37 and in fourth place, 8½ games behind the Boston Braves.

Following Stanky's trade to the Boston Braves in March 1948, Robinson took over second base where he logged a .980 fielding percentage (second in the National League at the position) fractionally behind Stanky. Robinson also had a batting average of .296 and 22 stolen bases for the season.

Racial pressure on Robinson eased a little in 1948 as a number of other black players entered the major leagues. In 1947, Larry Doby (who broke the color barrier in the American League on July 5, 1947, just 11 weeks after Robinson) and Hank Thompson, Willard Brown and Dan Bankhead joined the Major Leagues. In 1948 "Satchel" Paige played for the Cleveland Indians and Roy Campanella for the Dodgers.

In February 1948, Jackie signed a $12,500 contract (equal to $124,602 today) with the Dodgers; while a significant amount, this was less than Robinson made in the off-season from a vaudeville tour, where he answered preset baseball questions and participated in a speaking tour of the South. Between the tours, he underwent surgery on his right ankle. Due to his off-season activities, Robinson reported to training camp 30 pounds overweight. While he lost the weight during training camp, dieting left him weak at the plate. He batted .296 with 12 home runs and 85 RBI's in 1948.

After Burt Shotton returned as manager the Dodgers rallied to take the lead in the 1948 NL standings by the end of August, before they faltered in September to finish third, 7½ games behind Boston.

In the spring of 1949, Robinson turned to Hall of Famer George Sisler, working as an advisor to the Dodgers, for batting help. At Sisler's suggestion, Robinson spent hours at a batting tee, learning to hit the ball to right field. Sisler taught Robinson to anticipate a fastball on the theory that it is easier to adjust to a slower curveball.

This guidance helped Robinson raise his batting average from .296 in 1948 to .342 in 1949. In addition to his improved batting average, Robinson stole 37 bases that season, was second place in the league for both doubles and triples, and registered 124 runs batted in with 122 runs scored. For the performance, Robinson earned the Most Valuable Player Award for the National League. Baseball fans also voted Robinson as the starting second baseman for the 1949 All-Star Game—the first All-Star Game to include black players.

In 1949, Shotton won his second pennant, with Brooklyn capturing 97 regular-season victories to finish a game ahead of the Cardinals.

Ultimately, the Dodgers won the National League pennant but lost in five games to the New York Yankees in the 1949 World Series.

Despite Shotton's two pennants in three seasons, he continually faced criticism from Durocher loyalists who claimed that Shotton was a poor game strategist and lacked Durocher's competitive intensity. Because he avoided wearing a uniform, Shotton was prohibited from stepping onto the field of play during games and remained in the dugout during arguments with umpires and pitching changes while one of his uniformed coaches assumed those tasks.

Shotton also had severe critics within the press, notably *New York Daily News* baseball writer Dick Young, who came to refer to him in print only by the derisive acronym KOBS, short for "Kindly Old Burt Shotton."

In 1950, despite chronic pitching woes, Shotton guided the Dodgers to within a game of first place on the final day of the season. When

Dick Sisler's tenth-inning home run off Don Newcombe won the pennant for the Phillies the Dodgers season was over. So was Shotton's managerial career. Rickey was forced from the Brooklyn front office by new majority owner Walter O'Malley at the end of the 1950 season. O'Malley had already decided on Chuck Dressen as his new manager; his hiring was formally announced November 28, 1950. In contrast to Shotton, the fiery Dressen would be conspicuous on the field wearing uniform No. 7 and doubling as Brooklyn's 1951 third-base coach.

In 1950, Robinson led the National League in double plays made by a second baseman with 133. His salary that year was the highest any Dodger had been paid to that point: $35,000 ($348,402 in 2016 dollars). He finished the year with 99 runs scored, a .328 batting average, and 12 stolen bases.

1950 also saw the release of a film biography of Robinson's life, *The Jackie Robinson Story*, in which Robinson played himself, and actress Ruby Dee played Rachael Robinson. Robinson's Hollywood exploits, however, did not sit well with Dodgers co-owner Walter O'Malley, who referred to Robinson as "Rickey's prima donna.

In late 1950, Rickey's contract as the Dodgers' team president expired. Weary of constant disagreements with O'Malley, and with no hope of being reappointed as president of the Dodgers, Rickey cashed out his one-quarter financial interest in the team, leaving O'Malley in full control of the franchise. Rickey, shortly thereafter, became general manager of the Pittsburgh Pirates. Robinson was disappointed at the turn of events and wrote a sympathetic letter to Rickey, whom he considered a father figure, stating, "Regardless of what happens to me in the future, it all can be placed on what you have done and, believe me, I appreciate it."

Before the 1951 season, O'Malley reportedly offered Robinson the job of manager of the Montreal Royals, effective at the end of Robinson's playing career. O'Malley was quoted in the Montreal Standard as saying, "Jackie told me that he would be both delighted and honored to tackle this managerial post"—although reports differed as to whether a position was ever formally offered.

During the 1951 season, Robinson led the National League in double plays (137) made by a second baseman for the second year in a row. Jackie helped keep the Dodgers in contention for the 1951 pennant. During the last game of the regular season, in the thirteenth inning, he had a hit to tie the game and then won the game with a home run in the fourteenth. This forced a best of three playoff series against their crosstown rival New York Giants.

Despite Robinson's regular-season heroics, the Dodgers lost the pennant on Bobby Thomson's famous home run, known as the "Shot Heard 'Round the World," on October 3, 1951. He finished the 1951 season with 106 runs scored, a batting average of .335, and 25 stolen bases.

The 1952 season was the last year Robinson was an every day starter at second base.

Robinson had what was an average year for him in 1952. He finished the year with 104 runs, a .308 batting average, and 24 stolen bases. He did, however, record a career-high on-base percentage of .436.

The Dodgers improved on their performance from the year before, winning the National League pennant before losing the 1952 World Series to the New York Yankees in seven games.

In 1953 Robinson played sporadically at first, second, and third bases, shortstop, and in the outfield, with Jim Gilliam, another black player, taking over every day second base duties. He played in a total of 136 games with the most at 3rd base (44) and left field (75).

In 1953, Robinson had 109 runs, a .329 batting average, and 17 steals, leading the Dodgers to another National League pennant (and another World Series loss to the Yankees, this time in six games). Robinson's continued success spawned a string of death threats. He was not dissuaded, however, from addressing racial issues publicly. That year, he served as editor for *Our Sports* magazine, a periodical focusing on Negro sports issues; contributions to the magazine included an article on golf course segregation by Robinson's old friend Joe Louis. Robinson also openly criticized segregated hotels and restaurants that served the Dodger organization; a number of these establishments integrated as a result, including the five-star Chase Park Hotel in St. Louis.

The following year, in 1954, Robinson had 62 runs scored, a .311 batting average, and 7 steals.

During the autumn of 1955, Robinson won his only championship when the Dodgers beat the New York Yankees in the 1955 World Series. Although the team enjoyed ultimate success, 1955 was the worst year of Robinson's career. He hit .256 and stole only 12 bases. The Dodgers tried Robinson in the outfield and as a third baseman, both because of his diminishing abilities and because Gilliam was established at second base. Robinson, then 37 years old, missed 49 games and did not play in Game 7 of the World Series. Missing those games because manager Walter Alston decided to play Gilliam at second and Don Hoak at third base. That season, the Dodgers' Don Newcombe became the first black major-league pitcher to win 20 games in a year.

In 1956, Robinson had 61 runs scored, a .275 batting average, and 12 steals. By then, he had begun to exhibit the effects of diabetes and to lose interest in the prospect of playing or managing professional baseball.

After the season, Robinson was traded by the Dodgers to the archrival New York Giants for Dick Littlefield and $35,000 cash (equal to $308,317 today). The trade, however, was never completed as

Robinson refused to report, and the trade was voided. Jackie returned to the Dodgers and retired.

Beginning his major-league career at the relatively advanced age of 28, he played only 10 seasons from 1947 to 1956, all of them for the Brooklyn Dodgers. During his career, the Dodgers played in six World Series, and Robinson himself played in six All-Star Games.

Robinson had an exceptional 10-year baseball career. He was the recipient of the inaugural MLB Rookie of the Year Award in 1947, was an All-Star for six consecutive seasons from 1949 through 1954, and won the National League Most Valuable Player Award in 1949—the first black player so honored.

He scored more than 100 runs in six of his 10 seasons (averaging more than 110 runs from 1947 to 1953), had a .311 career batting average, a .409 career on-base percentage, a .474 slugging percentage, and substantially more walks than strikeouts (740 to 291). Robinson was one of only two players during 1947–'56 to accumulate at least 125 steals while registering a slugging percentage over .425 ("Minnie" Miñoso was the other). He accumulated 197 stolen bases in total, including 19 steals of home which places him in the top ten of lifetime steals of home.

Historical statistical analysis indicates Robinson was an outstanding fielder throughout his 10 years in the major leagues and at virtually every position he played. After playing his rookie season at first base, Robinson spent most of his career as a second baseman. He led the league in fielding, among second basemen, in 1950 and 1951. Toward the end of his career, he played about 2,000 innings at third base and about 1,175 innings in the outfield, excelling at both.

Robinson retired from baseball at age 37 on January 5, 1957. Later that year, after he complained of numerous physical ailments, his doctors diagnosed him with diabetes. Although Robinson adopted an insulin injection regimen, the state of medicine at the time could not prevent the continued deterioration of Robinson's physical condition from the disease.

In his first year of eligibility for the Baseball Hall of Fame in 1962, he was elected on the first ballot, becoming the **first black player inducted into the Cooperstown Hall of Fame Museum.**

In 1965, Robinson served as an analyst for ABC's major-league Baseball Game of the Week telecasts becoming the first black person to do so.

In 1966, Robinson protested against the major leagues' ongoing lack of minority managers and central office personnel, and turned down an invitation to appear in an old-timers' game at Yankee Stadium in 1969.

He made his final public appearance on October 15, 1972, throwing the ceremonial first pitch before Game 2 of the World Series at Riverfront Stadium in Cincinnati. He gratefully accepted a plaque honoring the twenty-fifth anniversary of his MLB debut, but also commented, "I'm going to be tremendously more pleased and more proud when I look at that third base coaching line one day and see a black face managing in baseball." This wish was only fulfilled after Robinson's death. Following the 1974 season, the Cleveland Indians gave their managerial post to Frank Robinson (no relation to Jackie), a Hall of Fame-bound player who would go on to manage three other teams. Despite the success of these two Robinsons and other black players, the number of African American players in major-league baseball has declined since the 1970s.

Complications from heart disease and diabetes weakened Robinson and made him almost blind by middle age. On October 24, 1972, 9 days after his appearance at the World Series, Robinson died of a heart attack at his home in Connecticut. Jackie was only 53 years old.

In 1997, MLB "universally" retired his uniform number, 42, across all major-league teams; he was the first pro athlete in any sport to be so honored. MLB also adopted a new annual tradition, "Jackie Robinson Day," for the first time on April 15, 2004, on which every player on every team wears No. 42.

After signing Jackie Robinson and "Johnny" Wright in 1945, Branch Rickey signed three additional players for the Brooklyn Dodgers and brought them through the minors to major-league baseball.

Those players and their first appearance in a MLB game were:

Dan Bankhead on 8/26/47

Roy Campanella, on 4/20/48

Don Newcombe on 5/20/49

Brooklyn Dodgers

Dan Bankhead

August 26, 1947

Daniel Robert Bankhead (May 3, 1920–May 2, 1976) was **the first African American pitcher in major-league baseball.** He played in Negro-league baseball for the Birmingham Black Barons and the Memphis Red Sox from 1940 to 1947, and then played for the Brooklyn Dodgers from 1947 to 1951. During World War II, he served in the Marine Corps from 1942 to 1945.

1947 was the first time African-Americans played in the World Series. Two men played for the Brooklyn Dodgers. Jackie Robinson would go on to win his place as a courageous American path breaker, but his teammate, Dan Bankhead, the first black major league pitcher in modern baseball, has been almost forgotten.

After the war, in 1946, ex-Sergeant Bankhead joined the Memphis Red Sox and excelled in two Negro leagues all-star games — a performance he repeated in another contest in July 1947, at Chicago's Comiskey Park. Bankhead was promoted as "the colored Bob Feller" or "the next Satchel Paige."

Two Dodger scouts saw Bankhead stand out at Comiskey. The following month, their boss, the Dodger president, Branch Rickey, flew to Memphis to watch Bankhead in action himself and in 1947 bought his contract from the Memphis Red Sox (for which he had been the best-paid player) for $15,000.

During 1947 the Dodgers at that moment were in close contention for the National League pennant and Rickey was badly in need of pitchers.

Rickey told a reporter: "I know this boy (Bankhead) has the physical equipment to help this club. The only question is whether he will be able to withstand the tremendous pressure under which he will work. His problem is greater than Robinson's — all eyes are on the pitcher."

Bankhead, an excellent hitter who was leading the Negro league with a .385 batting average in 1947 when purchased by the Dodgers. He finished the 1947 season having pitched in four games for the Dodgers with an earned run average (ERA) of 7.20.

Once Bankhead joined the Dodgers, when the team traveled, he would room with Robinson in segregated hotels. With so much in common and at stake, braving racist catcalls and death threats, the two pioneers quickly bonded.

In his first Dodgers appearance, on Tuesday, Aug. 26, 1947, against the Pirates at Brooklyn's Ebbets Field, Bankhead produced a home run, but the pitching for which Rickey had hired him was terrible.

"I was scared as hell," Bankhead later recalled. "When I stepped on the mound, I was perspiring all over and tight as a drum." His first pitch, a fastball, banged the Pirates batter Wally Westlake hard on the elbow.

Although the Dodgers made it to the 1947 Series, Bankhead never truly found his footing. In that seven-game series, which the Yankees won, he pinch ran but did not pitch. After it was over, an Associated Press sportswriter called Bankhead a "flash in the pan" and sarcastically recalled how some had called him a "gift to baseball."

Bankhead was shipped to the minor leagues for the 1948 and 1949 seasons. Pitching for clubs in Nashua, New Hampshire, and St. Paul, Minnesota, in 1948, he recorded 24 wins and six losses and in 1949 20 wins and 6 losses.

He returned to the Dodgers for the 1950 season, appearing in 41 games, with 12 starts, and finished with nine wins, four losses, and a 5.50 ERA.

In 1951, his final year in the majors, he appeared in seven games, losing his only decision, with an ERA of 15.43.

After his short Major League career was over, he struggled in Minor League ball in the United States, Dominican Republic and Canada before being destined to spend the rest of his career in Mexico through 1966. In Mexico Bankhead tried to reinvent himself as a first baseman and outfielder who could also pitch a little. Bankhead did meet with success as a hitter but never again showed the pitching skills that had him touted as "the next Satchel Paige" or "the colored Bob Feller."

Dan Bankhead died of cancer at a Veterans Administration hospital in Houston, Texas, on May 2, 1976, the day before his 56th birthday.

The Bankhead's Empire

There have been many brothers, fathers, and sons to play baseball or be involved in the business of the Negro leagues. However, no family was more involved than the Bankhead family of Empire, Alabama. Five brothers played in the Negro leagues.

The oldest and most prolific was **Sam Bankhead** (1905–1976), who played several positions and managed in the Negro leagues from 1930–1950. **Fred Bankhead** (1912–1972) played infield for many teams from 1936–1948.

Perhaps the most famous brother was **Dan Bankhead** (1920–1976), who was a pitcher in the Negro leagues from 1940–1947. In 1947, he became the first black pitcher to integrate the major leagues in the modern era when he pitched for the Brooklyn Dodgers, becoming Jackie Robinson's roommate.

Joe Bankhead (1926–1988) and **Garnett Bankhead** (1928–1991) both had brief careers in the leagues between 1947 and 1949. Yet, in spite of all this baseball experience, only Fred and Dan got to play on the same team together (the Memphis Red Sox) between 1946 and 1947.

Brooklyn Dodgers
Roy Campanella (HOF)
April 20, 1948

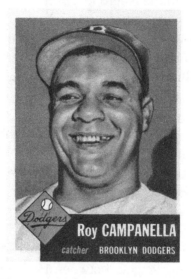

Roy Campanella (November 19, 1921–June 26, 1993), nicknamed "Campy," was an American baseball player, primarily as a catcher. The Philadelphia native played for the Negro leagues and Mexican League for several seasons before entering the minor leagues in 1946.

Widely considered to be one of the greatest catchers in the history of the game, Campanella played for the Brooklyn Dodgers in the 1940s and 1950s.

Campanella's father, John, was the son of Sicilian immigrants. His mother, Ida, was African American. Therefore, he was effectively prohibited from MLB play before 1947, the season that black players were admitted to the major leagues for the first time since the nineteenth century.

Campanella began playing Negro-league baseball for the Washington Elite Giants in 1937 after dropping out of school on his sixteenth birthday. The Elite Giants moved to Baltimore the following year, and Campanella became a star player with the team. He remained with Baltimore thru 1941, but few statistics were kept.

During the 1942 Negro League season, Campanella jumped to the Monterrey Sultans of the Mexican League after a contract dispute with the Elite Giants. He remained in Mexico for the 1943 season before returning to Baltimore for the 1944 and 1945 campaigns. Again, few statistics were kept.

In October 1945 Campanella caught for a black all-star team organized by Effa Manley against a squad of major leaguers managed by Charlie Dressen. In a five-game exhibition series at Ebbets Field, Dressen, a Dodgers coach at the time, approached Campanella to arrange a meeting with Dodgers general manager and part owner Branch Rickey later that month. Campanella spent four hours listening to Rickey, whom he later described as "the talkingest man I ever did see," and politely declined when Rickey asked if he was interested in playing in the Brooklyn organization. Campy thought he was being recruited for the Brooklyn Brown Dodgers, a new Negro League outfit that Rickey was supposedly starting. A few days later, however, he ran into Jackie Robinson in a Harlem hotel. After Robinson confidentially told him he'd already signed with the Dodgers, Campy realized that Rickey had been talking about a career in organized baseball. Afraid that he had blown his shot at the big leagues, he fired off a telegram to Rickey indicating his interest in playing for the Dodgers just before he left on a barnstorming tour through South America. The 1946 spring-training season was already under way by the time Campanella returned from South America and reported to the Dodgers office in Brooklyn.

Like most of the first generation of black players to cross the color line, Campanella took a steep pay cut to enter organized baseball and was forced to start at a level far below his ability. A top star in the

Negro leagues, he found himself competing against a bunch of inexperienced kids, most of whom would never play above Class A ball. Furthermore, he would be making only $185 a month for six months at Nashua rather than the $600 a month he'd been earning with the Baltimore Elite Giants.

Campanella moved into the Brooklyn Dodgers' minor-league system in 1946 as the Dodger organization began preparations to break the MLB color barrier with Jackie Robinson. The team looked to assign Campanella to a Class B league. The general manager of the Danville Dodgers of the Illinois–Indiana–Iowa league reported that he did not feel the league was ready for racial integration. The organization sent Campanella and pitcher Don Newcombe to the Nashua Dodgers of the Class B New England League, where the Dodgers felt the climate would be more tolerant. **The Nashua team thus became the first professional baseball team of the twentieth century to field a racially integrated lineup in the United States.**

Campanella's 1946 season proceeded largely without racist incidents, and in one game, Campanella assumed the managerial duties after manager Walter Alston was ejected. **This made Campanella the first African American to manage Caucasian players of an organized professional baseball team.** He batted .290 and had 96 RBI's in 1946 and was voted the Most Valuable Player in the New England League.

In 1947 he remained with Nashua again winning the Most Valuable Player Award while batting .273 with 13 home runs and 75 RBI's.

Roy's experience in Nashua also changed his parents' life. Home runs around the New England League were virtually impossible. A local poultry farmer offered 100 baby chicks for every Nashua home run. At the end of the season, Campy collected 1,400 chicks as reward for his 14 homers (a team-leading 13 in the regular season and one in the playoffs). He had them shipped to his father, who promptly began a farming business on the outskirts of Philadelphia.

Campanella went to spring training with the Dodgers in Havana before the 1948 season. He was listed on the Montreal roster, along with Robinson, Newcombe, and Roy Partlow, a left-handed pitcher. Jackie, of course, was promoted to the Dodgers, Newcombe was sent back to Nashua, and Partlow was released, leaving Campanella the only black player in the International League. Campanella won the International League MVP award batting .325. Veteran catcher Paul Richards, then managing Buffalo in the International League, called him "the best catcher in the business – major or minor leagues." With his extensive Negro League experience and a Triple-A MVP award under his belt, the 26-year-old receiver was ready for major-league duty.

Unfortunately, the Brooklyn Dodgers weren't yet ready for him. Brooklyn's regular catcher was Bruce Edwards, who in 1947 posted an excellent .295 batting mark, drove in 80 runs, and finished fourth in National League MVP balloting, the highest ranking of any Dodger. In addition, Edwards was a fine defensive backstop and was almost two years younger than Campy.

Edwards had injured his arm in the offseason, and it failed to come around in the spring of 1948. Manager Leo Durocher, back in command of the Dodgers after a year's suspension, fully appreciated Campanella's talents and wanted to insert him in Edwards' place behind the plate.

Though Campanella broke camp with the Dodgers, the plan was to send him down to their St. Paul American Association farm club when rosters had to be trimmed to 25 players on May 15. **He made his big-league debut against the New York Giants at the Polo Grounds on Opening Day April 20, 1948.** Gil Hodges, who hadn't made the move to first base yet, started behind the plate in place of Edwards, but went out for a pinch-hitter in the top of the seventh. In the bottom half of the inning, Campanella took over behind the plate with the Dodgers down 6-5. With ace reliever Hugh Casey on the mound, the Giants went scoreless for the final three innings while the Dodgers scored two runs to win the game. Campanella got to the plate in the top of the eighth inning and was promptly drilled by Giants re-liever Ken Trinkle – the type of welcome that many more black hitters would receive in the early days of baseball's integration era. He was sent to the minors in May as planned.

The American Association's first black player broke the color barrier with a disastrous performance, going hitless and fanning twice in four at-bats, and making an error on a pickoff attempt, but he was soon terrorizing the opposition. In 35 games, Campy batted .325, slammed 13 homers, and drove in 39 runs, forcing the struggling Dodgers to recall him.

When Campanella rejoined the Dodgers' lineup on July 2, 1948, the defending National League champions had lost five straight and were languishing in seventh place with a 27-34 record. From that point on they won 57 while losing 36, a .613 pace – better than the .591 overall winning percentage posted by the pennant-winning Braves. Even more remarkable was the fact that the Dodgers won 50 of the 73 games that Campanella started after his recall, an incredible .685 mark. His installation behind the plate was the last in a series of moves orchestrated by Durocher to turn the club around. Three days earlier Gil Hodges, who had acquitted himself well behind the plate filling in for the injured Edwards, was shifted to first base, allowing Jackie Robinson to move over to his natural second-base position. Unfortunately for Durocher, he didn't stay around long enough to enjoy the results, as he left the Dodgers to take over the reins of the New York Giants a week after Campanella's recall.

For his rookie year 1948, Campanella batted .258 with 9 homers in 83 games and led National League catchers in percentage of runners caught stealing. He even garnered eight points in the MVP voting despite playing only half the season.

In 1949 he batted .287 with 22 home runs and 82 RBI's.

In 1950 he batted .281 with 31 home runs and 89 RBI's.

In 1951, his first MVP Season he batted .325 with 33 home runs and 108 RBI's.

In 1952, partially due to injuries his batting average dropped to .269 but he still hit 22 home runs with 97 RBI's.

In 1953, his second MVP season, he batted .312 with 41 home runs and 142 RBI's

In 1954 he only played in 111 games due to injuries batting only .207 with 19 home runs and 51 RBI's.

In 1955 he rebounded for his third MVP batting .318 with 32 home runs and 107 RBI's.

In 1956 he batted only .219 with 20 home runs and 73 RBI's.

In 1957, his last season, he batted .246 with 13 home runs and 62 RBI's.

Campanella began his MLB career with the Brooklyn Dodgers playing **his first game on April 20, 1948.** He played for the Dodgers from 1948 through 1957 as their regular catcher. In 1948, he had three different uniform numbers (33, 39, and 56) before settling on 39 for the rest of his career. Campanella played in the All-Star Game every year from 1949 through 1956. His 1949 All-Star selection made him one of the first four African Americans so honored. (Jackie Robinson, Don Newcombe, and Larry Doby were also All-Stars in 1949.)

Campanella received the Most Valuable Player (MVP) Award in the National League three times: in 1951, 1953, and 1955. In each of his MVP seasons, he batted more than .300, hit more than 30 home runs, and had more than 100 runs batted in. His 142 RBI's during 1953 exceeded the franchise record of 130. That same year, Campanella hit 40 home runs in games in which he appeared as a catcher. **During his**

**career, he threw out 57 percent of the base runners that tried to steal
a base on him, the highest by any catcher in major-league history.**

In 1955 (Campanella's final MVP season), he helped Brooklyn win its
first-ever World Series championship. After the Dodgers lost the first two
games of the series to the Yankees, Campanella began Brooklyn's comeback by hitting a two-out, two-run home run in the first inning of Game
3. The Dodgers won that game, got another home run from Campanella
in a Game 4 victory that tied the series, then went on to claim the series
in seven games when Johnny Podres shut out the Yankees 2–0 in Game
7. After the 1957 season, the Brooklyn Dodgers relocated to Los Angeles
and became the Los Angeles Dodgers, but Campanella's playing career
came to an end as a result of an automobile accident.

He never played a game for Los Angeles.

After his playing career, Campanella remained involved with
the Dodgers. In January 1959, the Dodgers named him Assistant
Supervisor of Scouting for the eastern part of the United States and
special coach at the team's annual spring training camp in Vero
Beach, Florida, serving each year as a mentor and coach to young
catchers in the Dodger organization.

On June 4, 1972, the Dodgers retired Campanella's uniform number 39
alongside Jackie Robinson's number 42 and Sandy Koufax's number 32.

In 1978, he moved to California and accepted a job as assistant to the
Dodgers' Director of Community Relations, working for Campanella's
former teammate and longtime friend, Don Newcombe.

During 1969, Campanella was inducted into the Baseball Hall of Fame,
the second player of black heritage so honored, after Jackie Robinson.

Campanella died of heart failure at age 71 on June 26, 1993, at his
home in Woodland Hills, California.

Brooklyn Dodgers

Don Newcombe

May 20, 1949

Donald Newcombe (born June 14, 1926), nicknamed "Newk," was a major-league baseball right-handed starting pitcher who played for the Brooklyn/Los Angeles Dodgers (1949–'51 and 1954–'58), Cincinnati Reds (1958–'60), and Cleveland Indians (1960).

Until 2011, when Detroit Tigers pitcher Justin Verlander accomplished the feat, Newcombe was the only baseball player to have won the Rookie of the Year, Most Valuable Player, and CY Young awards in his career.

In 1949, he became the first black pitcher to start a World Series game.

In 1951, Newcombe was the first black pitcher to win 20 games in one season. He became the first pitcher to win the National League MVP and the CY Young in the same season.

After playing one season in 1946 with the Newark Eagles in the Negro leagues where he went 14 and 4, Newcombe signed with the Dodgers. Along with catcher Roy Campanella, Newcombe played for the first racially integrated baseball team based in the United States in the twentieth century, the 1946 Nashua Dodgers of the New England League. He continued to play for Nashua in 1947 where he went 19 and 6 before moving up through the minor leagues.

In 1948 in the minors he went 17 and 6 with 149 strikeouts.

He debuted for Brooklyn on May 20, 1949. He immediately helped the Dodgers to the league pennant as he earned 17 victories, led the league in shutouts and pitched 32 consecutive scoreless innings. Newcombe was named Rookie of the Year by both *The Sporting News* and the Baseball Writers' Association of America.

In 1950, he won 19 games and won 20 games in 1951 also leading the league in strikeouts with 164.

After 2 years of military duty in 1952 and 1953 during the Korean War, Newcombe suffered a disappointing season in 1954, going 9–8 with a 4.55 earned run average.

He returned to form in 1955 by finishing second in the NL in both wins and earned run average, with marks of 20–5 and 3.20 ERA, as the Dodgers won their first World Series in franchise history.

He had an even greater 1956 season, with marks of 27–7, 139 strikeouts and a 3.06 ERA, five shutouts and 18 complete games, leading the league in winning percentage for the second year in a row. He was named the National League's MVP and won the first ever CY Young Award, awarded to the best pitcher in the combined major leagues.

In 1957 he went 11 and 12 with an ERA of 3.49.

Following the Dodgers' move to Los Angeles, Newcombe got off to a 0–6 start in 1958 before being traded to the Reds for four players in midseason. He posted a record of 24–21 with Cincinnati until his contract was sold to Cleveland in mid-1960. He finished with a 2–3 mark in Cleveland in 1960 before being released to end his major-league career.

He played in the Minor Leagues in 1961 with a 9-8 record.

On May 28, 1962, Newcombe signed with the Chunichi Dragons of Japan's Nippon Professional Baseball. Doby would join him the same year. Newcombe played one season in Japan, splitting time as an out-fielder and a first baseman, only pitching in one game. In 81 games, he hit .262, with 12 home runs and 43 RBI.

Newcombe acknowledges that alcoholism played a significant role in the decline of his career. In his 10-year major-league career, Newcombe registered a record of 149–90, with 1,129 strikeouts and a 3.56 ERA, 136 complete games, and 24 shutouts in 2,154 innings pitched.

In addition to his pitching abilities, Newcombe was a dangerous hitter, hitting seven homers one season. He batted .271 (ninth-best average in history among pitchers), with 15 home runs, 108 runs batted in, 238 hits, 33 doubles, 3 triples, 94 runs scored, and 8 stolen bases.

Newcombe rejoined the Dodger organization in the late 1970s and served as the team's Director of Community Affairs.

In March 2009, he was named Special Adviser to the chairman of the team and remains in that position today.

CHAPTER 2

Cleveland Indians

The Indians were the second team in major-league baseball to promote a black ballplayer to their major-league roster.

The Indians would bring up the second black player to MLB (Doby), the seventh (Paige), the eighth (Miñoso), the eleventh (Easter), the sixteenth (Simpson), and the twentieth (Jones) from 1947 to 1951.

Bill Veeck proposed integrating baseball in 1942, which had been informally segregated since the turn of the century, but Commissioner Kenesaw Mountain Landis rejected it.

In 1946, Bill Veeck formed an investment group that purchased the Cleveland Indians for a reported $1.6 million. Among the investors was Bob Hope, who had grown up in Cleveland, and former Tigers slugger, Hank Greenberg.

Veeck then began the process of finding a young, talented player from the Negro leagues and told a reporter in Cleveland that he would integrate the Indians' roster if he could find a black player with the necessary talent level who could withstand the taunts and pressure of being the first black athlete in the American League.

Several reporters suggested Doby including reporters who covered the Negro leagues. Indians scout Bill Killefer rated Doby favorably and perhaps just as important for Veeck, reported Doby's off-field behavior was not a concern.

Mr. Veeck hired Abe Saperstein, known mostly for owning and coaching the Harlem Globetrotters, as a baseball scout. Saperstein was a leading figure in black baseball leagues. At various times, he owned the Chicago Brown Bombers, the Birmingham Black Barons, and Cincinnati Crescents baseball teams.

At Saperstein's suggestions, Veeck eventually signed "Luke" Easter, Larry Doby, "Minnie" Miñoso, Harry Simpson, "Satchel" Paige, and others.

By 1947, the Indians had signed 14 black players and invited six to spring training in 1948

Veeck attempted to sign Ray Dandridge (future MLB HOF) in 1947 with the thought of bringing him up as the first American-League player, but Ray was making more money playing in Mexico than Veeck could afford, plus Ray was treated as a fan favorite in Mexico, so he declined the offer.

Under Veeck's leadership, the Indians signed Larry Doby, formerly a player for the Negro league's Newark Eagles in 1947, eleven weeks after Jackie Robinson signed with the Dodgers.

Unlike the Brooklyn Dodgers' Branch Rickey, who signed Robinson one full season before bringing him to the National League, Veeck used a different strategy, letting Doby remain with the Eagles instead of bringing him through the Indians' farm system. While Rickey declined to pay for the purchasing rights of Robinson while he played for the Kansas City Monarchs, Veeck was determined to buy Doby's contract from the Eagles and had no problem paying purchasing rights. Effa Manley, business manager for the Eagles, believed her club's close relationship with the New York Yankees might put Doby in a Yankees uniform, but they did not take an interest in him. Veeck finalized a contract deal for Doby with Manley on July 3. Veeck paid her a total of $15,000 for the second baseman ($10,000 for taking him from the Eagles and another $5,000 once it was determined he would stay with the Indians for at least 30 days). After Manley agreed to Veeck's offer, she stated to him, "If Larry Doby were white and a free agent, you'd give him $100,000 to sign as a bonus." The press was not told that the Indians had signed Doby as Veeck wanted to manage how fans in Cleveland would be introduced to him.

On July 5th of 1947, less than 3 months after Jackie Robinson entered major-league baseball as the first black player, Larry Doby became the first black player in the American League when he joined the Cleveland Indians.

In 1959, Larry would become the first black American player for the Detroit Tigers.

Similar to Robinson, Doby battled racism on and off the field. In 1947 he appeared in 32 games.

He posted a .301 batting average in 1948, his first full season.

In 1948, needing pitching for the stretch run of the pennant race, Veeck turned to the Negro league again and signed pitching great "Satchel" Paige amid much controversy. Barred from major-league baseball during his prime, Veeck's signing of the aging star in 1948 was viewed by many as another publicity stunt. At an official age of 42, Paige became the oldest rookie in major-league baseball. Paige ended the year with a 6–1 record, with a 2.48 ERA, 45 strikeouts, and two shutouts.

Cleveland Indians

Larry Doby (HOF)

July 5, 1947

**The first black player in the American League
The second black player in the major leagues,
The second black manager in the major leagues**

Lawrence Eugene Doby (December 13, 1923–June 18, 2003) was an American professional baseball player in the Negro leagues and major-league baseball (MLB) and was the second black player to break baseball's color barrier in July 1947.

In 1942 Negro-league umpire Henry Moore advised Newark Eagles' owners Abe and Effa Manley to give Doby a tryout at Hinchliffe Stadium in Paterson, NJ, which was successful.

Doby joined the Eagles in 1942 at the young age of 18 for $300 a month. The contract stated Doby would play until September when he would start classes in college. To protect his amateur status, he signed using the alias "Larry Walker," and local reporters were told he originated from Los Angeles, California.

On May 31, 1942, Doby appeared in his first professional game when the Eagles played against the New York Cubans at Yankee Stadium. In the 26 games where box scores have been found, Doby's batting average was .391.

Doby's career in Newark was interrupted for service in the United States Navy. Doby spent 1943 and part of 1944 at Camp Robert Smalls at the Great Lakes Naval Training School near Chicago. He then went to Treasure Island Naval Base in San Francisco Bay, California, before serving in the Pacific Theater of World War II. He was discharged in January 1946.

Doby rejoined the Eagles in 1946. He made the All-Star roster, batted .360 (fourth in the NNL), hit five home runs (fifth), and led the NNL in triples (six). Manager Biz Mackey led the Eagles, including Doby, "Monte" Irvin, and Johnny Davis, to the Negro World Series championship over "Satchel" Paige and the Kansas City Monarchs in seven games to conclude the 1946 season.

In July 1947, three months after Jackie Robinson made history with the Brooklyn Dodgers, Doby broke the MLB color barrier in the American League when he signed a contract to play with Bill Veeck's Cleveland Indians.

Doby was the first player to go directly to the majors from the Negro leagues. On July 5, 1947, with the Indians in Chicago in the midst of a road trip, Doby made his debut as the second black baseball player. Veeck hired two plainclothes police officers to accompany Doby as he went to Comiskey Park. Player-manager Lou Boudreau initially had a hard time finding a place in the lineup for Doby, who had played second base and shortstop for most of his career. Boudreau himself was the regular shortstop, while Joe Gordon was the second baseman. That day, Doby met his new teammates for the first time. "I walked down that line, stuck out my hand, and a few hands came back in return. Most of the ones that did were cold-fish handshakes, along with a look that said, 'you don't belong here,'" Doby reminisced years later.

Four of Doby's teammates did not shake his hand, and of those, two turned their backs to him when he tried to introduce himself. Doby entered the game in the seventh inning as a pinch hitter for relief pitcher Bryan Stephens and recorded a strikeout.

After the game, Doby quickly showered and dressed without incident in the Cleveland clubhouse. His escort, Louis Jones, then took him not to the Del Prado Hotel downtown, where the Indians players stayed, but to the black DuSable Hotel in Chicago's predominantly black South Side, near Comiskey Park. The segregated arrangement established a pattern that he would be compelled to follow in spring training and during the regular season in many cities throughout his playing career.

The Indians had a doubleheader against the White Sox on Sunday, July 6, where 31,566 were in attendance; it was estimated that approximately 30 percent of the crowd was black. Boudreau had Doby pinch-hit in the first game, but for the second, listed him a starter at first base, a position Doby was not expected to fill when the Indians brought him up to play at second base. It was the only game Doby started for the remainder of the season.

In his rookie year 1947, Doby hit 5-for-32 in 29 games. He played four games at second base and one each at first base and shortstop.

In 1948, Doby experienced his first spring training with the Indians in Tucson, Arizona. Bill Veeck the Indians owner moved the team to Arizona from Florida for spring training because of the Jim Crow laws, local and state laws that enforced racial segregation, still in place in Florida. Veeck hoped that Arizona would be more hospitable to players like Doby, Minoso and others.

Unlike their white teammates, Doby, along with "Satchel" Paige and "Minnie" Miñoso, were not permitted to stay at the nearby Santa Rita Hotel but instead, stayed with a local black family and used a rental car provided by the Indians for transportation.

In 1948, he played in 121 games and hit .301 for the season with 14 home runs and 66 RBI.

Throughout the regular 1948 season, opposing teams racially abused Doby, and Veeck asked AL president Will Harridge for support in getting players to rein in their animosity toward Doby. No action was taken.

In 1949 he batted .280 and, his home run (24) and RBI (85) totals increased from 1948.

In 1950, he was considered the best center fielder in the game by *The Sporting News*. At the end of the season, Cleveland signed him to a new, more lucrative contract. In 1950 he batted .326 with 25 home runs and 102 RBI's.

In 1951, Doby hit 20 home runs and 69 RBI, both fewer than the past season, while batting .295. Indians general manager Hank Greenberg reduced Doby's salary due to the lower home run numbers.

One month before spring training for the 1952 season, Doby employed former Olympic track and field athlete Harrison Dillard to come to his home in New Jersey to prepare his legs in hopes of eliminating injuries, which had affected him the previous season.

By the end of the 1952 season, Doby was second in the AL in RBI to teammate Al Rosen by one, 105 to 104. His .541 slugging percentage, runs scored (104), strikeout (111), and home run (32) totals were all the highest in the AL.

Leading up to the 1953 season, Doby asked Greenberg and Indians management for a pay raise after earning $22,000 the previous season. In early March, the raise was granted and he was slated to make $28,000 in 1953.

For 1953, Doby had a .263 batting average, which was his lowest since joining the league in 1947. He led the AL in strikeouts for the second and final time in his career, a career-high 121 times, but hit 29 home runs and 102 RBI on the year. He also had 96 walks, which was third in the AL.

In 1954, Doby helped the Indians to win a franchise-record 111 games and the AL pennant. His regular-season 32 home runs and career-high 126 RBI were highest in the AL. The Indians were swept in the 1954 World Series by Doby's former Eagles teammate "Monte" Irvin and the New York Giants.

The year 1955 was his last full season with the Indians. He finished with 26 home runs and 75 RBI while hitting .291 in 131 games, his fewest played since 1948.

After spending nine seasons with Cleveland, Doby was traded on October 25, 1955, to the Chicago White Sox for Chico Carrasquel and Jim Busby. Chicago was looking for a consistent home run hitter after finishing the season with 116 home runs as a team. "The search is over for a long ball hitter. We've certainly needed a consistent one—and we've been eying Doby for some time," said White Sox vice president Chuck Comiskey.

Doby finished the 1956 season with a .268 batting average and led the team with 24 home runs and 102 RBI. Chicago finished 1956 in third place in the AL with an 85–69 record.

His 1957 home run total of 14 tied for the team-high, as he managed a .288 average and recorded 79 RBI, second highest on the team after former Indians teammate "Minnie" Miñoso.

Doby was part of a December 3, 1957, multiplayer trade between the White Sox and Baltimore Orioles. He then was traded again on April 1 to Cleveland along with Don Ferrarese for Gene Woodling, Bud Daley, and Dick Williams.

In 1958, he appeared in 89 games with the Indians and had a .289 batting average, 13 home runs, and 45 RBI. He was sent to the Detroit Tigers on March 21, 1959, in exchange for Tito Francona.

With the Tigers, he appeared in 18 games and was the first African American player to play for the Tiger franchise. He hit .218 with four RBI before Detroit sold the 35-year-old Doby to the White Sox on May 13 for $20,000.

After 21 games with the White Sox in 1959,he was sent to Triple-A affiliate San Diego Padres of the Pacific Coast League. Doby fractured an ankle while sliding into third base after hitting a triple during a road game the Padres played against Sacramento, and was sent to a local hospital in Sacramento before going to Johns Hopkins Hospital for further evaluation. Doby worked out with the White Sox before the 1960 season, but due to nagging injuries, did not earn a roster spot. In late April he joined the Toronto Maple Leafs of the International League on a trial basis, but was released by the team on May 6, 1960 after X-rays showed bone deterioration in his affected ankle.

Doby had participated in baseball clinics as a member of a travel delegation from the State Department to Japan. In 1962, Doby came out of retirement and became one of the first Americans to play professional baseball in Japan's Nippon Professional Baseball league when he and Don Newcombe, a former teammate with the Newark Eagles, signed contracts with the Chunichi Dragons. After the 1962 season, Doby returned to the U.S. in October and resumed his work as a liquor retailer.

Doby finished his 13-year major-league career with a .283 batting average, accumulated 1,515 hits, 253 home runs, and 970 RBI in 1,533 games and 5,348 at-bats. Of his 1,533 career games, 1,146 of them were spent with the Indians.

After retiring as a player, Doby became a scout with the Montreal Expos in 1969 and served as a minor league instructor with the organization in 1970. He was batting coach under manager Gene Mauch from 1971 to 1973. He managed various teams during five seasons of winter league baseball in Venezuela.

Doby rejoined the Indians for the 1974 season as the first-base coach for manager Ken Aspromonte. When Aspromonte was fired after the 1974 season, the Indians named Frank Robinson the club's player-manager and baseball's first black manager. After Robinson's hire as manager, Doby returned to work for the Expos as a coach.

In 1976, Bill Veeck purchased the White Sox for a second time and hired Doby to be the team's batting coach. After firing the White Sox's manager and former Doby teammate Bob Lemon, Veeck replaced him with Doby on June 30, 1978. **At age 53, Doby became the second black manager in the majors after Robinson.**

The White Sox finished 71–90, including 37–50 under Doby, in what would be Doby's sole managerial role. Veeck hired player-manager Don Kessinger to succeed Doby. After removing Doby from the manager's role and reassigning him to batting coach, the position Doby held before being named manager, Veeck said, "Larry will always have a role on this team in some capacity." He served in that role for one additional season and resigned in October 1979.

The New York Times wrote, "In glorifying those who are first, the second is often forgotten. " Larry Doby integrated all those American League ballparks where Jackie Robinson never appeared. And he did it with class. During the 1997 season, when the long-departed Jackie

Robinson's number 42 was being retired throughout baseball, and the media were virtually ignoring the still-living Doby, an editorial in *Sports Illustrated* pointed out that Doby had to suffer the same indignities that Robinson did, and with nowhere near the media attention and implicit support.

Scoop Jackson in 2007 wrote, in response to the tradition of MLB players wearing jerseys in homage to Robinson, "Second place finishers in America are suckers". And so are those who make the story of history less simple than it needs to be. This sometimes happens in America. Those who don't come first or don't do things a certain way gets lost. They disappear. Jackie got all the publicity for putting up with it (racial slurs).

The Veterans Committee elected Doby at the age of 74 into the National Baseball Hall of Fame on March 3, 1998. Upon hearing of Doby's election, Gene Mauch said, "You have to be some kind of special person to go through what Larry and Jackie Robinson went through. I'm not too sure there's a player in the game today who could handle it."

Doby died on June 18, 2003, at his home in Montclair, New Jersey, at age 79 after suffering from cancer.

Leroy "Satchel" Paige (HOF)

Cleveland Indians

July 9, 1948

Leroy Robert "Satchel" Paige (July 7, 1906–June 8, 1982) was an American Negro-league baseball and major-league baseball (MLB) pitcher who became a legend in his own lifetime by being considered by some as perhaps the best pitcher in baseball history.

Paige was a right-handed pitcher, and **at age 42 in 1948, he was the oldest major-league rookie** while playing for the Cleveland Indians. He played with the St. Louis Browns until age 47, and represented them in the All-Star Game in 1952 and 1953. At that time, he was the first player who had played in the Negro leagues to pitch in the World Series.

Additionally, he was the first black player elected by the Committee on Negro Baseball Leagues to be inducted in the National Baseball Hall of Fame, in 1971.

Paige began his career for the semiprofessional Mobile Tigers from 1924 to 1926. He began his professional baseball career in 1926 with the Chattanooga Black Lookouts of the Negro Southern League and became one of the most famous and successful players from the Negro leagues. While his outstanding control as a pitcher first got him noticed, it was his infectious, cocky, enthusiastic personality and his love for the game that made him a star.

Part way through the 1927 season, Paige's contract was sold to the Birmingham Black Barons of the major Negro National League (NNL). According to Paige's first memoir, his contract was for $450 per month, but in his second memoir he said it was for $275.

He finished the 1927 season with a 7–1 record including 69 strike-outs and 26 walks in 89⅓ innings.

Over the next two seasons (1928–'29), Paige went 12–5 and 10–9 while recording 176 strikeouts.

In 1929, due to his increased earning potential, Barons owner R. T. Jackson would "rent" Paige out to other ball clubs for a game or two to draw a decent crowd with both Jackson and Paige taking a cut.

In the spring of 1930, Jackson leased him to the Baltimore Black Sox, who had won the 1929 American Negro League championship. Paige, as a Southerner, found that he was an outsider on the Black Sox, and his teammates considered him a hick.

In midsummer of 1930, Paige returned to Birmingham, where he pitched well the rest of the summer, going 7–4.

In September 1931, Paige joined a Negro All-Star team organized by Tom Wilson, called the Philadelphia Giants, to play in the California Winter League. This was the first of nine winters that he played in a league that provided ongoing competition between elite black and white baseball players, including major- and minor-league players. He finished the winter with a 6–0 record and 70 strikeouts in 58 innings.

In 1932, Gus Greenlee signed Josh Gibson, Oscar Charleston, and Ted "Double Duty" Radcliffe away from Cumberland Posey's Homestead Grays to assemble one of the finest baseball clubs in history the Pittsburgh Crawfords. Paige took the mound when the Crawfords opened the season on April 30th in their newly built stadium, Greenlee Field, the first completely black-owned stadium in the country.

In 1933 Paige went 10–4, allowing 3.19 runs per game and striking out 92 in $132\frac{2}{3}$ innings.

In the 1933 season, Greenlee organized a new Negro National League, which survived for 16 years. Despite Greenlee's efforts to control his biggest star, Paige followed his own schedule and was often late to games when he was scheduled to pitch. In August, he jumped the Crawfords, accepting an offer from Neil Churchill's North Dakota semipro team, the Bismarcks (sometimes known as the "Bismarck Churchills" today), of $400 and a late-model car for just 1 month of work.

Back with the Crawfords 1934 was perhaps the best season of Paige's career, as he went 14–2 in league games while allowing 2.16 runs per game, recording 144 strikeouts, and giving up only 26 walks·

In 1934 The Denver Post conducted an annual baseball tournament (sometimes known as the "Little World Series") that attracted semi-pro and independent professional teams from across the country. In 1934 it was open, for the first time, to black players. Greenlee leased Paige to the Colored House of David, a prominent barnstorming team of white men who represented a religious commune and wore beards. Their manager was Hall of Fame pitcher Grover Cleveland Alexander. Paige pitched shutouts in his first two starts, striking out 14 and 18. The final, championship game was his third start in five days and he faced the Kansas City Monarchs, at the time an independent, barnstorming team who were participating in the tournament with a lineup augmented by Negro league stars Turkey Stearnes and Sam Bankhead. Paige faced Chet Brewer before a crowd of 11,120. Paige won the pitchers' duel 2–1, striking out 12 Monarchs for a tournament total of 44 strikeouts in 28 innings. The 1934 tournament was Paige's first major exposure in front of the white press.

Paige received his first East–West All Star Game selection in 1934. Playing for the East, Paige came in during the sixth inning with a man on second and the score tied 0–0 and proceeded to strike out Alec Radcliffe as well as retire Turkey Stearnes and Mule Suttles on soft fly balls. The East scored one run in the top of the eighth and Paige held the West scoreless the rest of the game, giving him his first All-Star Game victory. Twenty-seven years after winning the second ever East-West All-Star Game, Paige was also the winning pitcher of the 1961 East-West Game, that being the next to last in the series.

Despite an outstanding season, Paige had a strong competitor for best Negro league pitcher of 1934, the 21-year-old Slim Jones of the Philadelphia Stars, who went 22–3 in league games. In September, a four-team charity benefit doubleheader was played at Yankee Stadium, with the second game featuring a faceoff between Paige and Jones. Paige recalled driving all night from Pittsburgh and parking near the stadium, then falling asleep in the car. A batboy found and woke him and he got into uniform just in time for his scheduled start. In a game that was sometimes described as the greatest game in Negro league history, Paige and Jones battled to a 1–1 tie that was called because of darkness. A rematch was scheduled and this time Paige and the Crawfords beat Jones and the Stars 3–1.

That fall, Paige faced off against major league star Dizzy Dean, who that season had won 30 regular season games plus two more in the World Series. In an exhibition game in Cleveland, Paige struck out 13 while beating Dean 4–1, although for that game Dean was playing with a minor league team. Later, while playing in the California Winter

League, Paige faced Dean in front of 18,000 fans in Los Angeles with Dean's team, including major league stars like Wally Berger. The two teams battled for thirteen innings with Paige's team finally winning 1–0. Bill Veeck, future owner of the Cleveland Indians, St. Louis Browns, and Chicago White Sox, was watching the game and many years later described it as "the greatest pitchers' battle I have ever seen. Paige and Dean would continue to barnstorm against each other until 1945.

In the spring of 1935, Greenlee refused Paige's request to raise his $250 per month salary, so Paige decided to return to Bismarck for the same $400 per month and late model used car that he got before. Paige dominated the competition, with a 29–2 record, 321 strikeouts, and only 16 walks.

Later that season, in September, Paige could not return to the NNL because he was banned from the league for the 1935 season for jumping to the Bismarck team. J. L. Wilkinson, owner of the independent Kansas City Monarchs, signed Paige on a game-by-game basis through the end of the season.

In 1936, Paige returned to Pittsburgh where Greenlee agreed to Paige's salary demands and gave him a $600-per-month contract, by far the highest at that time in the Negro leagues. In games for which complete box scores are available, Paige went 5–0, allowed 3.21 runs per game, and struck out 47 in $47\frac{2}{3}$ innings.

In 1937, Paige and several Negro-league stars such as Sam Bankhead and "Cool Papa" Bell left the Negro leagues to play in the Dominican Republic for more money. Paige had an 8–2 record, and his team won the championship.

In 1938, Greenlee, who still held Paige's NNL contract, again made an unsuccessful attempt to sign Paige. Greenlee then sold his contract to the Newark Eagles for $5,000, but they could not sign him either. Paige instead went to play in the Mexican League.

In 1939, with his arm injured, Paige suddenly found himself unemployable. One ball club owner was willing to give him a chance to play ball again—J. L. Wilkinson of the Monarchs. Wilkinson offered him the modest opportunity to play, not for the Negro American League Monarchs, but for a second-string barnstorming team called the Travelers, which was now renamed the Satchel Paige All-Stars. Paige would pitch when he could and play first base when he could not. Managed by Newt Joseph, large crowds turned out to see Paige throw an inning or two. Relying on junk balls, Paige recalled, "Everybody'd heard I was a fast baller, and here I was throwing Alley Oops and bloopers and underhand and sidearm and any way I could to get the ball up to the plate and get it over, maybe even for a strike."

Sometime that summer Paige's fastball returned.

Because of Paige's strong gate appeal, there was considerable demand by outside teams for leasing Paige's services to pitch for a single game. With infrequent league games, Wilkinson booked Paige to pitch for small-town teams or other Negro-league teams at rates ranging from a third of the total receipts to a fixed fee $250 to $2,000 per game, plus expenses. Wilkinson purchased a Douglas DC-3 airplane to ferry Paige around to these outside appearances. Because of the larger gate when Paige pitched, the Monarchs' owners could also insist on a larger share of the receipts from their road games. Wilkinson and Paige each kept a share of the fees. By the early 1940s, Paige's estimated annual earnings were $40,000, which was four times the pay of the average player on the major-league New York Yankees and nearly matched the pay of their top star, Joe DiMaggio.

Hoping for some publicity for Paige, who had received relatively little coverage while pitching in the surrounding area with the Travelers, Wilkinson arranged for Paige to pitch on opening day of 1941 for the New York Black Yankees. Appearing in front of a crowd of 20,000 fans at Yankee Stadium, Paige pitched a complete game, 5–3 victory, striking out eight players. As intended, the contest brought considerable coverage from both the black and white media, including a pictorial by *Life* magazine.

On July 4,1941 some Negro League promoters rented Sportsman's Park in St. Louis for a game between the two marquee African Americans teams in the country, the Chicago American Giants and Paige's Kansas City Monarchs. The major attraction was Paige, the cocky hurler, who at 35 was already a legend. As game time approached Paige delivered a bold ultimatum. He would refuse to pitch unless the stands were desegregated. After a contentious standoff the promoters relented and 20,000 integrated fans watched the game. Three months later Paige again demanded integration for a tour with Bob Fellers barnstorming team. In 1944 Browns and Cardinals games at Sportsman's Park were officially desegregated.

From 1940-1947 Satchel played for the Kansas City Monarchs. The Monarchs won the Negro American League pennant again in 1942. For the first time since 1927, the champions of the two leagues, Kansas City and Washington/Homestead, met in the Negro World Series. Paige started game one in Washington and pitched five shutout innings. The Monarchs scored their first run in the top of the sixth. In the bottom of 6th inning Jack Matchett relieved Paige and finished the game with Kansas City adding seven more runs to win 8–0

Paige was the West's starting pitcher in the 1943 East-West All-Star Game, played before a record 51,723 fans in Comiskey Park. He pitched three scoreless innings without giving up a hit, struck out four, walked one and was credited as the winning pitcher in the West's 2–1 victory. As a batter, he hit a double to lead off the bottom of the third inning and then was lifted for a pitch runner to "thunderous applause".

World War II caused a large number of baseball players to be inducted into military service. Among Paige's Kansas City teammates, Connie Johnson, Buck O'Neil, and Ted Strong entered military service and Willard Brown followed them the following season. Paige's

Selective Service records show that during the war his draft status evolved from 1-A (available to be drafted) to 2-A (deferred in support of national health, safety, or interest) to the final 4-A (too old for service, even though when he registered he gave a birth date of 1908, two years younger than his actual birth date).

Paige continued to play and the available statistics show a slip in performance in 1943, with a 6–8 record and a 4.59 run average for the Monarchs. The Monarchs' string of four straight pennants ended, as the Negro American League title was captured by the Birmingham Black Barons in 1943 and 1944 and by the Cleveland Buckeyes in 1945.

Before the 1944 East-West All-Star Game, black baseball's most lucrative event, Paige grabbed headlines when he demanded that the owners contribute the receipts to the war relief fund, thus threatening a player strike if they did not agree. The owners were able to turn the other players and fans against Paige, however, when they revealed that Paige had received $800 for participating in the 1943 game (in contrast to the $50 paid to the other players) and had demanded an extra cut for the 1944 game as well, Paige was removed from the roster and the strike was averted when the owners agreed to raise the player payments (the East's team accepted $200 each, while the West's players agreed to $100).

In 1946, many of the Monarchs' players, including Willard Brown, Connie Johnson, Buck O'Neil, Ford Smith, and Ted Strong, returned from military service and the team led the NAL in both the first and second halves, capturing the league pennant. O'Neil led the league in batting average, Brown in home runs, Johnson in wins, and Paige in earned run average.

The Monarchs faced the Newark Eagles in the 1946 Negro World Series. The first game was played at the Polo Grounds and Hilton Smith started for the Monarchs. The Monarchs held a 1–0 lead in the bottom of the sixth when Smith walked Larry Doby to lead off the inning. Paige was called in to relieve. Paige struck out Monte Irvin and Lenny Pearson, but Doby stole second and Paige gave up a single to Johnny Davis, which tied the game. In the top of the seventh, the Monarchs got the lead back when Paige hit a single, advanced to second on an error, and scored on a hit by Herb Souell. Paige shut down the Eagles for the rest of the game, striking out eight and allowing four hits over four innings, and was credited with the win.

In 1946, Bob Feller organized the first whistle-stop tour to use airplanes to travel from site to site. His tour has been described as "the most ambitious baseball undertaking since John McGraw and Charles Comiskey dreamed up their round-the-world junket in 1913. For his team, Feller recruited all-stars from both major leagues. As his main opponent, he asked Paige to head a team of Negro league all-stars.

Feller's team included 1946 American League batting champion, Mickey Vernon at first base, Johnny Beradino at second, Phil Rizzuto at shortstop, and Ken Keltner at third. The outfielders were Jeff Heath, Charlie Keller, and Sam Chapman. After the World Series was over, National League batting champion Stan Musial would also join the tour. Catching was shared by Jim Hegan and Frankie Hayes. In addition to Feller, the pitching staff included Bob Lemon, Dutch Leonard, Johnny Sain, Spud Chandler, and Fred Hutchinson

With help from J.L. Wilkinson and Tom Baird, Paige assembled a team that included first baseman Buck O'Neil, second baseman Hank Thompson, shortstops Chico Renfroe and Artie Wilson, third basemen Howard Easterling and Herb Souell, outfielders Gene Benson and Johnny Davis, catcher Quincy Trouppe and pitchers Barney Brown, Gentry Jessup, Rufus Lewis, Hilton Smith and Neck Stanley.

Feller scheduled 35 games in 31 cities in 17 different states, all to be played in 27 days. The tour would require 13,000 miles of travel. Several same-day multi-city doubleheaders were to be played. Feller leased two DC-3 airplanes, with "Bob Feller All-Stars" painted on one fuselage and "Satchel Paige All-Stars" on the other. While Feller's team would face several other opponents, the majority of the games were against Paige's team. Feller and Paige would start each game whenever possible and usually pitch one to five innings.

In 1947 and 1948 Satchel played for the Kansas City Monarchs and also continued to barnstorm.

Finally, on July 7, 1948, with his Cleveland Indians in a pennant race and in desperate need of pitching, Indians owner Bill Veeck brought Paige in to try out with Indians player-manager Lou Boudreau.

On that same day, his 42nd birthday, Paige signed his first major-league contract, for $40,000 for the 3 months remaining in the season, becoming the first Negro pitcher in the American League and the seventh Negro big leaguer overall. Larry Doby, who broke the color barrier in the American League at the age of 23 in 1947, would be a teammate of Paige.

On July 9, 1948, Paige became the oldest man ever to debut in the major leagues, at the age of 42 years and 2 days.

Paige got his first big-league victory on July 15, 1948, the night after he pitched in an exhibition game against the Brooklyn Dodgers in front of 65,000 people in Cleveland's Municipal Stadium.

On August 3, 1948, with the Indians one game behind the Athletics, Boudreau started Paige against the Washington Senators in Cleveland. The 72,562 people in attendance set a record for a major-league night game. Although a nervous Paige walked two of the first three batters and gave up a triple to Bud Stewart to fall behind 2–0, by the time he left in the seventh, the Indians were up 4–2 and held on to give him his second victory.

His next start was at Comiskey Park in Chicago. Approximately 51,013 people paid to see the game, but many thousands more stormed the turnstiles and crashed into the park, overwhelming the few dozen ticket takers. Paige went the distance, shutting out the White Sox, 5–0, debunking the assumption that nine innings of pitching were now beyond his capabilities.

Some 201,829 people had come to see his last three starts. For his game in Cleveland, 78,382 people came to see Paige, a full 6,000 more people than the previous night game attendance record. Paige went the distance, giving up two singles and one double for his second consecutive three-hit shutout. At that point in the season, Paige was 5–1 with an astoundingly low 1.33 ERA.

He made one appearance in the 1948 World Series. He pitched two-thirds of an inning in game five.

Paige ended the 1948 season with a 6–1 record with a 2.48 ERA, 2 shutouts, 43 strikeouts, 22 walks and 61 base hits allowed in 72⅔ innings.

The following year was not nearly as good for Paige as his previous season. He ended the 1949 season with a 4–7 record and was 1–3 in his starts with a 3.04 ERA. After the season, with Veeck selling the team to pay for his divorce, the Indians gave Paige his unconditional release.

Penniless, Paige returned to his barnstorming days after being released from the Indians. In 1950, he signed with the Philadelphia Stars in the Eastern Division of the NAL for $800 per game. When Veeck bought an 80 percent interest in the St. Louis Browns, he soon signed Paige.

In his first game back in the major leagues, on July 18, 1951 against the Washington Senators, Paige pitched six innings of shutout baseball until the seventh when he gave up three runs. He ended the season with a 3–4 record and a 4.79 ERA.

By July 4, 1952 with Paige having worked in 25 games, Casey Stengel named him to the American League All-Star team, making him **the first black pitcher on an AL All-Star team.** Paige finished the year 12–10 with a 3.07 ERA for a team that lost 90 games.

Paige ended 1953 with a disappointing 3–9 record, but a respectable 3.53 ERA. Paige was released after the season when Veeck once again had to sell the team.

Paige then signed for $300 a month and a percentage of the gate to play for the Monarchs again in winter ball.

In 1954 and 1955, Paige, along with Sam Bankhead, "Cool Papa" Bell, and other black stars, played in the Dominican Republic, where Paige went 8–1, and his team won the championship.

In 1956, Veeck once again came to Paige's rescue when, after taking control of the Phillies' Triple-A farm team, the Miami Marlins of the International League, he signed Paige to a contract for $15,000 and a percentage of the gate.

In Paige's first game as a Marlin, he pitched a complete game, four-hit shutout. Paige finished the season 11–4 with an ERA of 1.86 with 79 strikeouts and only 28 walks. This time, when Veeck left the team, Paige was allowed to stay on for 2 more years.

In 1957, the Marlins finished in sixth place, but Paige had a 10–8 record with 76 strikeouts versus 11 walks and 2.42 ERA.

In 1958, he was fined several times throughout the year, for being late and missing practices, and finished 10–10, saying that he would not return to Miami the following season.

In 1959, Paige returned to his barnstorming roots and signed a pitching contract with the Havana Cuban Stars who were owned by Dempsey Hovland. Paige was in and out of baseball, pitching sporadically over the next decade.

In 1961, at the age of 55, Paige signed on with the Triple-A Portland Beavers of the Pacific Coast League, pitching 25 innings, striking out 19, and giving up eight earned runs.

In 1965, Kansas City Athletics owner Charles O. Finley signed Paige, 59 at the time, for one game. On September 25th against the Boston Red Sox, Finley invited several Negro-league veterans including "Cool Papa" Bell to be introduced before the game. In the fourth inning, Paige took the mound to be removed according to the plan by Haywood Sullivan. He walked off to a standing ovation from the small crowd of 9,289. The lights dimmed and, led by the PA announcer, the fans lit matches and cigarette lighters while singing "The Old Gray Mare."

In 1966, Paige pitched in his last game in organized baseball when he pitched for the Carolina League's Peninsula Grays of Hampton, Virginia, against Greensboro Patriots. Interestingly, Peninsula used their backup catcher that day, rather than play their regular starter, a young Johnny Bench.

Bill Veeck learned Paige could not collect any pension money because he was 30 days short of having enough time to qualify. He called Tommy Reynolds, who owned the Atlanta Braves, and told him he had a moral obligation to hire the pitcher as a coach for 30 days. Paige needed the money badly. Tommy hired Paige despite his coach's cautions that "Satchel" was very old and might have a heart attack on the field. Mr. Paige survived and drew his pension.

Bowie Kuhn replaced William Eckert as the commissioner of baseball in 1969. In the wake of Ted Williams's 1966 Hall of Fame induction speech urging the induction of Negro leaguers, and on the recommendation of the Baseball Writers' Association of America, Kuhn empowered a 10-man committee to sift through hundreds of names and nominate the first group of four Negro-league players to go to the Hall of Fame. Because Paige pitched in Greensboro in 1966, he would not have been eligible for enshrinement until 1971, as players have to be out of professional baseball for at least 5 years before they can be elected. All of the men on the committee agreed that Paige had to be the first Negro-league player to get elected, so this gave Kuhn plenty of time to create some sort of Negro-league branch in the Hall of Fame. On February 9, 1971, Kuhn announced that Paige would be the first member of the Negro wing of the Hall of Fame. Because many in the press saw the suggestion of a "Negro wing" as separate-but-equal and denounced major-league baseball for the idea, by the time that Paige's induction came around on August 9, Kuhn convinced the owners and the private trust of the Hall of Fame that there should be no separate wing after all. It was decided that all who had been chosen and all who would be chosen would get their plaques in the "regular" section of the Hall of Fame.

Paige died of a heart attack at the age of 75 at his home in Kansas City on June 8, 1982.

Cleveland Indians

"Minnie" Miñoso

April 19, 1949

First black Cuban to play in the major leagues

Miñoso only had 16 at-bats with Cleveland in 1949 due to their very strong lineup. He was sent down to the minors and then traded to the Chicago White Sox in 1951 and became the first black player that year for the White Sox.

See Chapter 6 for more details on Miñoso.

Cleveland Indians

"Luke" Easter

August 11, 1949

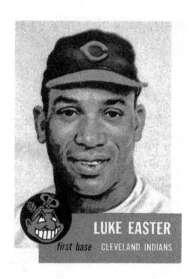

LUKE EASTER
first base CLEVELAND INDIANS

Luscious "Luke" Easter (August 4, 1915–March 29, 1979) was a professional baseball player in major-league baseball and the Negro leagues. He batted left-handed, threw right-handed. The birth year listed here is drawn from census data. Easter himself listed multiple birth years ranging from 1911 to 1921 on different occasions, so some ambiguity as to the correct year exists for his birth year.

"Luke" Easter attended the same high school as fellow Negro-league star Quincy Trouppe before dropping out in the ninth grade.

In 1937, Easter joined the top team in the area, a semipro outfit called the St. Louis Titanium Giants. The team was made up of African Americans employed by the National Lead Company. Players would work their factory job during the week, often with time off to practice, then play baseball for the company on weekends. Easter earned $20 per week, plus another ten to twenty on the weekends for baseball games. A left-handed hitting first baseman, he was known for towering home runs. During his 5 years with the Giants, they fielded a very competitive team. Also featuring Sam Jethroe (see Boston Braves), they went 6–0 in exhibitions against teams from the Negro American League in 1940.

With World War II raging and America soon to enter the fray, Luscious "Luke" Easter, serial number 37 368 805, was inducted into the army of the United States at Jefferson Barracks in St. Louis on June 22, 1942. Easter was separated from the army at Fort Leonard Wood on July 3, 1943, and thereafter, worked in the defense industry.

Following the war's end in 1945, "Luke" Easter had tryouts with two Negro National League teams, the Kansas City Monarchs and the Chicago American Giants. Both teams felt he was too big and awkward to be a good ballplayer despite his previous success with the Titanium Giants.

Manager "Candy Jim" Taylor of the American Giants elected not to sign Easter but referred him to promoter Abe Saperstein—famous as the founder of the Harlem Globetrotters. At that time, Saperstein was founding a new touring baseball team, the Cincinnati Crescents. Saperstein signed Easter, and after a successful 1946 season, sold him to the Homestead Grays in Washington DC.

Easter was a solid contributor to the Grays in 1947 and excelled in 1948.

His success attracted the attention of Bill Veeck, owner of the Cleveland Indians, who purchased his contract from the Grays. A knee injury in spring training in 1949 cost Easter a spot on the major league roster at the start of the season. He batted .363, along with 25 home runs and 80 RBI playing in the Indians minor league. This performance impressed the Indians so much that they called Easter up for a brief appearance at the end of the season, and early in 1950, traded All-Star Mickey Vernon to open up first base for him.

In 1950, as a 34-year-old rookie, Easter continued his power hitting, ranking among the league leaders in home runs and RBI. He batted .280 with 28 home runs and 107 RBI's.

He continued to produce in 1951 batting .270 with 27 home runs and 103 RBI's.

In 1952 he batted .263 with 31 home runs and 97 RBI's while finishing thirteenth in Most Valuable Player voting.

He played in only 68 MLB games in 1953, spending part of the year at AAA, and finished his major-league career with six games in 1954 as continuing knee and ankle problems, as well as advancing age, brought his major-league career to an end.

Easter continued to play professionally at AAA, even though his leg injuries had reduced his running speed to a limp. He played regularly for the Ottawa Athletics, Charleston Senators, Buffalo Bisons, and Rochester Red Wings, and won the International League's MVP Award with the Bison's in 1957 while batting .279 with 40 home runs and 128 RBI's.

He ultimately retired as a player in 1963, at the age of 48, and worked for several years after that as a coach. He became a 2008 inductee in the International League Hall of Fame.

After his days as a coach, Easter returned to the Cleveland area. On March 29, 1979, he was shot and killed by two thugs outside a bank at East 260th Street and Euclid Avenue in Cleveland while transporting over $35,000 from payroll checks. Police reports indicated that two robbers armed with shotguns approached Easter and after refusing to turn over the funds, he was shot twice at close range.

Cleveland Indians

Harry "Suitcase" Simpson

April 21, 1951

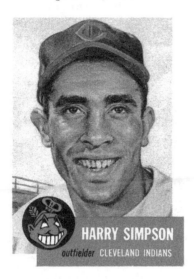

Harry Leon "Suitcase" Simpson (December 3, 1925–April 3, 1979) was an African American outfielder and first baseman in major-league baseball that played for the Cleveland Indians, Kansas City Athletics, New York Yankees, Chicago White Sox, and Pittsburgh Pirates in his 8-year career. He played in the World Series with the New York Yankees in 1957.

He was one of the earliest black players in the American League, playing first with the Cleveland Indians in 1951. His nickname of "Suitcase" originated from his being frequently traded during his playing career is a common misconception. According to the 1951 *Cleveland Indians Sketch Book*, he was called "Suitcase" by sportswriters after the *Toonerville Trolley* character, "Suitcase" Simpson, because of his size 13 shoes with feet as large as suitcases.

In September of 1941, with conflict escalating in Europe, Harry enlisted in the army and was assigned to Fort Benning, Georgia, for basic training serving until the war ended in 1945.

Goose Curry, manager of the Philadelphia Stars of the Negro National League, signed Simpson for his team in 1946. Originally a right-handed pitcher, Simpson moved to the outfield and hit a respectable .333 in 52 games.

With the Stars in 1947, his average slipped to .244, and a dejected Simpson started to second-guess his career choice. Life in the Negro leagues was hard, and Simpson became discouraged. He left the Stars and got a sales job outside of baseball. Johnnie, his wife, convinced Harry that his future was in baseball. She pleaded with him to return to the diamond and he followed her wishes.

In 1948, Simpson caught the eye of NBA coach Eddie Gottlieb, who doubled as an unofficial baseball scout. Gottlieb was greatly impressed. Based on glowing recommendations, eight major-league scouts offered a tryout; all declined the opportunity to sign the prospect. At his own expense, Gottlieb financed a trip to Arizona for Simpson to get a look-see by Cleveland Indians general manager Hank Greenberg. The Indians, owned by Bill Veeck, had signed Larry Doby to be the first black player in the American League and were one of the first major-league teams to scout and sign black players. During a split-squad game, Harry went 4-for-4, including two home runs, and Greenberg hustled to sign Gottlieb's protégé.

In 1949, Simpson was assigned to the Wilkes-Barre Indians of the Class-A Eastern League. He hit .305, leading the league with 31 home runs, 120 runs batted in, and 125 runs scored.

In 1950, Simpson was promoted to the San Diego Padres of the Pacific Coast League. He hit .323 and led the loop with 156 RBI in the 200-game season, also contributing 19 triples and 33 home runs.

Harry reported to the Indians' 1951 training camp in Tucson, Arizona. The Indians roster included four black players: Larry Doby, "Luke" Easter, "Minnie" Miñoso, and Simpson. According to several sources, including *The Sporting News*, Indians management wondered if four Negroes on the club were too many.

When it came time to trim the roster, Greenberg decided to stick with Simpson and peddle "Minnie" Miñoso to the Chicago White Sox. Harry hit over .400 during spring training but wound up having a disappointing 1951 season, with 332 at-bats, hitting only .229 while driving in a measly 24 runs. The pressure on Simpson was magnified when Miñoso went on to become an All Star with the White Sox.

Experiencing a hot start in 1952 (.347 by May 10th), he cooled to .266 by season's end with 10 home runs and 65 RBI. Simpson was a durable player participating in 146 of Cleveland's 155 games. His .266 average was slightly above the Indians' team average of .262.

In spring training of 1953, the Indians changed Simpson's stance. Simpson ultimately saw his average dip to .227 in 82 games with the Indians.

The 1954 Cleveland Indians won 111 games while claiming the American League flag, but it was without the services of Simpson. On March 24, he broke his wrist on a close play at the plate. Doctors predicted a recovery period of 6 weeks and the club decided to send Simpson back to the minors. The wrist healed, and Harry returned to the lineup with the Indianapolis Indians, playing in an even 100 games. The club finished at the top of the American Association, and Simpson contributed a .282 average with 12 home runs.

Spring training of 1955 and the arrival of Ralph Kiner proved that room no longer existed on the Indians' roster for the trim out-fielder. Simpson was sold to the Kansas City Athletics on May 11th and he hit for a 301 average, making him a fan favorite. He also showed his versatility by playing all three outfield positions as well as first base.

The year 1956 was a banner one for Simpson. He hit .293 with 21 homers and 105 RBI's. Naming him to the All-Star team, Yankees manager Casey Stengel took note of his long, smooth stride in the outfield and strong throwing arm and called him the best right fielder in the league.

In 1957, Simpson was traded to the Yankees. Simpson was hitting .296 when traded to the Yankees on June 15th, along with pitcher Ryne Duren and outfielder Jim Pisoni in exchange for infielder Billy Martin, pitcher Ralph Terry, infielder-outfielder Woody Held, and outfielder Bob Martyn. He knew he'd platoon with the Yankees, and history showed that he wasn't at his best coming off the bench. He ended the season hitting .250 in 75 games.

During the 1957 World Series, Simpson and Elston Howard alternated at first base, playing for an injured "Moose" Skowron. Simpson hit a disappointing .083 in the Fall Classic as the Milwaukee Braves prevailed over the Yankees in seven games.

Simpson was hitting a mere .216 on June 15, 1958, when the Yankees traded him back to Kansas City, along with pitcher Bob Grim for A's hurlers Duke Maas and Virgil Trucks. The deal was announced during a Yankees game against the Detroit Tigers, but Casey Stengel decided to send Harry up as a pinch hitter anyway. Back in Kansas City, he posted a .264 average in 78 games.

Simpson signed a contact with the A's for the 1959 season. On May 2nd, Harry was hitting a solid .286, but the A's sent him to the Chicago White Sox in exchange for infielder Ray Boone. Simpson batted only .187 in 38 games with the White Sox before being dealt to the Pittsburgh Pirates on August 25th for slugging infielder Ted Kluszewski, a 34-year-old veteran of 13 National League seasons. Simpson got into only nine games with the Pirates, hitting .267 in 15 at-bats.

In 1959 the White Sox bought Simpson back from the Pirates on October 13th. Simpson was about the unluckiest player in all of major-league baseball during 1959; his timing in and out of Chicago cost him a World Series check.

In 1960, Simpson saw action with the PCL San Diego Padres, batting .222 in 95 games.

Back with the Padres in 1961, he appeared in 146 games, hitting .303 with 24 home runs and 105 RBI's.

In 1962, the veteran was back with the Indianapolis Indians, where he hit .279 in 132 games with 24 home runs.

He started 1963 in Indianapolis, hitting .382 in 11 games, before moving on to the Mexican League, Diablo Rojos, where he hit .334 with 21 home runs.

He continued with the Mexican team the Red Devils in 1964, hitting .306 with 14 homers.

He retired as a player in 1964.

All told, Simpson hit a respectable .266 in a career spanning 1951 through 1959 in 888 major-league games, 2,829 at bats; his on-base percentage registered a respectable .331. The versatile outfielder/first baseman had a career-fielding average of .984. All of these factors certainly contributed to his longevity in the days when each league had eight teams.

Harry Simpson died in Akron, Ohio, on April 3, 1979, at the age of 53 of a heart attack.

Cleveland Indians

Sam Jones

September 22, 1951

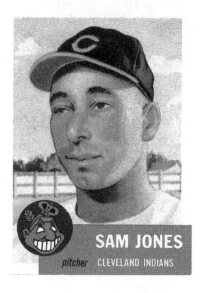

Samuel "Toothpick" Jones (December 14, 1925–November 5, 1971) was an American major-league baseball pitcher with the Cleveland Indians, Chicago Cubs, St. Louis Cardinals, San Francisco Giants, Detroit Tigers, and the Baltimore Orioles between 1951 and 1964.

Jones began his major-league career with the Cleveland Indians in 1951. When he entered a game on May 3, 1952, 39-year-old rookie Quincy Trouppe, a Negro-league veteran, was behind the plate. **Together, they formed the first black battery in American League history.**

In a pro-career that spanned 21 years (1947–67), Jones played in the Negro leagues and four Caribbean nations: Panama, Venezuela, Dominican Republic and Nicaragua. He was in the major leagues for eight full seasons (1955–62) and parts of four others (1951–52,

1963–64). His last four summers were spent as a player-coach in the minor leagues.

Samuel Jones was born Daniel Pore Franklin in Stewartsville, Ohio, on December 14, 1925. Although the Social Security Death Index gives the year as 1923, census records and Sam's gravestone show 1925, in line with baseball reference books.

He joined the army around 1943 (records have been lost). He was stationed in Orlando, Florida during World War II while considering making the Army his career.

Quincy Trouppe (Negro league player and manager) was the man who got Sam to leave the army and turn pro. He promised the soldier $550 a month, more than five times his army salary, and painted a colorful picture of the baseball life.

Jones signed, in 1947 to play with the Cleveland Buckeyes of the Negro American League. Veteran catcher Quincy Trouppe was the club's manager. In July 1947, Sam became a Buckeye and a full-time pitcher. He was 4–2 for Buckeyes that year. However, almost no box scores of these games were published, and only limited statistics were kept. A Sporting News feature on Sam in June 1951 gave his '47 record as 6–3.

Returning to the Buckeyes in 1948, Jones posted a 9–8 record—or possibly 13–8, as noted in the June 1951 *Sporting News* article.

Sam himself got a first look from the Indians in 1948, but an unnamed scout dismissed him with a brief "won't do."

After the '48 season ended, Sam joined the Kansas City Royals, a touring Negro-league squad, handpicked by "Satchel" Paige.

In November 1948, Sam signed to pitch in Panama with the Spur Cola Colonites, one of four teams in that nation's former pro league. Edric "León" Kellman, the Panamanian third baseman of the Buckeyes, managed the team and was almost certainly the man who brought Jones to play in Panama.

In 1949, the Negro National League had disbanded and the Negro American League was declining. Jones left for the Southern Minnesota League, a strong semipro circuit. Ben Sternberg, manager of the Rochester Royals, signed Sam thanks to his connections with Abe Saperstein. Saperstein, owner of the Harlem Globetrotters basketball team, was also active as owner and booking agent in the Negro leagues.

Jones became the Southern Minny's most feared pitcher. He won 10 and lost just 2 during the 1949 regular season.

That fall of 1949, Jones entered "organized baseball." Wilbur Hayes, business manager of the Buckeyes, had kept lobbying Hank Greenberg of the Indians on his pitcher's behalf. Greenberg, then farm director and later general manager, remained doubtful but agreed to bring Sam in for a tryout in November. His eyes were quickly opened.

Jones pitched for Spur Cola again in the winter of 1949–'50.

In 1950, Jones helped the Wilkes-Barre Barons win the championship of the Class A Eastern League. His 17–8 record included a 9–0 start. He led the league in strikeouts with 169, and his 2.71 ERA ranked second.

Spring 1951 saw Jones in camp with the Indians, but on March 9, he was assigned to the San Diego Padres of the Pacific Coast League. Jones did have a strong if not an extraordinary year. After a 9–4 start, which included a couple of tough shutout losses, he finished 16–13 with a 2.76 ERA. He struck out a league-leading 246 batters in 266 innings, and his 21 complete games also led the PCL.

The Indians called up Sam in September 1951. **He made his debut on September 22nd** in relief at Detroit, getting the last two outs in the eighth inning as the Indians lost, 9–4. His first major-league start came on the last day of the season against Detroit. Sam lost a tough 2–1 duel as he walked the bases loaded in the seventh inning.

Jones pitched in the Puerto Rican Winter League in the winter of 1951–52 with the San Juan Senadores. Sam had a fine season, tallying 13–5 with a 2.51 ERA. His 146 strikeouts in 167 innings led the league.

In 1952, Jones reported for spring training, but he left camp for a while to rest his arm. Upon his return, he remained on Cleveland's roster until being optioned to Triple-A Indianapolis on August 18th. With Cleveland he was seldom used, starting just four times in 14 outings. The results were poor with his statistics 2–3, 7.25 ERA, 37 walks and six homers during 36 innings.

Sam pitched the 1953 season with Indianapolis in the American Association. Jones posted a so-so record in '53 (10–12, 3.32) and did not see any major-league action.

Sam returned to better form in 1954 with a 15–8 record, and with a 3.75 ERA, despite four shutouts. Yet, he remained stuck at Indianapolis and grew disenchanted.

On September 30th the Indians finally traded Jones sending him to the Chicago Cubs (along with $60,000 and Gale Wade) for a player to be named later. That player turned out to be Ralph Kiner, Hall of Fame slugger, who had just one season left in him due to a bad back. Kiner was also an old teammate and friend of Hank Greenberg's.

In the winter of 1954–55, Sam returned to Puerto Rico, this time playing for Santurce. Sam won the Triple Crown of pitching that season with his 14–4 record, 168 strikeouts in 158 innings and 1.77 ERA.

In 1955, near if not yet over 30, Jones finally got his chance in a major-league rotation. The Cubs were a sub-.500 team at 72–81. This had a bearing on Sam's record of 14 wins, 20 losses (most in the majors), and a 4.10 ERA. He walked 185 and hit 14 batters in 241⅔ innings pitched, leading in both categories as well as in strikeouts (198). **On May 12th, before a sparse crowd of 2,918 at Wrigley Field, he threw a no-hitter against the Pittsburgh Pirates.**

The 1956 campaign was subpar for Sam (9–14, 3.91), even though he led the NL again in strikeouts. On December 11th of that year the Cubs sent him to the St. Louis Cardinals in a nine-player deal.

With the Cards, although a sore elbow troubled him, he enjoyed a fairly good season in 1957 with a record of 12–9 and ERA of 3.60.

He went on to record 14–13 in 1958 with a club-record 225 strikeouts, breaking "Dizzy" Dean's 1933 mark. His 2.88 ERA was second in the NL behind Stu Miller.

On March 25, 1959, Devine traded Sam to San Francisco in a four-player swap. Budding star Bill White, who was stuck behind Orlando Cepeda with the Giants came to St. Louis. The Cards were looking to the future; the Giants wanted to win right then.

Jones went on to win 21 games that year against 15 losses, the second black (after Don Newcombe) to have a 20-win season. His 2.83 ERA was the NL's best. He started 35 games and relieved in 15 more, with four saves.

In 1960, the Giants gave their ace a raise to $35,000. On Opening Day (April 12th), Jones started the first game at the new Candlestick Park. With Vice President Richard Nixon in attendance, San Francisco beat St. Louis 3–1. The 1960 season was the last in which Jones was a big winner. His 18–14, 3.19 mark included yet another brush with a no-hitter.

In 1961, Jones dropped off to 8–8, 4.49. He was no longer a full-time starter, coming out of the bullpen 20 times in 37 games. The Giants left him available in the expansion draft after the season, and the Houston Colt .45's made him their thirteenth selection on October 10th. However, the Colts traded him to Detroit on December 1st.

Sam played in 1962 under a cloud of cancer. The radiation must have been draining, yet Jones still pitched in 30 games (2–4, 3.65), making six spot starts. He got the sense as the season wound down that the Tigers would release him. They did so, on September 28th, with only two games left to play.

However, Jones signed "for peanuts" with Toronto, the top farm club of the Milwaukee Braves, on April 26, 1963.

Sam spent a couple of months with the Maple Leafs, and then the Cardinals organization obtained him in late June of 1963. They assigned him to their Atlanta Crackers affiliate. Sam remained an effective pitcher at the Triple-A level (9–4, 2.57 between Toronto and Atlanta), and the Cards called him up that August. Sam won both his decisions and had two saves in 11 appearances for the Cardinals. He was released shortly after the 1963 season ended.

However, he did enjoy a last fling in the majors with the Baltimore Orioles in September of the 1964 season. The Orioles' Hank Bauer used Jones in short and long relief and he went 0–0, 2.61 in seven games.

The Orioles released Jones on October 20, closing out his major-league career. Sam's final marks were 102 wins and 101 losses, with a 3.59 ERA, and nine saves. He notched 1,376 strikeouts in 1,643⅓ innings, for an imposing ratio of 7.54 per nine innings. Among his 76 complete games, Jones threw 17 shutouts.

Sam did play in the minor leagues in 1965 thru 1967 totaling 26 wins.

In 1970, Jones died from a recurrence of neck cancer first diagnosed in 1962, in Morgantown, West Virginia, at the age of 45.

CHAPTER 3

St. Louis Browns

The Browns were cash-strapped and struggling to survive as the second team in one of the smallest cities in the Major Leagues. They had drawn only 93,267 fans during the entire 1936 season. Those numbers rose from 1940 to 1951 averaging about 350,000 per season.

In 1947 the St. Louis Browns brought up the third (Hank Thompson) and fourth (Willard Brown) black players to the major leagues in July. Many believe these two were solely financial promotions in hopes of increasing game attendance and that did not happen.

Thompson played decently for the last-place Browns, hitting .256, while Brown struggled, hitting under .200. The Browns showed no patience with either man sending both back to the Negro leagues in August 1947.

Thompson went on have a solid career with the New York Giants, while Brown, a negro-league star and a future Hall of Famer, never played in the majors again.

In 1951, after Bill Veeck purchased the team, he signed "Satchel" Paige to play for the Browns.

In 1954, the Browns moved to Baltimore and were renamed the Orioles. The next black players were Chuck Diering in 1954 who played in 128 games and in 1955, Dave Pope, who played in 86 games as members of the Baltimore Orioles.

St. Louis Browns

Hank Thompson

July 17, 1947

Hank Thompson played in only 27 games in 1947 for the Browns, hitting .256 in 78 at-bats. He was released and later signed by the New York Giants and became the first black player for the Giants playing on the same day as "Monte" Irvin.

See Chapter 4 (NY Giants) for more details on Hank.

The .256 batting average Thompson had in 1946 was considerably better than the Browns team batting average of .241 for the year. Thompson was returned to the Kansas City Monarchs. Bill DeWitt told the media they "had failed to reach major-league standards." When viewed from afar, the trial appeared to be solely a quick attempt to increase attendance, and when that failed, the two were dumped.

DeWitt was a man of questionable racial tendencies who later, as the owner of the Cincinnati Reds, allegedly ordered rookie Pete Rose to stop hanging around the colored players and demonstrated his ability to judge "major-league standards" when he pawned off Frank Robinson for Milt Pappas, Jack Baldschun, and Dick Simpson in one of the worst trades in baseball history.

St. Louis Browns

Willard Brown (HOF)

July 19, 1947

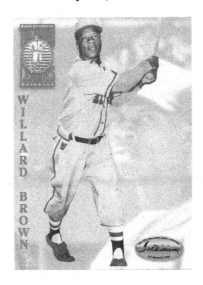

When Jackie Robinson broke into the Major Leagues in 1947, Willard was already 36 years old. His professional baseball career had begun in 1934 with the Monroe Monarchs. Willard was still a highly regarded hitter in the Negro Leagues in the mid 1940's, so much that the St. Louis Browns signed him as one of their first black ball players and immediately promoted him to their Major League roster. Brown's stay in the Major Leagues was short lived. He appeared in only 21 games, hit one home run, registered 6 runs batted in and posted a lowly .179 batting average.

As Brown shared with his best friend Bill Beverly (Negro League pitcher from 1950-1955) during an interview in Houston, Texas: "The pressure and indignities were unbearable, I was unhappy. I wasn't willing to put up with all that crap just to say I played Major League baseball. I knew I was a good player and that was enough for me." After his stint with the

St. Louis Browns, Brown went back to the Kansas City Monarchs and picked up where he had left off as the most dominant hitter in Negro League baseball.

Willard was considered one of black baseball's premier home-run hitter of the 1940s

Willard Brown was a slugger who was exceptionally fast on the field, a good base runner, and an excellent glove man with a great arm. Noted as a big-game player, he was at his best in front of a large crowd.

Brown first began playing baseball as a youngster in Shreveport, Louisiana and in 1934,he signed with the Negro Southern League's Monroe Monarchs for $10 a week as a shortstop and pitcher. After only 1 year, he was signed by Kansas City Monarchs' owner, J. L. Wilkinson, who offered Brown a $250 bonus, $125 per month, and $1 day meal money.

He began his Puerto Rican career in 1941–1942 with Humacao team as a second baseman and batted .410. Nicknamed "Esse Hombre" (The Man) in Puerto Rico, where he played winter ball, he hit for a lifetime .350 batting average and won three consecutive batting titles (1946–1950), with averages of .390, .432, and .353. During this span, he also won three home-run titles, establishing the all-time record of 27 home runs in the winter of 1947–1948 and following with totals of 18, 16, and 14.

After serving in World War II he returned to Puerto Rico as an outfielder with Santurce team for the rest of his career. Beginning in 1946, he had consecutive averages of .390, .432, .323, .353, .325, .295, .342, and .265. After a 2-year absence, he played a final season with Santurce in 1956–1957, but hit only .261.

In the United States, "Home Run" Brown played on the great Monarch teams that dominated the Negro American League from 1937 to 1942, winning five pennants in 6 years, contributing averages of .371, .356, .336, .337, and .365 to the pennant efforts, exclusive of 1940, when he opted to play in Mexico.

In 1942, one of his best years, Willard was hitting .429 at the All-Star break and batted cleanup for the West squad in the East-West All-Star game. After the midseason classic, he continued his slugging as the Monarchs captured another pennant and met the Negro National League champion Homestead Grays in the first World Series between the Negro American League and the Negro National League. With Brown continuing his hot bat, hitting .412 and a home run, the Monarchs swept the Grays four straight.

In 1943, Brown hit .345 and made another All-Star appearance before entering military service for 2 years (1944–1945), but the Monarchs had lost too many players to the service to secure another pennant.

In the army Brown was among those in the 5,000 ships that crossed the English Channel during the Normandy invasion.

After his discharge in 1946, Brown had little difficulty readjusting to baseball, batting .348 and clubbing a Negro league high 13 home runs in while leading the Monarchs to another pennant.

The following year, 1947, Jackie Robinson made his major-league debut with the Brooklyn Dodgers, and once the color barrier was lifted, Brown and Hank Thompson were signed by the St. Louis Browns.

At that time in the minors, Brown was labeled a "can't miss" prospect by major-league scouts and sent directly to the Browns without an adjustment period in the minor leagues. After playing briefly (21 games) and hitting only .179 with one homer, he was released.

Brown thought that they should have been farmed out after their release and given another chance after a period of adjustment. Thompson did get a second chance with the New York Giants and made good on his second opportunity, but Brown never received a second chance. A highlight to his major-league career was that his lone **home run was the first ever hit in the American League by a black player**.

After his release in 1947, he returned to the Monarchs, where he hit .336 for the remainder of the year.

In 1948, he resumed his barrage on Negro American League pitching with a .374 average while slugging a league-leading 18 home runs.

In 1949, he hit .371, ending his career in the Negro leagues with a .355 lifetime batting average and six All-Star appearances.

In 1950, he played in the Border League with Ottawa, where he hit .352. In the twilight of his career, then moving to the Texas League for 4 years (1953–1956), where he hit .310, .314, .301, and .299 with 23, 35, 19, and 14 home runs, respectively.

Willard gave organized baseball one more try when he spent four seasons in the Texas League from 1953 through 1956. During these seasons, Brown put up very respectable numbers during his Texas League career. He hit over 96 home runs with 405 RBI's and batted over .300 during his years in the Texas League but was not given an opportunity to return to Major League baseball.

His final appearance in professional baseball was with Santurce in Puerto Rico during the following winter (1956–1957), only hitting .261 with two home runs in 23 at-bats.

He was inducted into the National Baseball Hall of Fame in 2006. His big-league statistics—21 games, a .179 batting average tells the most incomplete story possible of the player who was Willard Brown.

His Hall of Fame plaque, however, speaks volumes about the pioneer who was one of the Negro leagues' greatest power hitters. In his minor-league career, he averaged about .342, with an average of 23 home runs and 125 RBI.

Willard Brown passed away on August 4, 1996, in Houston. He was 81, had been suffering from Alzheimer's disease since 1989, and had entered a Veteran's Administration hospital in the early '90s.

St. Louis Browns

Leroy "Satchel" Paige (HOF)

July 18, 1951

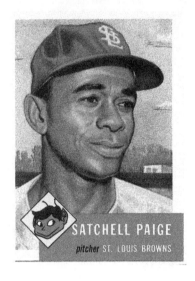

Leroy "Satchel" Paige played for the Cleveland Indians in 1947–'48 **(see Chapter 2 for more details),** but after Bill Veeck sold the team, he was released.

In 1951 when Veeck purchased the Browns, Satchel was signed again with them.

In 1971, "Satchel" was elected to the National Baseball Hall of Fame becoming the first player elected from the Negro leagues.

CHAPTER 4

New York Giants

The New York Giants were very aggressive in signing and bringing black players to the major leagues. Starting with "Monte" Irvin and Hank Thompson who appeared on the same day (7/8/49), with "Monte" appearing first in the game.

The Giants also promoted the fourteenth player (Ray Noble) and the fifteenth (Artie Wilson), who both appeared on the same day (4/8/51), with Ray appearing first.

On May 25, 1951, Willie Mays made his first appearance in major-league baseball.

New York Giants

"Monte" Irvin (HOF)

July 8, 1949

First black player on the New York Giants
(He played the same day, however two innings sooner than
Hank Thompson.)

Monford "Monte" Irvin (February 25, 1919–January 11, 2016) was an American left fielder and right fielder in the Negro leagues and major-league baseball (MLB) who played with the Newark Eagles (1938–'42 and '1946–'48), New York Giants (1949–'55), and Chicago Cubs (1956).

Irvin played for the Newark Eagles of the Negro National League in 1938. Larry Doby, the first player to break the color barrier in the American League was Irvin's double play partner with Newark at one time. After hitting high batting averages of .422 and .396 (1940–'41), Irvin asked for a raise before the 1942 season. When that was denied, he left the Negro leagues for the Mexican League, where he won a triple crown; he had a .397 batting average and 20 home runs in 63 games.

Following the 1942 Mexican-League season, Irvin was drafted into the military, interrupting his career by military service from 1943 to 1945.

Joining the army's GS Engineers, 13th Battalion, for the next 3 years, Irvin was deployed to England, France, and Belgium where he served in the Battle of the Bulge. Irvin's military service left him with ringing in his ears, which ultimately affected his coordination.

After World War II, Irvin was approached by Brooklyn Dodgers executive Branch Rickey about being signed for the major leagues, but Rickey was unwilling to pay Newark any compensation.

He returned to the Newark Eagles in 1946 to lead his team to a league pennant. Irvin won his second batting championship, hitting .401. He remained with Newark through 1948, but no stats exist.

In 1949, the New York Giants paid $5,000 for his contract and Monte was assigned to Jersey City of the International League, where he batted .373.

He debuted with the Giants on July 8, 1949, as a pinch hitter and appeared in 38 games batting .224

Back with Jersey City in 1950, he was called up to the Giants after hitting .510 with 10 HRs in 18 games.

In 1950 appearing in 110 games, Irvin batted .299 with15 home runs and 66 RBI's for the Giants, playing first base and the outfield.

In 1951, Irvin helped spark the Giants' miraculous comeback to overtake the Dodgers in the pennant race, batting .312 with 24 homers and a league-best 121 RBI's, ending in the World Series (he went 11–24 batting .458). **During the same year Irvin teamed with Hank Thompson and Willie Mays to form the first all-black outfield in the majors.**

In 1952, having sustained a broken leg in April, he appeared in only 46 games that season, hitting .310 with four home runs and 21 RBI.

In 1953, he hit .329 with 21 HRs and 97 RBI.

During the 1954 season, he hit .262 with 19 HRs and 64 RBI. The Giants won that year's World Series in four games, while Irvin collected two hits in nine at-bats.

In 1955, Irvin had been sent down to the minor leagues, where he hit 14 home runs in 75 games for the Minneapolis Millers.

The Chicago Cubs drafted Monte from the Giants and signed him before the 1956 season. Irvin appeared in 111 games for the Cubs that year, hitting .271 with 15 home runs.

In his major-league career, Irvin batted .293, with 99 home runs, 443 RBI, 366 runs scored, 731 hits, 97 doubles, 31 triples, and 28 stolen bases, with 351 walks for a .383 on-base percentage, and 1,187 total bases for a .475 slugging average in 764 games played.

A back injury led to Irvin's retirement as a player in 1957.

In 1973, he was inducted into the Baseball Hall of Fame, primarily on the basis of his play in the Negro leagues.

On January 11, 2016, Irvin died of natural causes in Houston at the age of 96. At the time of his death, Irvin was the oldest living African American to have played in the major leagues, as well as the oldest living member of a World Series winning team.

New York Giants

Hank Thompson

July 8, 1949

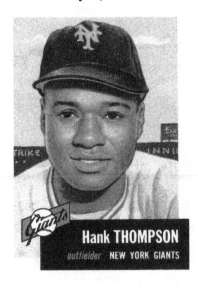

Hank THOMPSON
outfielder NEW YORK GIANTS

(He played same day as "Monte" Irvin, but two innings later).

Henry Curtis Thompson (December 8, 1925–September 30, 1969), best known as **Hank Thompson,** was an American player in the Negro leagues and major-league baseball who played primarily as a third baseman, becoming the second black player on the New York Giants team. As a left-handed batter, he played with the Dallas Green Monarchs (1941), Kansas City Monarchs (1943, 1946–48), St. Louis Browns (1947), and New York Giants (1949–56). **He was the first black baseball player to play in both the National and American leagues**

By the young age of 17 in 1943, Hank was playing professionally for the Kansas City Monarchs. He was given the nickname "Machine Gun" due to the rapid-fire line drives that flew off his bat in practice.

After a solid first season, he was drafted into the army in March of 1944. Hank served in an all-black engineering unit. His unit made it to Europe in time to participate in heavy action, particularly during the Battle of the Bulge, where he handled a machine gun.

Discharged from the army in 1946, Thompson returned to the Monarchs and became one of their star players. The 5′ 9″, 170-pound player generated serious power and consistently hit between .300 and .350 as he returned to playing.

Thompson played his first game with the Browns on July 17, 1947, integrating the Browns' lineup 2 days before Willard Brown made his debut as the second black player on the Browns. The following day, July 20th, Thompson played second base and Brown played center field for the Browns in a game against the Boston Red Sox. **That game marked the first time that two black players appeared in the same major league lineup.**

Thompson was with the Browns a little over a month and hit only .256 in 27 games, mainly at second base. On August 23rd, he was released, and he rejoined the Monarchs through the '48 season. Thompson batted .375 in his last year with Kansas City, finishing third in the batting race and leading the league in steals with 20.

On July 4, 1949, the New York Giants called Thompson up from the Giants' Jersey City farm club. He received $2,500 over the league minimum of $5,000. By signing with the Giants, Thompson earned a unique place in baseball history becoming the first black baseball player to play in both the National and American leagues.

Thompson and Irvin began the 1949 campaign with the Jersey City Giants and spent the first half of the year tearing up the international league. Irvin, being the bigger Negro-league name, outshined Thompson with Jersey City, although Hank's .296 batting average, 14 homers, and .447 on-base percentage, and .565 slugging average in

68 games were impressive. When the pair was called up to the parent club in July, Hank, who'd bounced between shortstop and left field with Jersey City, took over the Giants' regular second-base job. While Irvin stumbled in his first big-league exposure, Thompson hit a credible .280 and belted nine homers in 75 games.

In 1950, the Giants shifted Thompson to third base to clear second base for newly acquired Eddie Stanky. Often hitting in the cleanup spot, Hank enjoyed an excellent all around season, batting .289, smacking 20 homers and driving in a team-leading 91 runs in 148 games. In the field, he participated in 43 twin killings in 138 appearances at third base breaking Pie Traynor's 25-year-old National League record for double plays by a third baseman.

On a team filled with pleasant surprises, unsung veterans enjoying career years and unheralded rookies making headlines, Hank Thompson was the 1951 Giants' biggest disappointment. After his strong 1950 performance, the 25-year-old third baseman had been counted on to be a force in the middle of the New York lineup. Instead, he lost his regular job midseason and ended up watching the club's sensational stretch run for the pennant from the bench. Opening Day of that fateful 1951 season found Thompson manning third base and hitting in the third spot against the Boston Braves. He got off to a horrible start, but by June 4th his average was up to a respectable .278, and his seven home runs were the second-highest total on the club. However, by July 18th, the Giants eighty-eighth game of the season, Hank's average was down to .239, and he'd added only one homer to his total.

A few days later, it was announced that Thompson had been optioned to the Giants' Ottawa International League farm club with pitcher Al Corwin coming up to take his place. Hank never actually reported to Ottawa, instead, spending his time with the Giants working himself back into shape. Over the next 2 weeks, he made five pinch-hitting appearances with a lone single before he was optioned to the Giants' Minneapolis Millers farm team in the American Association.

Hank found his batting eye in Minneapolis, slamming seven homers and hitting .340 with a torrid 1.209 OPS (on-base percentage plus slugging average) in 14 games. Thanks largely to his phenomenal hitting; the Millers won 12 of the games in which he participated to climb back into the American Association pennant race before his recall to New York on August 28th.

In 1951, back with the Giants, Thompson resumed his place on the bench behind hot-hitting Bobby Thomson. After starting 68 of the Giants' first 88 games at third base, he didn't start another game for the remainder of the season. In fact, his only notable contribution to the "Miracle of Coogan's Bluff" came on September 16th when he replaced Bobby Thompson at third base after Bobby was ejected in the fourth inning of the second game of a doubleheader with the Pirates. Hank banged out two hits and drove in the go ahead run with a ninth-inning fly ball in a 6–4 Giants victory. His only other action after his recall was seven unsuccessful pinch-hitting appearances.

After finishing the 1951 season with a .235 batting average and only eight homers in 87 games, there did not appear to be a regular role for Thompson with the Giants the following season in 1952.

Left fielder "Monte" Irvin, the reigning National League RBI king, broke his leg before the start of the season. Thus, the Giants began their defense of the National League pennant with Thompson and newly acquired veteran Bob Elliott sharing play in left field. Hank handled his assignment well enough that he was entrusted with the Giants' center field job when Willie Mays was inducted into the army in late May. Eventually, Hank moved back to third base for the last third of the season, swapping positions with Bobby Thomson.

For the 1952 season, Hank started 51 games in center field, 43 at third base, and 17 in left field, while also filling in at second base and right field. He finished with a .260 batting average, 17 homers, and 67 RBI in 128 contests, while recording a solid .798 OPS.

Thompson spent the first month of the 1953 campaign warming the Giants' bench while highly touted rookie Daryl Spencer was tried at third base. Finally inserted back into the hot corner spot in mid-May, he responded with his finest big-league season. He appeared in only 114 games, sitting out most of the first month of the season and missing most of the last month after suffering a concussion when a bad-hop grounder knocked him out. Yet, he slammed 24 homers and drove in 74 runs while hitting .302. His .567 slugging average was the seventh highest in the National League that year, and his outstanding .967 OPS was the sixth-highest mark.

In 1954, Hank shook off a painful chipped kneecap suffered early in the campaign to set a career high with 26 homers, while hitting .263 and driving in 86 runs in 136 games for the world champion Giants. He also walked 90 times, finishing ninth in the league in on-base percentage and tenth in OPS.

In the Giants' four-game World Series sweep of the heavily favored Cleveland Indians, Hank posted an amazing .611 on-base percentage, hitting for a .364 average and breaking Lou Gehrig's record by drawing seven base on balls.

At only 29 years old with two fine seasons behind him going into the 1955 campaign, Thompson should have been at the peak of his career, but his average dropped to .245, and his home run output fell to 17.

In 1956, he injured his shoulder in spring training and lost his regular job to light-hitting rookie Foster Castleman. For the season, he hit only .235 with eight homers in 83 games, although he excelled as a pinch hitter, hitting .333 with a pair of homers in 24 pinch at-bats.

In 1957, his contract was sold to the minor-league Minneapolis Millers of the American Association, where he finished his career playing in 78 games while batting .243 with only 2 home runs and 19 RBI's.

In his 9-year career, Thompson batted .267, with 129 home runs, 482 runs batted in, 492 runs scored, 801 hits, 104 doubles, 34 triples, 33 stolen bases, 493 walks for a .372 on-base percentage, and 1,360 total bases for a .453 slugging average.

Thompson died at the young age of 43 following a seizure on September 30, 1969, 13 years to the day of his last game in the majors.

New York Giants

Ray Noble

April 18, 1951

Ray Noble
1951 NEW YORK GIANTS

Rafael "Ray" Noble Magee (March 15, 1919–May 8, 1998) was a Cuban catcher in the Negro leagues and major-league baseball.

In the winter of 1946–47, Noble played in the Cuban Winter League, joining the Cienfuegos Elefantes, playing with that team for 14 seasons. The Cuban league overlapped his time in the major leagues. Few statistics are available.

In that first winter-league season in 1946 he had only 82 at bats in 42 games. The Cubans became an informal Giants farm team when the first transactions between the clubs came in June 1949. The owner of the Cubans, Alex Pómpez, sold Noble, player-manager Ray Dandridge, and pitcher Dave Barnhill to the Giants for $21,000. It was the beginning of the end for the Cubans with the franchise going defunct after the 1950 season.

Noble finished the 1949 season with Jersey City, the Giants' Triple-A affiliate in the International League, where he batted .259 in 67 games.

In 1950, he was assigned to the Oakland Oaks of the Pacific Coast League and had a very strong year, hitting .316 with 15 homers and 76 RBI in 110 games for the PCL pennant-winners.

On October 11, 1950, Oakland and the Giants swung a deal in which Noble, shortstop Artie Wilson (another Negro-league star), and pitcher Al Gettel went to the New York Giants in exchange for four players and $125,000. Noble made the Giants' roster for 1951.

Noble was 32 years old when he broke into the big leagues with the New York Giants. **Making his big-league debut on April 18, 1951**, when he caught the ninth inning of a game at Braves Field in Boston. By coincidence, that inning also marked the debut in the majors of another notable Latino player, Luis Márquez from Puerto Rico for the Braves.

During the 1951 season, Noble appeared in 41 games behind the plate, with 26 starts. He hit .234 with five homers in 141 at-bats.

The winter of 1951–'52 was one of Noble's best. He hit .321-7-39 for Cienfuegos, finishing second in the batting race.

In 1953 with the Giants, he started well at the plate but slumped, finishing at .206 in 119 at-bats over 46 games. He then went back to play with Cienfuegos in Cuba. In the 1953–'54 season he tied for the league lead in homers with 10, while batting .281 and matching his winter high with 39 RBI. In late 1954 Cincinnati obtained Ray from the Havana Cuba club.

In 1955 he played for their minor league team batting .253.

In September 1955, Cincinnati traded Noble to the Kansas City Athletics for third baseman Hal Bevan. He spent the next three seasons in the A's organization as their starting catcher in Triple-A. He went on to spend 1956 at Columbus, 1957 and 1958 at Buffalo, hitting 21 and 20 homers consecutively in his 2 years with the Bisons.

Noble hit just .218 in his sporadic big-league opportunities yet, he continued in Triple-A as late as 1961. As did the other players of African descent in his era, Noble had to contend with racism in various ways. The unspoken practice of racial quotas influenced the Giants' roster in the early 1950s.

Noble's last season as a full-time player was 1959 when at 40 years of age, he hit .294 in 138 games for Houston of the American Association, which, at that time, was not affiliated with any major-league club.

Noble died in Cabrini Medical Center in Manhattan on May 9, 1998. The cause of death was from complications of diabetes. Noble was buried in Brooklyn's Cypress Hills Cemetery, which is also the resting place of Jackie Robinson.

New York Giants

Artie Wilson

April 18, 1951

Arthur Lee Wilson (October 28, 1920–October 31, 2010) was an all-star for the Birmingham Black Barons of Negro-league baseball before playing part of one season in major-league baseball for the New York Giants in 1951.

Artie appeared in the same game as Ray Noble. He only appeared in 19 games with 22 at-bats for the Giants despite his strong minor-league career.

Wilson played for the Birmingham Black Barons of the Negro American League from 1942 to 1948, where he was considered the league's best shortstop. During his time with the Black Barons, the team won the league championship in 1943, 1944, and 1948, advancing to, but never winning the Negro League World Series.

In the 1948 regular season, Wilson, who was known as an opposite field hitter, batted .402.

In 1948, the New York Yankees purchased Wilson's contract, and he was assigned to their Newark Bears minor-league team; but since his salary would have been less than he was making with Birmingham, he negotiated another contract with the San Diego Padres of the Pacific Coast League. The Yankees protested to baseball commissioner "Happy" Chandler, who voided Wilson's Padres' contract. The Yankees then sold Wilson to the Oakland Oaks of the Pacific Coast League, where he was the team's first black player and the roommate of Billy Martin. With Oakland, Wilson won the PCL batting title with a .348 average and also led in stolen bases with 47 in 1948.

In 1949 with Oakland he batted .350.

In 1950, Wilson went on to lead the PCL in runs with 168 and hits with 264, helping Oakland to the 1950 PCL Championship.

The New York Giants noticed Wilson's accomplishments, and he was called up for the 1951 season, where he was used as a utility infielder, a pinch runner and pinch hitter. But Wilson struggled in the big leagues, hitting only .182 in 22 at-bats. They sent him back to Oakland, ending his major-league career.

Back in the PCL, Wilson finished the 1951 season with Oakland and was sold to the Seattle Rainiers in 1952. Wilson also played with the Portland Beavers and Sacramento Solons of the PCL, winning three more PCL batting titles (with averages of .316, .332 and .336) in 1952-1954 before leaving baseball in 1957.

His career ultimately ended with a short comeback for the Beavers in 1962.

Wilson died in Portland, Oregon, on October 31, 2010, 3 days after celebrating his 90th birthday while suffering from Alzheimer's disease.

New York Giants

Willie Mays

May 25, 1951

Willie Mays Jr. (born May 6, 1931) is an American former major league baseball (MLB) center fielder who spent almost all of his 22-season career playing for the New York/San Francisco Giants, before finishing with the New York Mets.

Mays' professional baseball career began in 1947, while he was still in high school; he played briefly with the Chattanooga Choo-Choos in Tennessee during the summer. A short time later, Mays left the Choo-Choos and returned to his home state to join the Birmingham Black Barons of the Negro American League. Mays hit a respectable .262 for the 1949 season, but it was also his excellent fielding and base running that made him a standout.

The Brooklyn Dodgers scouted him and wanted Ray Blades (a Dodger scout) to negotiate a deal, but were too late. The New York Giants had already signed Mays on June 20, 1950 for $4,000 and assigned him to their Class-B affiliate in Trenton, New Jersey.

After Mays batted .353 in Trenton in 1950, he began the 1951 season with the class AAA Minneapolis Millers of the American Association. During his short time in Minneapolis, he batted .477 in 35 games and played excellent defense.

Mays was called up to the Giants on May 24, 1951, and **played in his first game for them on May 25, 1951.** Mays began his major-league career on a sour note, with no hits in his first 12 at-bats. Although his .274 average, 68 RBI, and 20 homers (in 121 games) were among the lowest of his career, he still won the 1951 Rookie of the Year Award.

The Giants went on to meet the New York Yankees in the 1951 World Series. **In Game 1, Mays, Hank Thompson, and Monte Irvin comprised the first all-African American outfield in major-league history** 4 years after the color line was broken.

The United States Army drafted Mays in 1952 during the Korean War and he subsequently missed most of that season and all of the 1953 season.

In 1954, Mays returned to the Giants and hit for a league-leading .345 batting average while slugging 41 home runs. Mays won the National League Most Valuable Player Award and the Hickok Belt as top professional athlete of the year.

The Giants won the National League pennant and the 1954 World Series, sweeping the Cleveland Indians in four games. The 1954 series is perhaps best remembered for "The Catch," an over-the-shoulder running grab by Mays in deep center field of the Polo Grounds of a long drive off the bat of Vic Wertz during the eighth inning of Game 1.

Mays went on to perform at a high level each of the last 3 years the Giants were in New York. In 1955, he led the league with 51 home runs.

In 1956, he hit 36 homers and stole 40 bases, being only the second player and first National League player to join the "30–30 club", which signifies 30 stolen bases and 30 home runs in the same season.

In 1957, the first season the Gold Glove Award was presented, he won the first of 12 consecutive Gold Glove Awards. In 1957, Mays became the fourth player in major-league history to join the 20-20-20 club (20 doubles, triples and home runs in the same season), something no player had accomplished since 1941. He batted .333 with 35 home runs, 97 RBI's and led the league in stolen bases with 38.

After the 1957 season, the Giants' franchise relocated to San Francisco, California.

In 1958, Mays vied for the National League batting title until the final game of the season. Mays collected three hits in that game to finish with a career-high .347, but Philadelphia Phillies' Richie Ashburn won the title with a .350 batting average.

In 1959, the Giants led by two games with only eight games to play, but only won two of their remaining games, finishing in fourth place. Willie batted .313 with 34 home runs and 104 RBI's. He also led the National League in stolen bases for the 4th consecutive year with 27.

In 1960 Mays batted .308 with 29 home runs and 103 RBI's.

Alvin Dark was hired to manage the Giants before the start of the 1961 season and named Mays team captain. Willie batted .308 with 40 home runs and 123 RBI's.

The Giants won the National League pennant in 1962, with Mays leading the team in eight offensive categories. He batted .304 with 141 RBI's and led the League in home runs with 49. The 1963 and 1964 seasons saw Mays batting in over 100 runs each year and hitting 97 total home runs, which led the League both years in home runs.

Mays won his second MVP Award in 1965 with a career-high 52 home runs. On September 13, 1965, he hit his 500th career home run off Don Nottebart. Mays played in over 150 games for 13 consecutive years (a major-league record) from 1954 to 1966.

The year 1966 was his last with 100 RBI's. Plagued by injuries that season, he managed only 13 home runs while batting .288

In 1967 through 1969, the stats for Willie Mays were not great, but still considered good.

In 1967, he had a .263 batting average with 22 homers and 70 RBI's.

In 1968, .he batted 289 with 23 homers and 79 RBI's.

In 1969 he batted 283 with 13 homers and 58 RBI's.

Mays enjoyed a good year in 1970, hitting 28 homers and batting .291.

He got off to a fast start in 1971, the year he turned 40. He had 15 home runs at the All-Star break but faded down the stretch and finished with only 18 for a season total while batting .271.

In May 1972, 41-year-old Mays was traded to the Mets for pitcher Charlie Williams and $50,000 ($292,522 in today standards).

At the time, the Giants' franchise was losing money. Owner Horace Stoneham could not guarantee Mays a pension after retirement, and the Mets offered Mays a coaching position upon his retirement.

Mays played a season and a half with the Mets before retiring. He played in 135 games. He batted .239 with 14 homers and 44 RBI's in 1972-1973.

He finished his career in the 1973 World Series, which the Mets lost to the Oakland Athletics in seven games.

Mays retired after the 1973 season with an impressive lifetime batting average of .302 and 660 home runs. His lifetime total of 7,095 outfield putouts remains the major-league record to this day.

Mays won two National League (NL) Most Valuable Player (MVP) awards, ended his career with 660 home runs (third at the time of his retirement) and won a record tying 12 Gold Glove Awards beginning in 1957 when the award was first introduced. Mays shares the record of most All-Star Games played with 24, along with Hank Aaron and Stan Musial.

Mays' career statistics and his longevity have led many to conclude that he may be the finest five-tool player ever. His ability to hit for average, run, field, throw and hit for power has been matched by very few.

He was elected to the Baseball Hall of Fame in 1979, his first year of eligibility.

CHAPTER 5

Boston Braves

In 1948, the Braves won the pennant behind the pitching of Warren Spahn and Johnny Sain who won 39 games between them. They lost the World Series to Cleveland 4-3. This may have been one of the reasons they did not look to integrate earlier. They also drew over 1,000,000 fans each year from 1946 thru 1949.

The Braves were not very active in the black player market until 1950 when their attendance dropped to less than 400,000.

In the 1950's many major-league baseball franchises sent scouts to watch Willie Mays play, but the Boston Braves were the first. The Browns scout who discovered him, Bud Maughn, had been following him for over a year and referred him to the Braves, who then packaged a deal that called for $7,500 down and $7,500 in 30 days for the Barons. They also planned to give Mays $6,000 in salary. The Giants signed Willie in June of 1950. Had the Browns been able to act more quickly, the Braves' franchise might have had both Mays and Hank Aaron in their outfield from 1954 to 1973.

Boston Braves

Sam Jethroe

April 18, 1950

Sam Jethroe *Boston Braves*™

Samuel Jethroe, nicknamed **"The Jet"** (January 20, 1918–June 18, 2001), was an American center fielder in the Negro league and Major League Baseball. He was the oldest Rookie of the Year at 33 in 1950 when he was honored.

From 1942 to 1948, Jethroe played for the Cleveland Buckeyes of the Negro American League, leading the league in stolen bases three times and Sam helped the team to two pennants as well as participating in the 1945 Negro World Series.

In 1943, Jethroe batted .291 while leading the league in both doubles (8) and triples (4).

During the 1944 season he won his first batting title with a .353 average and led the league with 14 doubles and 18 steals.

On April 16, 1945, following pressure from a Boston city councilman, Jethroe was one of three black players to try out for the Boston Red Sox on the recommendation of black sportswriter, Wendell Smith. After coaches Hugh Duffy and Larry Woodall observed the tryout, he was turned away along with Marvin Williams and Jackie Robinson, as the Red Sox had no plans to integrate their roster.

In 1945, Jethroe returned to the Buckeyes and won his second consecutive batting title with a .314 average, again leading the league with 10 triples and 21 stolen bases. The Buckeyes won the pennant under player-manager Quincy Trouppe with a 53–16 record and swept the Homestead Grays. In the Negro World Series, Jethroe hit .333, and Cleveland's pitching dominated the series as the Buckeyes outscored the Grays 15–3.

In 1946, Jethroe batted .310 and led the league in steals for the third straight year with 20 stolen bases.

He went on to bat .340 in 1947 as the Buckeyes took another pennant, but lost the Negro World Series to the New York Cubans. He was named to the East-West All-Star team five times (1942, 1944–47), and ended his Cleveland career with a .296 average in 1948.

Dodgers' general manager Branch Rickey acquired Jethroe's services from the Cleveland Buckeyes for a reported $5,000.

During the 1948–'49 seasons, Jethroe played for the Dodgers' Montreal Royals minor-league team in the International League. Jethroe took a pay cut from $700 a month to $400 when he joined Montreal Royals late in 1948. He batted .322 for them.

For Montreal in 1949, Sam dazzled the International League. The 32-year-old hit .326 and led the league in runs (154 in 153 games), hits (207), triples (19) and steals (89). He also hit 17 homers and drew

79 walks. The run, triple and steal totals were phenomenally high for the era.

In October 1949, he was sold to the Boston Braves for $150,000 by the Brooklyn Dodgers and added to the Braves' major league roster. The Dodgers had another young outfielder named Duke Snider rising in their system.

On April 18, 1950, Jethroe became the first black player on the Boston Braves' roster and contributed two hits, including a home run. He was named Rookie of the Year that season at age 33 (although he was believed to be 28) after hitting .273 with 100 runs, 18 home runs, and 58 runs batted in with 35 stolen bases topping the National League. He remains the oldest player to have won Rookie of the Year honors.

Jethroe enjoyed an almost identical, but perhaps slightly improved season in 1951 when he posted better figures in batting (.280), runs (101), RBI (65), hits (160), doubles (29), and triples (10), while hitting 18 homers. He also repeated his 35 steals, once again to lead the league.

In 1952, he experienced a bad slump, hitting .232, reportedly due to vision problems. Rumors were also circulating that he was older than his listed age. In addition, he was among the NL's top four batters in strikeouts each year.

Jethroe then spent 1953 with Triple-A Toledo, hitting .307. Before the 1954 season, he was one of six players acquired by the Pittsburgh Pirates in exchange for infielder Danny O'Connell, but Jethroe played only two games for the team, the last on April 15, 1954.

After that, he spent the next five seasons at Toronto in the International League. Despite being among the league leaders in hits, runs, and stolen bases during that period, his batting averages generally declined, and he never did get another chance in the majors.

During his four season major league career, he was a .261 hitter with 460 hits, 49 home runs, 280 runs, 181 RBI's, and 98 stolen bases during 442 games.

In 1994, Jethroe sued major-league baseball in an attempt to collect pension payments, being one of many former Negro leaguers who could not qualify for benefits due to the racial discrimination in the 1940's and 1950's. In 1997 major-league baseball decided to award a yearly payment plan of $10,000 to Negro league veterans, including Jethroe. This benefitted about 80-90 players.

Mr. Jethroe died of a heart attack in 2001 in Erie, Pa at the age of 82.

Boston Braves
Luis Márquez
April 18, 1951

Luis Márquez Sánchez (October 28, 1925–March 1, 1988,) was from Aguadilla, Puerto Rico becoming the third Puerto Rican to play in major-league baseball (after Hiram Bithorn and Luis Olmo) and was the second black player on the Boston Braves.

Márquez played in a total of 68 games in the major leagues, splitting his time in two seasons between the Boston Braves, the Chicago Cubs, and the Pittsburgh Pirates.

Márquez had begun playing professional baseball at the age 18 in the winter Puerto Rican League. He was voted as Rookie of the Year in the 1944–'45 season with the Mayaguez Indians.

He then led the league in 1945–'46 with 10 triples, while the following season (1947) he topped the circuit with 27 doubles, 14 home runs, and

69 runs scored. He also led the league in stolen bases in 1947–'48 (20) and 1948–'49 (29), the year Mayaguez won the PRL Championship.

While playing in his native country of Puerto Rico during the winter months, Márquez also played three seasons in the Negro National League. He was with the Baltimore Elite Giants and the Homestead Grays in 1946.

In 1947, he led the league with a .341 average for Homestead. He was playing for Homestead in 1948 when the league folded, and his contract reverted to the Elite Giants, which joined the Negro American League.

Márquez became a sought-after commodity among major-league teams, with both the New York Yankees and Cleveland Indians courting him during the winter of 1948–'49.

In late November, Cleveland Indians owner Bill Veeck paid Seeford Posey, secretary of the defunct Grays, $25,000 for a 120-day option on Márquez's contract. Meanwhile, the New York Yankees paid Baltimore $10,000 for Márquez's contract; proposing half down and half if he made the roster of their AAA International League team at Newark. **Márquez was the first black player signed by the Yankees organization.**

On March 14, 1949, Márquez reported to Newark's spring training site at Haines City, Fla. When Newark opened the International League season on April 21st, Márquez was in the Bears' lineup, along with Panamanian Negro second baseman, Frankie Austin.

Márquez's goal with Newark was to play well enough to get a spring training tryout with the Yankees for 1950.

In an unprecedented ruling in early May, however, Commissioner Albert B. Chandler ruled that Cleveland's option on Márquez was valid when New York bought him from the Elite Giants. Chandler ordered New York and Cleveland to make a trade with the Indians' Artie Wilson for the Yankees' Luis Márquez.

Devastated at being taken from the Yankees' organization, Márquez threatened to return to Puerto Rico, but Veeck was able to persuade him to report to Portland in the Pacific Coast League.

Márquez finished the 1949 season with the Beavers batting at .294. He had 32 stolen bases, and no doubt would have contended for the PCL lead if he'd been there for the league's complete season.

In 1950 Luis played for the Portland Beavers. Márquez earned the bases stolen title in 1950, with 38 swipes. He also led the league with 19 triples wile hitting .311.

In the Rule 5 draft (which allows teams to draft minor league players who have over 4 years of only minor league service) after the 1950 season, the Boston Braves claimed Márquez from Cleveland.

The Braves had visions of creating the fastest outfield in the majors by pairing Márquez with Sam Jethroe. If nothing else, the addition of another black player gave Jethroe a roommate on the road.

Major league competition was too fast for the speedy Márquez, however, and he was never able to earn a regular spot in the Braves' lineup.

In 1951, he appeared in 68 games, often used as a pinch runner. During the season he only hit .196 and was just 4-for-8 in stealing bases.

The Braves returned Márquez to the minors for 1952. He was integral to the Milwaukee Brewers' winning the American Association Championship in '52, batting .345 (third-best in the league) with 14 HRs and 99 RBI's.

When the Braves moved their AAA club to Toledo in 1953, Márquez once again teamed with Sam Jethroe as the Sox again won the AA title.

In the Rule 5 draft, the Cubs claimed Márquez for 1954. During a mere 6-week timeline, he batted .083 with Chicago, who then traded him to the Pirates in mid-June. Márquez faired a little better with Pittsburgh, batting .111 before the Bucs turned him back to the Braves and he was sent once again to Toledo. He never returned to the majors.

Márquez continued to play in the high minors through the 1963 season. In 1959, with Dallas, he led the American Association with a .345 batting mark.

He remained active in the Puerto Rican League ball, playing some 20 seasons in all. He retired as the league's all-time leader in hits (1,206), runs (768), and doubles (235).

Márquez was murdered in Puerto Rico during a domestic dispute on March 1, 1988.

CHAPTER 6

Chicago White Sox

The White Sox, due to large debt and ownership problems were a team with no black players on their roster until 1951. It was not until they realized the potential financial gains that they began to integrate aggressively.

In 1950–'51, they started to acquire black players via trades (Mi.oso), signings of (Hairston and Boyd), and purchase (Connie Johnson and Hector Rodriquez).

In 1951 thru 1957 they had attendance of over 1,000,000 fans each year.

From 1951 to 1967, the White Sox had their longest period of sustained success, scoring a winning record for 17 straight seasons. Known as the "Go-Go White Sox" for their tendency to focus on speed and getting on base, versus power hitting.

The 1950s saw several ownership changes within the Comiskey family due to deaths and lawsuits until the club was sold in 1958 to Bill Veeck.

Chicago White Sox

Orestes "Minnie" Miñoso

May 1, 1951

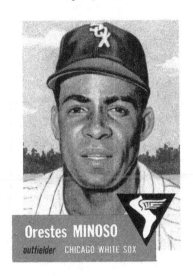

Orestes "Minnie" Miñoso November 29, 1925–March 1, 2015), was a Cuban Negro league and major-league baseball (MLB) player. His career included that he was the first black Cuban in the major leagues, the first black White Sox player and was voted Sporting News Rookie of the Year in 1951.

Minoso signed a contract with the team from the region of Marianao in Cuba in 1945 for $150 per month and moved into the Negro leagues with the New York Cubans in 1946, doubling his monthly salary.

He began his professional baseball career in 1946 and became an All-Star third baseman with the New York Cubans. Batting leadoff for the Cubans, he hit .309 in 1946 and followed up with a .356 average in 1947. He helped lead to Cubans to the Negro World Series title in 1947.

Miñoso remained with the Cubans until signing with the Cleveland Indians organization during the 1948 season, which started his minor-league career with the Dayton Indians of the Central League, batting .525 in 11 games.

On April 19, 1949, Miñoso made his major-league debut with the Cleveland Indians, becoming the first Black Cuban in the major leagues. During his debut in the big leagues he drew a walk as a pinch hitter in the seventh inning of a 5–1 road loss, then having his first hit in his next game on May 4th.

Miñoso had little further chance to make an impression. He had only 16 at-bats through May 13th before being sent back to the minor leagues.

Although the Indians were signing black players more aggressively than any other team in the American League, coming off their victory in the 1948 World Series, they were one of the strongest team in baseball.

Miñoso was then sent to the San Diego Padres of the Pacific Coast League for the rest of the 1949 season and all of 1950, batting .297 the first year and following up with a .339 average and 115 runs batted in 1950.

In 1951, Miñoso rejoined the Indians to start the season, but the team still could not find a spot for him in the lineup, as the Indians had Al Rosen at third base and Larry Doby, Dale Mitchell, and Bob Kennedy in the outfield. He consequently had only 14 at bats in 8 games during the month of April.

On April 30, 1951, the Indians sent Miñoso to the White Sox in a three team trade, getting relief pitcher Lou Brissie from the Athletics in exchange.

On May 1, 1951, Miñoso became the first black player on the White Sox. He was an instant star, maintaining a batting average over .350 through most of the first half of the season and finished the season hitting .324, second in the AL behind the .344 mark of the Athletics' Ferris Fain.

During the 1951 season he scored 112 runs (one short of Dom DiMaggio's league-leading total) in 138 games played, topping the league with 14 triples and 31 stolen bases.

Following the '51 season, he finished second in the American League's Rookie of the Year voting behind the Yankees' Gil McDougal, drawing a protest by the White Sox who stated Miñoso had better statistics in nearly every category. Additionally, Miñoso also finished fourth in the year's Most Valuable Player voting that same year.

Miñoso continued the next several years with outstanding play for Chicago. He led the American League in steals both in 1952 (with 22) and 1953 (with 25, also topping the league with 18 triples and 304 total bases) and batted .313 in 1953.

In 1954 Miñoso again finished second in the batting race with a .320 mark, trailing the .341 average by the Indians' Bobby Ávila.

In 1955, he finished the season with a .288 average, his lowest from 1953 through 1960.

In 1956, Miñoso topped American League left fielders again with 282 putouts and 10 assists. He continued to lead the league in triples again in 1956 with 11 while batting .316.

The 1957 season marked the first in which Gold Glove Awards were awarded, with Miñoso being chosen as the first honoree in left field. He also led the league in doubles with 36 and batted .310.

The White Sox traded Miñoso back to the Indians after the 1957 season in a four-player deal, with the White Sox getting pitcher Early

Wynn and outfielder Al Smith in exchange for Miñoso and third baseman Fred Hatfield.

With Cleveland, Miñoso hit career high 24 home runs in 1958 and
again led American League left fielders with 13 assists. He batted
.302 in both 1958 and 1959.

In 1959 he led all major-league left fielders with a career high 317
putouts and also led the American League again with 14 assists, re-
ceiving his second Gold Glove Award.

Miñoso was deeply disappointed missing the opportunity to play
for the White Sox during their 1959 pennant-winning season and
was thrilled to be traded back to Chicago in a seven-player deal in
December of '59, with Norm Cash being the top player sent in return.

Miñoso had his last great season in 1960 as he participated in his
last All-Star appearance (being a starter in both games), led the
American League with 184 hits, 105 RBI's, batting over .300 for the
eighth and final time and finished respectfully in fourth of the MVP
voting. He also had perhaps his best defensive season, leading all
major-league left fielders in putouts (277), assists (14), and double
plays (3), ultimately winning his third and final Gold Glove Award.

After the 1961 season with the White Sox where his average dropped
to .280, Miñoso was traded to the St. Louis Cardinals in exchange
for Joe Cunningham. During the 1962 season, he played in only 39
games, batting .196.

His contract was sold to the Washington Senators before the 1963
season, and after hitting .229, he was released that October of 1963.

He signed with the White Sox before the 1964 campaign but appeared in only 30 games that year, batting .226, almost exclusively
as a pinch hitter.

He retired from major league baseball after the 1964 season.

Starting in 1965, Miñoso played for the Charros de Jalisco of the Mexican League. Playing first base, he batted .360 in his first season, leading the league with 35 doubles and 106 runs scored. He continued to play in the Mexican League for the next eight seasons. He hit .265 with 12 home runs and 83 RBI in 1973 when he was 50 years old.

In 1976, Miñoso was called out of retirement, becoming a first- and third-base coach for three seasons for the White Sox. He also made three game appearances for the Sox that September in games against the California Angels, picking up one single in eight at bats, becoming at age 50, the fourth-oldest player ever to get a base hit in the major leagues.

In 1980, Miñoso at age 54, was activated again to play for the White Sox, and was a pinch hitter in two games, again against the Angels.

Miñoso was an American League (AL) All-Star for seven seasons and a Gold Glove winner for three seasons when he was in his 30's. He batted over .300 for eight seasons. He was the AL leader in triples and stolen bases three times each and in hits, doubles, and total bases once each. Minnie also led the American League in being hit by a pitch a record 10 years.

Miñoso became eligible for election to the National Baseball Hall of Fame in 1970, a year before the Hall began considering players from the Negro leagues or taking into account the accomplishments of major leaguers in the Negro leagues. He was ultimately dropped from the ballot for insufficient support.

He was then restored to the ballot 5 years after his final 1980 appearances as a player and finally began to receive support as a candidate, remaining on the ballot for 14 years before his eligibility expired; however, most of the writers voting by that point had little memory of him during his prime.

In 2001, historian Bill James selected Miñoso as the tenth-greatest left fielder of all time; based on the then-general belief that Miñoso was born in 1922 rather than 1925. James wrote, "Had he gotten the chance to play when he was 21 years old, I think he'd probably be rated among the top thirty players of all time."

Minnie Miñoso was the last Negro league player to play in a Major League game, appearing in two games for the 1980 Chicago White Sox.

Miñoso was found dead from pulmonary disease, at age of 90, in the driver's seat of his car in Chicago March 1, 2015, after attending a friend's birthday party.

Chicago White Sox

Sam Hairston

July 21, 1951

Samuel Harding Hairston (January 20, 1920–October 31, 1997) was a Negro-league baseball and major-league baseball player. He played for the Birmingham Black Barons and the Indianapolis Clowns of the Negro leagues and played part of one season (1951) with the Chicago White Sox as a catcher.

Sam only appeared in four games for the White Sox in 1951, but to some baseball purists, he is the first black player on the White Sox as he was the first Black African American.

In 1944, Hairston joined the Black Barons. He was a third baseman by trade, and one account held that he volunteered to back up starting catcher Ted "Double Duty" Radcliffe after "Duty" broke a finger.

In 1945, the Barons traded Sam to the Cincinnati-Indianapolis Clowns for Pepper Bassett. He spent the next six seasons with the Clowns, mainly as a catcher. During this time, Sam matured into a solid .300 hitter.

Sam won the Triple Crown for the Indianapolis Clowns in the Negro American League (NAL) in 1950 with a .424 batting average, 17 homers, and 71 RBI in 70 games.

Then in 1949–'50, he joined the Vargas Sabios (Wise Men) in the Venezuelan League to play winter ball.

The scout who signed Hairston was John Wesley Donaldson, the former star pitcher who became the first African American to join a big-league scouting staff when the White Sox hired him in June 1949. That summer, Donaldson also signed first baseman Bob "The Rope" Boyd from the Memphis Red Sox. Hairston and Boyd went on to finish the 1950 season with Colorado Springs in the Western League.

Sam then returned in 1950 to Venezuela and the Vargas club. He had an excellent winter season, hitting .375, including a 26-game hitting streak, which was then a league record.

Hairston and Boyd received a fair amount of press coverage during camp, but they were assigned to Triple-A Sacramento. Meanwhile, the White Sox obtained Orestes "Minnie" Miñoso in a three-way deal at the end of April, and the Cuban became their first player of African descent to appear in a regular season game.

The White Sox gave Sam his shot that July 1951 after backup catcher Gus Niarhos suffered a broken wrist on a foul tip. Hairston remained on the roster for approximately 5 weeks, appearing in just four games between July 21 and August 26. When Niarhos returned to action in early September, Sam was sent back to the minors.

Sam played nine more summers in the minors after that, all in the White Sox chain except for a portion of the 1958 season when he was with the Baltimore organization. Most of that time was spent at Class A, except for the 1954, 1957, and 1958 seasons when he played at AA and AAA levels hitting on average at a .260 level.

Hairston remained a very effective line-drive hitter, batting .304 lifetime in the minors with 53 homers. He was well over .300 in the four additional seasons he played for Colorado Springs (1952–'53; 1955–'56), including a league-leading .350 in 1955.

In May 1960, Sam retired as an active player to scout the Alabama area for the White Sox.

In the June 1967 issue, *Ebony* magazine noted that Hairston was one of eight full-time black scouts in the majors. In addition to him and Buck O'Neil, the others were Charles Gault (also of the White Sox), Quincy Trouppe and David "Showboat" Thomas (Cardinals), Hiram "Jack" Braithwaite (Senators), Alex Pómpez (Giants), and Bob Thurman (Reds).

Bill Veeck saw to it that Sam was hired as the White Sox bullpen coach in 1978.

For the last 12 years of his life, Sam was on the staff of the Birmingham Barons in the Double-A Southern League as a coach.

Hairston comes from a very large family of MLB players. As the father of MLB players Jerry Hairston Sr. and Johnny Hairston, He is also the respected grandfather of Jerry Hairston Jr. and Scott Hairston. A son, Sammy Hairston Jr., and three grandsons, Johnny Hairston Jr., Jeff Hairston, and Jason Hairston, also played in the minor leagues. The five Hairstons who have played in the majors are tied for the most ever with the Delahanty brothers. The two other three-generation MLB families have four members each: the Boone family (Ray, Bob, Bret, and Aaron) and the Bell family (Gus, Buddy, David, and Mike).

On October 31 1997 Hairston died from pulmonary cardiac arrest at the age of 77.

Chicago White Sox
Bob Boyd
September 8, 1951

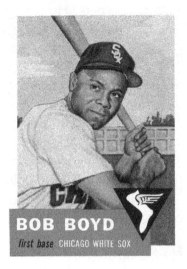

Robert Boyd (October 1, 1919- September 7, 2004) was an American first baseman in the Negro leagues and major-league baseball.

Nicknamed "Rope" for his line drive hitting, Boyd played in the Negro leagues with the Memphis Red Sox (1947–'49), and in the major leagues for the Chicago White Sox (1951, 1953–'54), Baltimore Orioles (1956–'60), Kansas City Athletics (1961), and Milwaukee Braves (1961).

It was in Mississippi and later in Memphis that Bobby developed the smooth swing that would lead to a .327 batting average in 4,337 Negro, minor, and major league times at bat.

He started his professional career in the Negro leagues with the Memphis Red Sox and played three seasons for them between 1947 and 1949, batting .352, .369, and .371, respectively.

World War II took Bobby from home where he served 2 years in the Quartermaster Corps.

Freed from the service in 1947, he went to work in a united warehouse but also decided to give baseball a serious try. He "walked on" to the Memphis Red Sox, a Negro American League team, where he was paid $175 a month. The team traveled and partly lived in a bus as it played both league games with a barnstorming schedule over a generous part of the eastern United States.

Boyd was in Negro baseball until 1950, never hitting under .352, playing in two East-West All-Star Games, and leading the league in hitting in 1947. By his final season, he was earning $500 a month and selling beer in the off-season.

It was White Sox scout John Donaldson, who arranged for Boyd to leave Memphis In 1950. Boyd became the first black player to sign with the Chicago White Sox. **He made his debut on September 8, 1951,** as the third black on the White Sox, basically a backup player and pinch hitter with the Sox.

Boyd never quite made it with the White Sox, bouncing back and forth from the minors to the White Sox. In Seattle Bobby hit .342 in the Pacific Coast League before playing his first dozen games with Chicago in September 1951.

Sent back to Seattle for 1952, he hit a league-leading .320 and stole 33 bases. That same year, he led the Winter League in Puerto Rico in hitting, giving him two league batting titles for the year, but he was still stuck in the minors.

After hitting .297 for one-third of a season in Chicago in 1953, he was still demoted to the minor leagues. In 1954, he was sent to the St. Louis Cardinals and played in their minor leagues batting .321 in 94 games.

He was in Cuba in 1956 when he learned he was to be given another chance in the majors. The Orioles General Manager Paul Richards had purchased his contract from the Houston minor league team, where he had hit .321 and .309 over two seasons (1953 and 1955).

Richards had been the White Sox manager and remembered Bobby's potential when he took over in Baltimore. He had the Birds draft Boyd from Houston in the Texas League, where he had gone reluctantly after the Cardinals obtained him from Chicago in 1954. Boyd was Richards' only draft choice in 1956. Bobby felt he owed much of his major-league career to Paul Richards, the Texas born manager who many believe may have been the most prejudiced against blacks of any he encountered but gave him a chance to play Major League Baseball.

In five seasons at Baltimore, all after his thirtieth birthday, he responded with averages above .300 four times. The one miss was a summer he was ill from a chronic ulcer that wasn't cured until after he left organized baseball.

In 1956 with the Orioles, he hit .311 with two homers and 11 RBI in 70 games.

With the Orioles Boyd enjoyed a career season in 1957. He finished fourth in the batting race with a .318 average. As the shortest first baseman at 5' 10" in the majors in 1957, Boyd led the league in putouts with 1,073 and his .991 was the third-best fielding percentage among American League regulars. Boyd's relatively small size also could have affected his power output. In his best major-league season, Boyd hit only seven home runs and had a total of just 19 in 1,936 major-league games, but he made up for that in part with speed as he hit 23 triples and 81 doubles.

In 1958, at Baltimore he batted .309 with a career-high seven home runs.

In 1959 he batted only .269 at Baltimore.

In 1960, the Orioles came up with a power-hitting first baseman, Jim Gentile, and Bobby was demoted to pinch-hit duty. He batted .321 in 71 games but only had 9 RBI's.

In 1961 he was traded to the Kansas City A's, who had Norm Siebern playing at first base. Norm was having a good year in 1961. Bobby did not, hitting only .229 in 26 games for Kansas City.

In 1961 Milwaukee purchased his contract from Kansas City for his only playing time in the National League where he batted .244 in 36 games.

Boyd ended his major-league career in 1961. He compiled a .293 batting average with 19 home runs and 175 RBI in 693 games.

Bob spent 2 more years trying. At Louisville and Oklahoma City in the American Association, he regained his batting eye, batting over .300 again. Even with the increase to his batting average, he did not receive a return call to the major leagues and retired after the 1963 season in the minor leagues.

Over the course of 14 years in organized baseball, he played in Colorado Springs, Sacramento, Seattle, Charleston, Toronto, Houston, Oklahoma City, Louisville, and San Antonio, as well as for Winter League teams in Puerto Rico and Cuba.

Bob is a member both of the Negro League Hall of Fame and of the National Baseball Congress Hall of Fame.

Bob Boyd died at age 84 in Wichita, Kansas on September 7, 2004 after a long battle with cancer.

CHAPTER 7

Philadelphia Athletics

The outlook in the 1940's was not bright for the Philadelphia Athletics. In fact, it was downright bleak. Problems from all sides beset the franchise. A bad team, sparse crowds, burdensome debt and internal strife all were set against the backdrop of playing in an old ballpark located in a declining neighborhood with limited parking and bad transportation. Grumblings were being heard from other American League clubs that were dissatisfied with the paltry receipts they were getting from games played in Philadelphia.

Philadelphia was a team owned by Connie Mack and family. Mack, several times, sold or traded his best players to reduce costs as his only income was from the baseball team.

In September 1932, Mack sold Al Simmons, Jimmy Dykes, and Mule Haas to the Chicago White Sox for $100,000.

In December 1933, Mack sent Lefty Grove, Rube Walberg, and Max Bishop to the Boston Red Sox for Bob Kline, "Rabbit" Warstler, and $125,000. Also in 1933, Connie Mack sold Mickey Cochrane to the Detroit Tigers for $100,000.

Mack has been accused of being a racist and hurting the quality of his team by turning down opportunities to acquire black stars. In the early years of integration he allowed black players to be prime targets for abuse by his Athletics. Larry Doby claimed that the Athletics engaged a professional heckler to torment him in Philadelphia and even paid the heckler to follow him to New York. Minnie Minoso remembered that Jimmy Dykes, who took over as A's manager in 1951, used to direct his pitchers to throw at him and called him names such as "black n----r so and so"and also "black dog".

The team and its fans appeared to have been as racist as the Philadelphia Phillies and had no desire for a black player on their team.

The Athletics brought up Bob Trice in 1953 as the first black player on the A's

The Athletics were sold and moved to Kansas City in 1954 due to poor attendance and other factors.

Philadelphia Athletics

Bob Trice

September 13, 1953

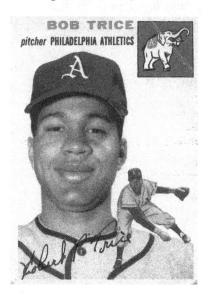

Robert Lee (Bob) Trice (August 28,1926-September 16, 1988) was a pitcher for 10 years (1949–1958); three in the Negro leagues (1949–1951); three in the majors (1953–1955); and eight in the minors (1951–1958). He was followed on the A's in 1954 by Vic Power (4/13/54) and Joe Taylor (8/6/54).

With the country embroiled in World War II, the 17-year-old Trice joined the US Navy on March 30, 1944. While in the Navy, the 6-foot-3, 190-pounder played first base for various base teams.

Discharged from the Navy on May 17, 1946, Trice went home to Weirton, where he joined his father working in a steel mill. According to Trice, he didn't last very long at the mill. "I worked there one day," said Trice, "and that was enough." He continued to play baseball, pitching for a nearby Steubenville, Ohio, semipro team. He also played left field and pitched for the Weirton Negro Stars.

In 1948 Trice caught the eye of the Homestead Grays. He loved to play in the field, but the Grays had different ideas. "I still thought I was a first baseman when I joined the Homestead Grays," said Trice. "They had such a team that the only place a fellow had a chance to break in was as a pitcher so I started pitching." That's when Sam Bankhead took the youngster under his wing. "(He) taught me about control at Homestead," said Trice. It wasn't until late in the 1948 season that Trice signed with the Grays, and he ended up playing sparingly thru 1950.

He was signed by the A's in 1951 and after poor minor-league numbers, ended up in Ottawa of the International League in 1952 and 1953. During the 1953 season at Ottawa, Trice had his one great season. He went 21–10, with a 3.10 ERA, and he earned a September call-up.

Trice was 27 years old when he broke into the big leagues on September 13, 1953 with Philadelphia, and in three games, he won two games with one loss.

Imagine it is 1953 in Philadelphia. You are on the mound for your major-league debut, and you walk out to a thunderous booing from the crowd. You begin your warm-ups and the booing continues. The game wears on, and nothing changes. You look at the opposing pitcher, Don Larsen of the St. Louis Browns and he is pitching out there, making your teammates work for every run. As the game comes to an end, the booing just does not wear down. You walk out of Connie Mack Stadium, and the people just will not stop harassing you with booing and threatening words. However, you continue on your path to the hotel room and realize that you just set the standard for integration for the Athletics organization.

This is the day that Bob Trice made history, on September 13, 1953. Trice went eight innings, giving up five runs, and striking out two. He lost to Don Larsen and the St. Louis Browns, 5–2.

In 1954, the A's brought him back. Trice went 7–8 with an ERA over 5.00 and 22 strikeouts in 119 innings.

In 1955, the Athletics moved to Kansas City, Missouri, and he had one last try in the major leagues, but pitched poorly without a decision in only four outings where he played his final big league game on May 2nd at age 28.

Trices's career totals for 27 games (26 as a pitcher) include a 9–9 record; 21 games started, nine complete games, one shutout and three games finished. He allowed 98 earned runs in 152 innings pitched, giving him a lifetime ERA of 5.80. He had a strong bat for a pitcher; at the plate he was 15-for-52 (.288) with one home run, six runs batted in, eight runs scored and a slugging percentage of .423.

Although his MLB career was short-lived, Trice's work challenging racial intolerance as an early African American professional baseball pioneer cannot be overemphasized.

Trice has shared that "black players encountered racial barriers, both on and off the field: teammates refusing to shake hands, fans shouting out insults, whites-only signs, and many other painful struggles just to play baseball. Today's black athletes and major-league players have no idea what we had to endure."

During his first spring training Bob and others were quartered at homes in the black section of town and had to walk to practice, as no cabs would stop to pick them up.

Eventually they were allowed to stay in the same hotels as the white players but were cautioned to not use the pool, look at white women or eat in the hotel restaurant. Even at the ballpark discrimination continued, as they were not allowed to use the same bathrooms or drinking fountains as the white players.

He died at age 62 of pancreatic cancer at Weirton Medical Center in Weirton, West Virginia, on September 16, 1988.

CHAPTER 8

Chicago Cubs

The Cubs were not very aggressive in bringing up black players to their roster until the White Sox starting drawing more fans after "Minnie" Miñoso and other black players on the White Sox made their debuts in 1951.

A telephone conversation was held on April 7, 1943 between Clarence "Pants" Rowland and P.K. Wrigley. Rowland worked for the Chicago Cubs overseeing farm teams and was serving as the General Manager of the Los Angeles Angels of the Pacific Coast League. P.K. Wrigley was the head of the Wm. Jr. Wrigley Company and also the owner of the Chicago Cubs of the National League. The purpose of the conversation was to discuss "the colored situation" as Rowland put it. The net result was that the Chicago Cubs recognized that integration was coming, but chose not to take a leadership role. The planned tryouts for the black ball players with the Cubs minor league team never did materialize. At the last moment the tryouts were cancelled with no reason given. The Negro League players who were supposed to be given a tryout were Chet Brewer (Cleveland Buckeyes), Howard Easterling (Homestead Grays) and Nate Moreland (Baltimore Elite Giants).

In 1953 the Cubs had two black shortstops (Ernie Banks and Gene Baker) in the minors that they considered bringing up to the majors.

Ernie Banks was not supposed to be the Chicago Cubs' first black player. Gene Baker, a fancy-fielding, 28-year-old shortstop with the Cubs' top farm team, was penciled in for that role in 1953. The previous year, Baker's manager with the Los Angeles Angels had pronounced him ready to make the jump to the big leagues. Banks was more of an unknown quantity in September 1953, coming from the Kansas City Monarchs of the Negro American League, and the team's interest in him was chiefly as a roommate for Baker.

By the luck of the draw, Baker was nursing a minor injury when the two arrived at Wrigley Field on Sept. 14, 1953, and Banks was chosen as the first to play. By season's end of 1954, Banks already was recognized as the shortstop of the future and well on his way to becoming Chicago's beloved "Mr. Cub" while Baker converted to a second baseman.

In 1954, the Cubs would add Luis Márquez (see Chapter 3, Boston Braves), and in 1955–'56, Gale Wade, an outfielder, would play in 19 games for the Cubs. Via trades, they added Sam Jones (see Chapter 2, Cleveland Indians), and "Monte" Irvin (see New York Giants, Chapter 4) to their roster.

Chicago Cubs

Ernie Banks

September 17, 1953

Ernest Banks (January 31, 1931–January 23, 2015) was an American professional baseball player who starred in major-league baseball (MLB) as a shortstop and first baseman for the Chicago Cubs between 1953 and 1971. He was inducted into the National Baseball Hall of Fame in 1977 and was named to the Major-League Baseball All-Century Team in 1999. Some regard Banks as one of the greatest players of all time.

He began playing professional baseball in 1950 with the Kansas City Monarchs in the Negro leagues.

In 1951, Banks was drafted into the U.S. Army and served in Germany during the Korean War. In 1953, he was discharged from the army and joined the Monarchs for the remainder of the 1953 season, achieving a .347 batting average.

Banks signed with the Chicago Cubs in late 1953, making his major-league debut on September 17 at age 22, playing in 10 games at Wrigley Field. **He was the Cubs' first black player.** Banks became one of several former Negro-league players who joined MLB teams without playing in the minor leagues.

In 1954, Banks' double play partner during his official rookie season was Gene Baker, the Cubs' second black player. Banks and Baker roomed together on road trips and became the first all-black double play combination in major-league history. Ernie batted .274 with 19 home runs and 79 RBI's in 1954.

In 1955, Banks hit 44 home runs, had 117 RBI while batting .295.

In 1956, Banks missed 18 games due to a hand infection, breaking his run of 424 consecutive games played. He batted .297 with 28 home runs and 85 RBI.

In 1957, Banks finished the season with 43 home runs, 102 RBI, and a .285 batting average.

In 1958 and 1959, Banks became the first NL player to be awarded back-to-back MVP Awards, leading the league in RBI's in both those seasons (with 129 and 143, respectively). Banks hit a major league leading 47 home runs in 1958 while batting .313, third best in the NL. In 1959, he hit .304 with 45 home runs.

In 1960, Banks hit a major league and NL leading 41 home runs, had 117 RBI and led the NL in games played for the sixth time in 7 years. He was also the first Cubs player to receive an NL Gold Glove Award for his solid play at shortstop.

In 1961, Banks experienced problems with a knee injury he had ac-quired while in the army. After 717 consecutive games, he removed himself from the Cubs' lineup for at least four games, ending his pursuit of the record for playing in the most consecutive NL games of 895 games set by Stan Musial. He batted .278 with 29 home runs and 80 RBI despite the injury.

In 1961 the Cubs announced that Jerry Kindall would replace Banks at shortstop and that Banks would move to left field. During the remaining 23 games, Banks committed only one error playing left field.

In 1962 he was moved to first base, learning that position from former first baseman and Cubs coach Charlie Grimm. He batted .269 with 37 home runs and 104 RBI that season.

In May 1963, Banks set a single-game record of 22 putouts by a first baseman and finished the season with 18 home runs, 64 RBI, and a .227 batting average.

In 1964, Banks finished the season with 23 home runs, 95 RBI, and a .264 batting average.

In 1965, Banks hit 28 home runs, had 107 RBI and a .265 batting average. On September 2, he hit his 400th home run.

In 1966, Banks hit only 15 home runs with 80 RBI and batted .272.

In 1967, the Cubs appointed Banks a player-coach. Banks competed with John Boccabella for a starting position at first base. Shortly there-after, manager Durocher named Banks the outright starter at first base. Banks hit 23 home runs and drove in 95 runs. He was also voted into the All-Star Game that year.

In 1968, the 37-year-old Banks hit 32 home runs, had 83 RBI and finished that season with a .246 batting average.

In 1969, he came the closest to helping the Cubs win the National League pennant but the Cubs fell from first place in September after holding an 8½ game lead. He batted .253 with 23 home runs and 106 RBI.

On May 12, 1970, Banks hit his 500th home run at Chicago's Wrigley Field. He played in only 72 games with 12 home runs and 44 RBI while batting .253.

In 1971 he played in only 39 games and on December 1, 1971 he retired as a player but continued to coach for the Cubs until 1973. He was an instructor in the minor leagues for the next three seasons and also worked in the Cubs' front office.

Banks finished his career with 512 home runs. He is the Cubs' all-time leader in games played (2,528), at-bats (9,421), home runs (512), total bases (4,706), and extra-base hits (1,009).

Banks was voted into the National Baseball Hall of Fame in 1977, his first year of eligibility. He received votes on 321 of the 383 ballots.

Banks was named to the Major-League Baseball All-Century Team in 1999. In the same year, the Society for American Baseball Research listed him twenty-seventh on a list of the 100 greatest baseball players.

Banks died of a heart attack at a Chicago hospital on January 23, 2015, eight days before his eighty-fourth birthday.

Chicago Cubs

Gene Baker

September 20, 1953

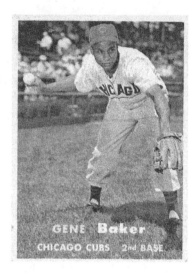

Eugene Walter Baker (June 15, 1925–December 1, 1999) was an American major-league baseball infielder who played for the Chicago Cubs and Pittsburgh Pirates during eight seasons between 1953 and 1961, Gene made his MLB debut **3 days after Ernie Banks on September 20,1953.**

In 1946, he joined the United States Navy being stationed at Ottumwa Naval Air Station and Iowa Pre-Flight School.

In 1947 with his service obligations fulfilled, Baker returned to Davenport, Iowa, where he played semipro baseball. His exploits on the diamond caught the attention of the Kansas City Monarchs of the Negro American League. He was the Monarchs' regular shortstop in 1948 and 1949 but no statistics are available for that period.

After the 1949 season, Gene returned to Davenport and played recreation league basketball, but the spring of 1950 found him in organized baseball in the Chicago Cubs organization that signed him as a free agent. After a few games with the Springfield Cubs in the International League, he was acquired by the Des Moines Bruins of the Western League as the team's first black player.

At the end of June, he moved up to the Los Angeles Angels of the Triple-A Pacific Coast League. California newspapers reported that the 25-year-old shortstop was regarded as one of the most promising players in the Cubs' farm system. He played in the PCL from 1950-1953 batting highs of .290 in 1950 and .284 in 1953.

On September 1, 1953, the Cubs purchased his contract from the Angels. It was reported that Baker was the first Negro player to ever appear on the Cubs' official roster. A week later, the Cubs purchased Ernie Banks from the Kansas City Monarchs. Both shortstops reported in Chicago on September 14th; Banks became the regular shortstop, and suddenly, Baker was a second baseman. **He made his major-league debut on September 20th,** striking out as a pinch hitter in the eighth inning of a Cubs 11–8 loss in St. Louis.

Baker hit .275 in 135 games in 1954 during his rookie season. Both he and Banks made *The Sporting News* all-rookie team.

Gene's best season came in 1955, when he hit .268, leading the league with 18 sacrifices and was named to the National League All-Star team.

In 1956 Gene batted .258 with 12 home runs and 57 RBI's.

On May 1, 1957, Baker was traded along with first baseman Dee Fondy to Pittsburgh for infielder Dale Long and infielder-outfielder Lee Walls. There was no way he could match the play of future Hall of Famer Bill Mazeroski at second base, so Baker played mainly third base for the Pirates. He played in 111 games batting .266

In 1958 he played in only 29 games as his knee was injured and required surgery. Baker was out of action for the remainder of the season. He spent the rest of 1958 back in Davenport on crutches.

The Pirates hoped to have Baker back in 1959, but when spring came he was unable to play. Pittsburgh placed him on the 30-day disabled list in April. In May, they restored him to the active list and immediately placed him on waivers for the purpose of giving him an unconditional release. Even so, they did not cast Baker aside. They signed him as an instructional assistant for their minor-league clubs. Baker worked predominantly with minor league players but also helped with the analysis of minor league clubs and scouting programs.

In January 1960, Baker began a series of exercises and tests on his injured left knee at Southern Illinois University's Physical Education Research Laboratory in Carbondale. Throughout his ordeal, the Pirates were compassionate, generous, and supportive of Baker—qualities not always evident in major-league clubs.

During 1960 spring training, Baker went with the club to Fort Myers, Florida, as a non-roster invitee. By late March he was playing well. He was the talk of the training camp and earned a big league contract. As it turned out, there was not much need for Baker's services and he became almost a forgotten man during the Pirates' drive to the 1960 pennant. Second baseman Mazeroski and third baseman Don Hoak each played more than 150 games. Baker played only one game at second and seven games at third base. All told, he appeared in 33 games during the season batting .243

In the 1960 World Series, Baker did not play in the field, but he came up three times as a pinch hitter and failed to make a hit.

During spring training in 1961, the club decided to keep Baker as a utility infielder and sent Dick Gray to the minors. Baker sat on the Pirates' bench almost all spring, getting into three games at third base and occasionally pinch-hitting. He played his last major-league game on June 10, 1961.

On June 20ᵗʰ of 1961 he was released as a player to make room for outfielder Walt Moryn, purchased from the St. Louis Cardinals. The Pirates kept their promise that there would always be room in the organization for Baker.

On the same day he was released, he was named player-manager of the Batavia Pirates of the Class D New York-Pennsylvania League. Baker found Class D pitching to his liking, hitting .387 in 55 games, by far the highest average in his career.

In 1961, Baker became the first African American manager in organized baseball when the Pirates named him skipper of their Batavia Pirates farm club in the New York-Penn League.

In 1962, he became the first black coach in organized baseball when the Pirates named him player-coach of their Triple-A International League affiliate Columbus Jets.

In 1963, the Pirates promoted him to coach on the major-league team. He was the second black coach in the big leagues following Buck O'Neil by a half season. Baker continued for many years as a scout for the Pirates.

He died in Davenport Iowa from a heart attack at the age of 74. He is buried in Rock Island National Cemetery.

CHAPTER 9

Pittsburgh Pirates

Bill Benswanger, the president of the Pittsburgh Pirates from 1932–1946, petitioned baseball's commissioner to integrate baseball in the early 1940s. He failed, of course, but he remains the only baseball owner (besides Bill Veeck) who challenged Judge Kenesaw Landis, who was then the game's commissioner.

On August 20, 1942, the New York Times officially reported that the Pittsburgh Pirates President Bill Benswanger had authorized Pittsburgh Courier sports writer Wendell Smith to recommend several Negro League players that the Pirates might want to tryout. Wendell Smith recommended the following players: Sam Bankhead (Homestead Grays), Leon Day (Newark Eagles), Josh Gibson (Homestead Grays) and Willie Wells (Newark Eagles). The initial report was that the try-outs would most likely be scheduled after the regular season. The tryouts unfortunately were never scheduled.

The first black players were not brought into the organization until 1953–'54 when Branch Rickey moved to the Pirates from the Dodgers as president.

Who was the Pirates' first black player?

Depending on who is asked, the seemingly simple question elicits various replies. The Pirates, the Hall of Fame and most Internet baseball sites claim that in 1954, second baseman "Curt" Roberts broke the Pirates' color line. Others say Carlos Bernier was first.

Early in his professional career, Carlos played in the Manitoba-Dakota League, a Canadian Negro league. By 1948, one year after Robinson appeared with the Brooklyn Dodgers, Bernier played in Class B Port Chester and was, one of organized baseball's early black players.

Why baseball will not acknowledge Bernier's status as the Pirates first black player remains a mystery to this day. In 1953, Bernier appeared in 105 games, two-thirds of the season, deserving a prominent place in the Pirates' lore as a courageous pioneer who deserves more than footnote status.

In 1954, Sam Jethroe (see Chapter 5, Boston Braves) and Luis Márquez (see Chapter 5, Boston Braves) joined the Pirates playing in just a few games.

In 1955, the great Roberto Clemente would join the Pirates and in 1957, Gene Baker.

On September 21, 1963, the Pirates were the first MLB team to have an African American Manager in Gene Baker, as Gene filled in for Danny Murtaugh after Danny was ejected from a game.

In 1971 Pirate Manager Murtaugh assembled a starting lineup that was completely composed of minorities for the first time in MLB history.

The first all-minority lineup in MLB history took the field on September 1, 1971. The lineup was Rennie Stennett, Gene Clines, Roberto Clemente, Willie Stargell, Manny Sanguillén, Dave Cash, Al Oliver, Jackie Hernandez, and Dock Ellis.

Pittsburgh Pirates

"Curt" Roberts

April 13, 1954

Curtis "Curt" Roberts (August 16, 1929–November 14, 1969) was an American baseball second baseman who played three seasons for the Pittsburgh Pirates in major-league baseball from 1954 to 1956.

"Curt" Roberts is considered by MLB to be the first black player on Pittsburgh, but some sources also include Carlos Bernier who was a black Latin player, appearing in a game on April 23, 1953.

After two seasons in the Pirates' farm system, Roberts was the first black American major-league player for the Pirates.

Soon after finishing high school at the age of 17, Roberts began his professional career with the Kansas City Monarchs in the Negro Leagues. He played four seasons (1947–1950) with the Monarchs, where his teammates included "Satchel" Paige, Hilton Smith, Buck O'Neil, and Elston Howard. Few statistics are available from that period

The Boston Braves signed Roberts in 1951 on the recommendation of scout Andy Cohen, who saw him play in the Mexican League during the 1950 off-season. They sent Roberts to their minor-league's affiliate in the Western League, the Denver Bears, and as part of a working agreement between the Braves and the Pirates, Roberts became a member of the Pirates organization for a sum of $10,000.

In 1951 he played in 132 games batting .281.

He stayed with the Denver Bears for the next two seasons, (1952 and 1953) playing a combined total of 280 games with 15 home runs and a .285 batting average.

Prior to the 1954 Pittsburgh Pirates' season, the local black community in Pittsburgh pressurized the team to integrate their roster as other teams such as the Brooklyn Dodgers and New York Giants had done. To speed up the integration, the black community began to protest against the Pirates and boycotted Pirate home games. The general manager of the Pirates at the time was Branch Rickey, who, 7 years earlier as general manager of the Dodgers, signed Jackie Robinson, the first black major-league baseball player. After playing 2 years in the Pirates' minor-league system, **Roberts made his major-league debut on April 13, 1954,** against the Philadelphia Phillies to become the first black American player in Pirates' history.

Roberts finished the 1954 season as the primary starter at second base, batting .232 with one home run and 36 runs batted in (RBI) in 134 games.

Roberts started the 1955 season in a slump. In his first six games, he only had two hits in 18 at-bats for a batting average of .118. Roberts was soon demoted back to the minor leagues and spent the rest of the 1955 season with the Hollywood Stars in the Pacific Coast League where he batted .321.

In 1956, Roberts played 31 games at the beginning of the year for Pittsburgh, hitting .177 with four runs batted in, mostly in a backup role.

On June 23,1956, Roberts was traded to the Kansas City Athletics with pitcher Jack McMahan for "Spook" Jacobs and $5,000 cash. He never played a game with the Athletics, who soon sent him to the Columbus Jets of the International League that same month.

On April 4, 1957 Roberts was traded to the New York Yankees as the player to be named later in a trade that sent former American League Most Valuable Player Bobby Shantz to the Yankees.

In 1957, Roberts played with the New York Yankees minor-league affiliate in Denver. Roberts never again reached the majors, becoming a journeyman in the minor leagues, and at one point, playing baseball in Nicaragua.

Roberts played with the Montreal Royals of the International League in 1959, where he led the league in fielding percentage with .987 being named the Royals' Most Valuable Player.

In 1960, Roberts was acquired by the Spokane Indians, a Dodger affiliate, after he was made expandable by the Royals when they acquired Chico Carrasquel. He played two more seasons in the minors, but an injury diminished his playing ability, and Roberts retired from baseball after the 1963 season.

Despite Roberts's short major-league career, he paved the way for other black players to debut for the Pirates, the most notable of whom was future Baseball Hall of Famer Roberto Clemente. He befriended Clemente, teaching him how to handle the racial abuse and the huge pressure that Roberts had suffered with the Pirates.

Roberts tragically died in 1969 when an automobile struck him while he was changing a tire on his car.

Pittsburgh Pirates

Carlos Bernier

April 22, 1953

Carlos Bernier Rodríguez (January 28, 1927–April 6, 1989) was an outfielder who played one full season of major-league baseball for the 1953 Pittsburgh Pirates.

Bernier's professional career extended for 17 seasons (1948–1964). In addition to the 105 games he played for the 1953 Pirates, he appeared in an even 2,200 games in minor-league baseball, with 1,725 games played at the highest levels (Triple-A and the Open Classification) then in existence. In his minor league career Bernier batted .298 with nearly 2,300 hits and exactly 200 home runs.

In 1948, his first season in organized baseball, he was struck by a pitch which fractured his skull and caused him to suffer from chronic headaches the rest of his life. The headaches were sometimes blamed for the quick temper that kept him in hot water much of the time. It was not just headaches that got him in trouble. Jackie Robinson was able to endure the slurs and indignities that came with being a racial pioneer, but Bernier was different. He was not one to take racial taunts lying down, whether from opponents, teammates, fans, or umpires. He was competitive and aggressive on the ball field and was suspended many times throughout his career.

Bernier's son, Dr. N. Bernier-Collazo, explained his father's behavior:

"He lived in an era when it was fashionable to discriminate; in fact, many states upheld laws that discriminated against people of color. My father's only shortfall was that he did not handle the injustices of society with the same grace as a Jackie Robinson or a Roberto Clemente. He was quite angry at the injustices and faced them head on, even if it meant challenging a white minor league umpire who made a racial slur. I have often wondered how different life would have been for him with all his talents if he had played now (2004), instead of then. His career would have been spent primarily in the majors, rather than in the minors. Despite his extremely competitive demeanor on the field, he was a gentle soul off the field with the greatest qualities kindness, compassionate, generous, responsible, and loving. Many people don't know what a wonderful person he was because they only witnessed his exploits and his aggressive style of play on the field."

In 1952, Bernier was named the PCL's Rookie of the Year by the Pacific Coast League Baseball Writers Association for his performance with the Hollywood Stars. He batted .301 with nine home runs, 79 RBI and a PCL-leading 105 runs and 65 stolen bases.

For the 1953 Pirates, Bernier collected 66 hits, including seven doubles, eight triples, and three home runs, while batting .213.

In 1954, Bernier went back to Hollywood quite willingly. Like Roberto Clemente after him, Bernier despised the racism he found prevalent throughout most of the major leagues and was happy to return to a more enlightened California. He batted .313 in 1954. Bernier earned as much money in minor-league Hollywood as he did in Pittsburgh.

He continued to play minor league baseball thru 1964 with various teams. Mostly Hawaii and Hollywood teams in the Pacific Coast league with a high batting average of .351 with Hawaii in 1961. Over more than 8 seasons in Triple AAA minors he averaged over .300

He never played another inning for any major-league team.

Sadly, in 1989, Bernier committed suicide.

CHAPTER **10**

St. Louis Cardinals

The Cardinals were the southern most major-league baseball team, and in no hurry to integrate.

The 1940's were one of the most successful decades in the Cardinals franchise history with 960 wins and 580 losses for a winning percentage higher than any other Major League team at .623.

With Billy Southworth managing, they won the World Series in 1942 and 1944 (in the only all-St. Louis series against the Browns), and won 105 or more games each in 1942, 1943, and 1944. Southworth's managerial winning percentage (.642) is St. Louis' highest since the franchise joined the National League.

In 1947 the St. Louis Cardinals, threatened to strike if Robinson played and also tried to spread the walkout across the entire National League. The existence of the plot was leaked by the Cardinals' team physician, Robert Hyland, to a friend, the *New York Herald Tribune*'s Rutherford "Rud" Rennie. The reporter, concerned about protecting Hyland's anonymity and job, in turn, leaked it to his *Tribune* colleague and editor, Stanley Woodward,

The Woodward article made national headlines. After the threat was exposed, National League President Ford Frick and Baseball Commissioner "Happy" Chandler let it be known that any striking players would be suspended. "You will find that the friends that you think you have in the press box will not support you, that you will be outcasts," threatened Chandler. "I do not care if half the league strikes. Those who do it will encounter quick retribution. All will be suspended, and I don't care if it wrecks the National League for five years. This is the United States of America, and one citizen has as much right to play as another." Woodward's article received the E. P. Dutton Award in 1947 for Best Sports Reporting.

Robinson, nonetheless, became the target of rough physical play by opponents (particularly the Cardinals). At one time, he received a seven-inch gash in his leg from Enos Slaughter of the Cardinals.

The Cardinals were the last team to abolish segregated seating in their ballpark.

According to Bing Devine, Fred Saigh (the owner from 1947-1953), refused to sign black players.

When Anheuser-Busch purchased the Cardinals in 1953 and saw that there were no black players on the roster, he hired Quincy Trouppe (a Negro-league veteran player) as a scout who signed more than a dozen black players to the Cardinals minor leagues.

Tom Alston was the fourteenth black player signed by the Cardinals' organization, but the first one on their major-league roster. Among the other blacks in the Cardinals' system in 1954 were pitchers Bill Greason, Brooks Lawrence, and John Wyatt who would eventually all pitch in the Major Leagues.

Devine then began to add talent and depth to the St. Louis roster, including African American and Latin players. In the first 5 years of his reign, he traded for or promoted players such as Bob Gibson, Bill White, Curt Flood, and Julián Javier.

St. Louis Cardinals

Tom Alston

April 13, 1954

Thomas Edison Alston (January 31, 1926–December 30, 1993) was a major-league baseball first baseman that played for the St. Louis Cardinals from 1954 to 1957.

Alston, the first African American player for the St. Louis Cardinals, spent most of his life in torment and poverty. He never escaped the grip of mental illness that ended his baseball career.

Besides the pressure to make it in the majors and to be "a credit to his race," Alston faced the added burden of being the most expensive black player ever. The Cardinals paid the Pacific Coast League's San Diego Padres more than $100,000, plus two players, for his contract.

Born in Greensboro, North Carolina, on January 31, 1926, Alston battled through racial tensions like most people in the south throughout his childhood. After high school, Alston joined the navy during World War II serving from 1944–1946 at various United States bases.

Following his military service, Alston moved on to college where he enrolled at North Carolina A&T and graduated with a degree in physical education in 1951.

After graduation in 1951, he played for the Jacksonville Eagles, a colored baseball team. His experience there led to the opportunity to sign with the Porterville Comets.

In 1952, Alston played organized professional baseball with the Porterville, California club in the Class C Southwestern International League. He hit .353 and slammed 12 home runs in 54 games, but the franchise and the league were limping toward collapse. San Diego of the Pacific Coast League bought his contract for $100.

The Pacific Coast League was on the level of the major leagues featuring players like the DiMaggio brothers, Ted Williams, and Bobby Doerr. The sun-soaked California coast was perfect for baseball.

The young first baseman was a very athletic player with a good glove.

The Padres thought they had a valuable prospect, but their new player was 27 years old. The Padres convinced him to go by the age of 22, because at that age, he would be more attractive to major-league buyers.

Early in the 1953 season, Alston hit 13 home runs in his first 50 games and was batting close to .300. The *San Diego Union*'s Jack Murphy hailed him as a top prospect while describing him in stereotypical terms as "a happy-hearted Negro with the build of a basketball goon and a get along borrowed from Step-in Fetchit."

In 1953, Alston put together a stellar season for San Diego. He had 207 hits in 180 games, with 101 runs scored, 23 home runs, 101 RBI, and a .297 batting average. The Cardinal scouts gave him rave reviews.

On Jan. 26, 1954, the Cardinals sent first baseman Dick Sisler, pitcher Eddie Erautt, and $100,000 to San Diego for Alston.

The Cardinals made their acquisition of Alston a media event. The team rented a suite at the Beverly Hills Hotel in Hollywood and Busch himself came out to sign the contract. "We took the viewpoint from the very beginning that we wanted the very best players we could get," Busch said, "that there would be no barriers in terms of race, religion or anything of that sort." He said the Cardinals had scouted the young player extensively and conducted a background check on his personal habits. "Our scouts, manager Eddie Stanky, and everyone on our staff are high on him. Now that I have met Alston in person and visited with him today, I'm more satisfied than ever that the Cardinals and all St. Louis will be proud of him."

When he made his major-league debut on April 13, 1954, at Sportsman's Park, he became the first black player in St. Louis Cardinals' history. On April 30, the Cardinals sent Bilko to the Cubs. Alston was their everyday first baseman.

In 1954 Alston hit .301 (37-for-123) in May and was at .285 overall for season but then slumped in June enduring a 2-for-27 stretch and batting .181 (15-for-83) for the month. He had seven RBI in his last 42 games.

On June 30, the Cardinals sent Alston to Class AAA Rochester and called up another rookie, Joe Cunningham, to replace him at first base.

He played in 66 games during his 1954 rookie season batting .246 with four home runs and 34 runs batted in. After that, he got into 25 more games over the course of the next three seasons.

He spent most of his major-league career splitting time between the majors and the Class AAA Omaha Cardinals. With Omaha, in 1955, he batted .274 and in 1956 he had a .306 batting average and 21 home runs with 80 RBI's.

Alston made brief appearances with the Cardinals in 1955, 1956 and 1957. His career totals for 91 games include a .244 batting average

(66-for-271), 4 home runs, 36 RBI, 30 runs scored, and an on-base percentage of .311.

Alston contracted prostate cancer and spent his final months in hospice care. He died at 67 on December 30, 1993.

Bill Greason

St. Louis Cardinals

May 31, 1954

William Greason (born September 3, 1924) is an American former professional baseball player who later became a Baptist minister.

Greason served in the United States Marine Corps during World War II in the 66th Supply Platoon, an all-black unit, in the Pacific Theater of Operations and took part in the Battle of Iwo Jima. After the war, he played professional baseball in the Negro leagues for the Nashville Black Vols, Asheville Blues, and Birmingham Black Barons.

His career in the Negro Leagues started in 1947, when he was picked up off of the sandlots of Atlanta, Georgia. "In 1947, the Nashville Black Vols heard about me and invited me to come and start playing with them. I played pretty good, I won 12 games and lost four," he said.

"The next year 1948 in spring training, I was in Ashville, North Carolina, and the Black Barons came through," he recalled. "Our pitcher started against them and they bombed him. They put me in and I shut them for seven innings. That was on a Monday night; Saturday morning, I was in Birmingham. I don't know how they got me, they bought me or whatever, but in 1948 I was with the Barons."

As a teammate of Willie Mays on the 1948 Birmingham Black Barons, Greason posted a 6–4 record with a 3.30 ERA for the Negro American League champions.

His expertise on the mound helped guide the Black Barons to the Negro World Series. They squared off against the Homestead Grays, who were led by future Hall of Famers "Cool Papa Bell", and Buck Leonard. Greason won the only game for the Black Barons in the 1948 series. "To have an opportunity to pitch in that environment, it was something exceptional," he said.

In 1949 he had stints in the Negro league and the Mexican League, but few statistics are available.

Bill served in the Korean War from 1950-1951

In 1952, he joined minor-league baseball as a member of the Oklahoma City Indians of the Double-A Texas League, where he won 9 of his 10 decisions and posted a sparkling 2.14 earned run average.

In 1953, he was 16–13 with a 3.61 ERA and 193 strikeouts in 240 innings for Oklahoma City, catching the attention of the Cardinals.

On Oct. 13, 1953, the Cardinals acquired Greason from Oklahoma City for three minor-league players. In 1954, as spring training ended, the Cardinals assigned Greason and another black pitcher, Brooks Lawrence, to Class AAA Columbus (Ohio), managed by Johnny Keane. At Columbus, Greason compiled a 4–5 record, winning his last three decisions.

On May 28,1954 the Cardinals sent pitcher Mel Wright to Columbus and called up Greason.

Bill Greason had a short but important stint with the Cardinals. **He was the first African American Cardinals' pitcher.**

Greason soon found out that integration did not yet mean equality to the Cardinals' front office. When St. Louis forced him to take a pay cut from the $1,200 per month he had been making in Triple-A to $900 per month, his promotion turned out not to be the exhilarating moment he had anticipated. Greason protested the pay cut and was given a "take it or leave it" ultimatum that made him bitter and dejected. He said, "I tried to get there for years, and then when I got there, I didn't want to stay."

Greason's already low spirits were not buoyed by the way Cardinals manager Eddie Stanky handled him, which was to remove him from games "faster than [he] could spew tobacco juice from his front teeth." His major-league debut came on **May 31, 1954** in the first game of a doubleheader against the Cubs at Wrigley Field. It was a brief start in which he surrendered five runs (all earned) and three homers in three innings of a 14-4 rain-shortened (seven-inning) loss.

Greason's second start was on June 6th against the Phillies in St. Louis, which was an even worse outing. He surrendered a leadoff homer and walked the next two batters before being pulled by Stanky. Greason knew his days in St. Louis were numbered when Stanky's only words to him were, "Get the damn ball over the plate."

His premonition was correct as he made one final appearance on June 20th and pitched a scoreless inning of relief against the New York Giants, though he did allow a single and a walk, before being sent back to the minors. After never really being given a chance in the majors, Greason was relieved to return to Columbus, where he finished the 1954 season with a 10-13 record. The major leagues never beckoned again, but Greason's final tally of 0-1 with a 13.50 ERA for the Cardinals fails to define him as a ballplayer.

Greason never appeared in the major leagues again. His career stats for four innings, eight runs (six earned), four home runs, eight hits, four walks, two strikeouts, 0–1 record, 13.50 ERA.

Greason pitched in the Cardinals' minor-league system until 1959 winning over 40 games.

After his playing career, Greason returned to Birmingham, worked in a department store and became a minister.

In September 2014, Greason, 90, was honored by the Cardinals at Busch Stadium for having been a pioneer in helping break the franchise's color barrier 60 years before.

Reverend Greason is one of the oldest living black players at 95.

Brooks Lawrence

St. Louis Cardinals

June 24, 1954

Brooks Lawrence (January 30, 1925–April 27, 2000) was a major-league baseball All-Star pitcher for the St. Louis Cardinals (1954–1955) and Cincinnati Redlegs (1956–1960).

In 1943, after graduating from high school, Lawrence was drafted and eventually sent to Guam as part of a segregated Army Engineers unit that built and repaired air bases in the Pacific. He and fellow soldiers were able to play baseball on company teams or on integrated teams composed of players from many units.

During a Japanese air assault on a base under repair by Lawrence's unit, he mounted a Jeep supporting a machine gun and began shooting at a low-flying plane firing upon soldiers. His action saved many lives, and when he was discharged in December 1945, he was awarded a Bronze Star medal.

Newly discharged in 1946, Lawrence debated with himself about whether to take a full-time job to support himself and his wife or go to school with the GI Bill. He decided to continue his education at

Miami University in Oxford Ohio as well as play baseball.

After playing less than two years at Miami and getting playing time with the Springfield Tigers when school was out, Lawrence attended a tryout in 1949 for the Dayton Indians of the Class A Central League, a farm team of the Cleveland Indians.

He showed enough ability to be signed to a contract and was sent to Zanesville with the Class D Ohio-Indiana League. He moved through the Indians' farm system until in 1953, at which time the Indians traded him to Portsmouth of the Class B Piedmont League, a step backward for Lawrence. About ready to change his career path entirely, Lawrence changed his mind when Mickey Owen, a major-league catcher who was managing the Caguas-Guayama team in the Puerto Rican League, recruited him for the winter-league team. Mentored by Owen, Lawrence developed a sinker, a slider, and a change-up to complement his strong curve and fastball.

Owen also served as Lawrence's promoter, encouraging the Cincinnati Reds to pick up his contract from Portsmouth where he went 18–13 in 1953.

The Reds planned to option Lawrence to their Oklahoma City farm team, but the St. Louis Cardinals drafted him and assigned him to the Triple-A Columbus Red Birds where, along with teammate Bill Greason, he broke the franchise's color barrier.

After going 6–4, Lawrence was called up by the Cardinals in June.

On **June 24, 1954 he launched his major-league career** with a 5–1 win over the Pittsburgh Pirates at Forbes Field in Pittsburgh. That victory set the pace for six more successive victories, an impressive start to his major league career. As a 29-year-old rookie, Lawrence went 15–6 with a 3.74 ERA while starting and relieving for the St. Louis Cardinals.

He struggled in 1955 and was demoted to Oakland (in the Pacific Coast League), but he went 5–1 down the stretch and earned a second chance with the big-league club where he went 3 and 8.

In January 1956, St. Louis sent Lawrence and Sonny Senerchia to the Cincinnati Reds in exchange for Jackie Collum.

In 1956 (his best season) with the Reds, Lawrence posted a 19–10 record and a 3.99 ERA. He opened the season with 13 consecutive wins and earned a spot on the National League All-Star team. That year, he led the Reds in wins, innings pitched, and shutouts.

In 1957, he went 16–13 with a 3.52 ERA.

In 1958, Bill was 8–13, and in 1959, 7–12 with an ERA over 4.00 each year.

Lawrence's career came to a close in 1960 as he only appeared in one game for the Reds. He retired with an overall record of 69–62 with a 4.25 ERA in 1,040.7 innings pitched.

Like other players during his era, Lawrence liked to spend the month after the close of the season on the barnstorming trail. For 30 days major leaguers were allowed to travel with a barnstorming team. In an interview, he recalled one such trip beginning in New York and ending in San Francisco, playing games on the coasts and across the South where professional baseball teams were not yet established. Along with Negro League players and teams who accompanied them, Lawrence remembered barnstorming with major-league stars like Roy Campanella, Ernie Banks, George Crowe, Hank Aaron, Willie Mays, Don Newcombe, Hank Thompson, Sad Sam Jones, and Joe Black among others.

Following his retirement from baseball in 1960, he worked 10 years for International Harvester in Springfield. He then worked for the Reds in scouting, minor league player development and radio and TV.

From 1988 to 1993 he coached the baseball team at Wilmington College in Wilmington,

Lawrence died on April 27, 2000 in his hometown of Springfield, Ohio at the age of 75.

CHAPTER 11

Cincinnati Reds

The Cincinnati Reds, like the St. Louis Cardinals, were a Southern team and in no hurry to bring black players to their major-league team.

When the Reds brought two Latino players into Major League Baseball in 1911, they were "light-skinned" Cubans. In a 1984 article on Cuban baseball by Bruce Brown in *The Atlantic* pointed out, the Reds "had affidavits prepared to 'prove' that only Caucasian blood flowed in the veins of Cubans Armando Marsans (who played 8 years in MLB) and Rafael Almeida (who played parts of 3 years in MLB), were referred to by the Cincinnati press as "two of the purest bars of Castille soap that ever floated to these shores."

Sportswriter Wendell Smith took a survey of Cincinnati players in 1939 and published several articles. When Smith asked Reds manager Bill McKechnie if he'd ever seen any black ballplayers good enough for the majors, McKechnie responded he had seen at least 25 and named some — Paige, Gibson, Oscar Charleston, Lefty Hamilton and more. "Some of the greatest ballplayers I have ever seen were Negroes, and those who I have named would have been stars on any major league team in the country," the manager said.

Smith asked the manager McKechnie a question that, he confessed to the reader, he was nervous to pose: Would the manager be willing to use a black player on the 1939 Reds? "Yes, if given permission, I would use a Negro player on my team," Not only were the Reds who

Smith interviewed strongly in favor of allowing black players, but also ultimately 75 percent of everyone he talked to felt the same way.

The players may have agreed that black players were good enough, but management took no action.

World War II and age finally caught up with the Reds. Throughout the 1940s and early 1950s, Cincinnati finished mostly in the second division. In 1944, Joe Nuxhall (who was later to become part of the radio broadcasting team), at age 15, pitched for the Reds on loan from Wilson Junior High School in Hamilton, Ohio. He became the youngest player ever to appear in a major league game—a record that still stands today. The Reds were desperate for players.

Bill DeWitt was a man of questionable racial tendencies who, as the owner of the Cincinnati Reds, is alleged to have ordered rookie Pete Rose to stop hanging around the colored players.

The Reds finally brought up two black players in 1954 (Nino Escalera and Chuck Harmon), almost 7 years after Jackie Robinson played his first game. They appeared in a game on the same day.

In 1955, they traded for Joe Black and brought up Bob Thurman after purchasing his contract in 1954 from the Cubs for a reported $2,000.

The year 1956 saw the arrival of Frank Robinson who would, in the future, be an MVP, Triple Crown Winner, Hall of Famer, and MLB's first black manager.

Cincinnati Reds

Nino Escalera

April 17, 1954

NINO ESCALERA outfield CINCINNATI REDLEGS

Saturnino Escalera Cuadrado (born December 1, 1929) is a former outfielder and first baseman in major-league baseball who played for the Cincinnati Redlegs in the 1954 season.

He started his baseball career at a very young age of 12 playing with his brothers and neighbors in Santurce, San Juan, Puerto Rico. In 1946 at the Amateur Baseball World Series held in the Latin American Republic of Colombia Escalera was named best first baseman and most valuable player (MVP) of the tournament.

He started his pro career on the mainland as a teenager (at least if his baseball age is accurate) in 1949 and got off to a promising start: .347 in the Colonial League in '49, .337 in the Canadian-American League and .389 in the Colonial in '50, .374 with 16 homers in the Central League in '51.

In 1952, he was purchased by the Toledo Mud Hens/Charleston Senators of the American Association where he batted .249.

He struggled to adjust to AAA pitching in 1952, but after hitting .305 in the Texas League in '53 he went north with the Reds as a 24-year-old rookie in '54.

On April 17, 1954, at Milwaukee County Stadium, a 24-year-old Escalera became the first black to play for the Cincinnati Redlegs. He entered the game as a pinch hitter and hit a single in a 5–1 loss to the Milwaukee Braves. Nino is one of only two players (Ozzie Virgil is the other) who entered the major leagues with no Negro league experience. Both of these black players came directly from Latin America.

He played in 73 games during his only big-league season, often as a pinch hitter. Season and career totals included a .159 batting average (11-for-69), three runs batted in, 15 runs scored and an on-base percentage of .234. He committed only one error in 49 total opportunities at OF/1B for a fielding percentage of .980.

On May 22 1954, Escalara became officially the last lefthanded player to field at shortstop in a National League game. Birdie Tebbetts, rookie Cincinnati manager, tried a novel four-man outfield against Stan Musial in a game at Busch Stadium, May 22, 1954. As a result, the box score of that contest and official National League score for the year show a left handed shortstop, Nino Escalera, in the Reds' lineup. Tebbetts pulled his surprise shift in the eighth inning. At the time Cincinnati owned a 4 to 2 lead, two were out and Red Schoendienst was on first for the Cards. With Musial coming to bat, the Redleg pilot removed Shortstop Roy McMillan from the game and called Escalera off the bench, stationing him in right-center between Outfielders Wally Post and Gus Bell. Tebbets explained later that he would rather risk a single through the vacated shortstop spot than an extra-base hit. The shift, however, wasn't needed, for Pitcher Art Fowler struck Musial out and emerged with a 4 to 2 victory.

Escalera didn't return to the majors after 1954, but played the next seven years at the AAA level in the international league where is batting average for those years was around .280. He continued to play and manage in winter ball and from 1966 to 1981.

Nino scouted in Puerto Rico for the Mets and Giants for more than a decade. Among the players he is credited with signing are Jerry Morales, Ed Figueroa, Benny Ayala, Jose Oquendo and Juan Berenguer.

Escalera is a member of the Puerto Rico Baseball Hall of Fame, Río Piedras Sport Hall of Fame, Puerto Rico Sport Hall of Fame and Santurce Sport Hall of Fame. He is considered alongside Victor Pellot and Orlando Cepeda among the best first basemen in Puerto Rico history. In 2015, he was also named as one of the best baseball players who ever played in Puerto Rico winter league history.

As of today he is one of the oldest living black players at age of 89.

Cincinnati Reds

Chuck Harmon

April 17, 1954

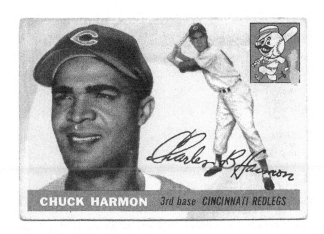

CHUCK HARMON 3rd base CINCINNATI REDLEGS

Charles Byron Harmon (born April 23, 1924) is an American former professional baseball utility player in major-league baseball who played for the Cincinnati Redlegs (1954–1956), St. Louis Cardinals (1956–1957), and Philadelphia Phillies (1957).

Harmon's basketball skills earned him a scholarship to the University of Toledo, where he was an All-American player. In 1943 Harmon scored six points in the Rockets' 48-27 loss to St. John's in the National Invitation Tournament (NIT) finals at Madison Square Garden. Perhaps more significantly, before the title game, Harmon met Babe Ruth and shook the hand of the "Sultan of Swat".

By the end of his freshman year, men of all ages were expected to serve their country and Harmon left school to serve in the Navy during World War II. Assigned to the Great Lakes Naval Station near Chicago, Harmon joined a black baseball team. He roomed with Larry Doby, who would later be the second African-American to play major-league baseball in the modern era.

Chuck served for 3 years in the Army being discharged in 1947 and he then returned to college.

In the summer of 1947, Harmon needed money to meet college and living expenses. He also wanted to maintain his NCAA eligibility, so he signed with the Indianapolis Clowns to play baseball under the name "Charlie Fine."

"Four games, four days on a bus," Harmon said about his short stint in the Negro leagues. "'Goose' Tatum, who played with the Harlem Globetrotters, took me under his wing. He liked me because he knew I played basketball. 'Goose' is the one who gave me the (alias) Charlie Fine. That's the name I played under."

Arriving home from a weekend road trip, Harmon had a telegram from the Toledo athletic director, who had found him a summer job on campus. His Negro-league career was over practically before it began.

In 1947 he was signed to a minor-league contract by the St. Louis Browns (today's Baltimore Orioles).

Assigned to the Browns' Gloversville-Johnstown team in upstate New York in 1947, he played 54 games in the outfield, batting .270.

In 1948, Harmon played baseball with the independent General Electric team out of Fort Wayne, Indiana, then returning to Gloversville in 1949. Later that summer, the Browns sent him to the Olean, New York, team in the Pennsylvania-Ontario-New York League, where he batted .351 in 31 games. It was the first of five consecutive seasons in the minors where Harmon batted .300-plus. He remained with Olean for the next two seasons.

In 1951, he hit .375 while leading the league with 143 RBI, as the team won the pennant. Despite his hot hitting, Harmon was not getting the call to the majors, so he also pursued a career in professional basketball. He was one of the final players cut by first-year coach Red Auerbach from the 1951 Boston Celtics. Had he made that team, he would have been one of the first African Americans in the NBA. He did, however, become the first African American to coach in integrated professional basketball, leading the Eastern League's Utica, New York, team as a player/coach in 1951

Harmon returned his focus to baseball in 1952, when the Cincinnati Reds acquired him. He spent 2 more years in the minors, including the 1952 season with the Burlington (Iowa) Flints of the Illinois-Indiana-Iowa League, batting .319 in 124 games.

In 1953, he was promoted to the AA Tulsa Oilers, becoming the **first African American player in the history of the Texas League's Tulsa franchise** and batted .311 with 83 RBI, 14 home runs, and 25 stolen bases in 143 games.

That winter, the Reds sent Harmon to Puerto Rico for winter ball, where Harmon was second in the league in hitting, beating out future home run king Hank Aaron. This performance was enough to be invited to Cincinnati's spring training in 1954, and in April, Harmon made the Reds' roster.

On April 17, 1954 at Milwaukee's County Stadium in the top of the seventh inning, manager "Birdie": Tebbetts needed a pinch hitter for pitcher Corky Valentine, Harmon got the call. His first major-league at-bat ended in a pop out but began an era for the Cincinnati Reds. **Harmon was the first African American to play for the Reds.**

However, Chuck was not the only player to make history for the team that day. Batting just before Harmon in the same game, Nino Escalera, a Puerto Rican of African descent, became the first black player for

Cincinnati. When asked who deserved credit for being the first player of color, Harmon said, "I was the first African-American; Nino was the first black. I don't know what difference it makes, but for history's sake, they might as well get it right."

Harmon hit over .300 during five consecutive minor-league seasons but never approached such numbers in the majors. He also played winter baseball in Puerto Rico winter baseball for 4 years.

In a four-season major-league career, Harmon was a .238 hitter with seven home runs and 59 RBI's in 289 games played. After his major-league career ended, he played four seasons in the minors from 1958 to 1961 in AAA leagues for five teams.

Following his playing career, Harmon worked as a scout with the Cleveland Indians and Atlanta Braves in baseball, and the Indiana Pacers in basketball.

With the death of "Monte" Irvin on January 11, 2016, Harmon is currently the oldest living African American to play in the major leagues at the age of 95.

CHAPTER 12

Washington Senators

In the early 1940s, although Washington, D.C. was moving toward an African American majority and Griffith Stadium stood in a largely black neighborhood near the predominantly black Howard University, the Senators' baseball crowds were still segregated.

"Sam" Lacy, a journalist for the *Washington Tribune*, held a meeting with the Senators owner Clark Griffith, in 1937, after Commissioner Landis refused his request to discuss integration. He stated that although Griffith earned praise for signing Cuban players, the Senators alienated black fans by banning interracial minor-league games at Griffith Stadium and maintaining segregated seating for white games. Griffith, like many other owners, saw integration as detrimental to his franchise. Lacy concluded that only economic forces (profits) would open the doors of major-league baseball to black players.

Clark Griffith held back from integrating his team. In 1953, he said, "Nobody is going to stampede me into signing Negro players merely for the sake of satisfying certain pressure groups."

Washington did sign many Cuban players in the 1950s, such as Connie Marrero, Camilo Pasquel, Pedro Ramos, Sandy Consuegra, and Julio Becquer, but none were black Cubans.

Senators' scout Joe Cambria scouted in Cuba under orders from the Senators' front office to recruit light-skinned Cubans. The year before,

Senators' farm director Ossie Bluege gave the written command, "If he's white, all is go, if not, he stays home."

In 1954, the Senators had not yet integrated. The press anticipated the Senators' color line would be broken in 1954, Cuban Angel Scull, the *Sporting News* reported, was "assured of an outfield berth and will be the first Negro ever to play for the Senators". Topps even included a baseball card of Scull in its 1954 set in anticipation of his major-league debut.

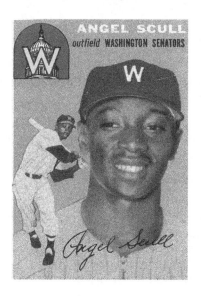

In 1954, Scull went to spring training with the Washington Senators, but by many accounts, the club simply wasn't yet willing to break the color line with a black American player. He was returned to the International League.

Scull never played in the major leagues. He was assigned to Class D Wellsville Rockets where he hit for a .329 average in 124 games and led the Pony League in stolen bases. He stayed in the minor leagues until 1969, which included 14 Triple-A seasons with the Atlanta Crackers, Charleston Senators, Havana Sugar Kings, Montreal Royals, Petroleros de Poza Rica, Syracuse Chiefs, Toronto Maple Leafs, and

Vancouver Mounties. In his minor league career he played over 1377 games with 1290 hits, a .254 batting average, 331 RBI's and 134 stolen bases.

After the Black Cuban-born Carlos Paula was signed and promoted to the major league roster, Shirley Povich complained in the *Washington Post* that Griffith would accept "dark players from other lands, but never an American Negro."

The first black African American player on the team was Joe Black who was signed as a free agent, but appeared in only seven games and pitched 12 innings in 1957.

In 1959, Washington traded for Lenny Green who played in 88 games in 1959 batting .246 and 127 games in 1960 batting .294. He remained with the team as they moved to Minnesota and then was traded to Baltimore in 1964.

In 1960, they traded Paula for catcher Earl Battey who played one year in Washington and then onto Minnesota when the Senators moved there in 1961.

In 1961, the Senators became the Minnesota Twins; it would be 1964 before black players such as Tony Olivia and "Mudcat" Grant joined the team.

Washington Senators

Carlos Paula

September 6, 1954

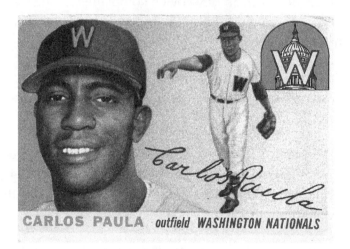

CARLOS PAULA *outfield* WASHINGTON NATIONALS

Carlos Paula Conill (November 28, 1927–April 25, 1983) was a major-league baseball right fielder who played for the Washington Senators from 1954 to 1956.

Carlos started his career with the Paris Texas Indians in 1952, where he batted .334. He continued with the Texas Indians in 1953 batting .300.

Washington acquired Paula via a transaction with the Paris Indians Big State League before the 1954 season.

The Senators decided Paula wasn't read and so they sent the Cuban down to the Senators' Charlotte Hornets farm team of the Class A Sally League on March 30, 1954.

The Washington *Post* assured readers that Paula would be called up if any of the Nationals' outfielders faltered. But, starting right fielder

Tom Umphlett hit .219 in 1954 (with a .255 on-base percentage) and left fielder Roy Sievers was not much better at .232. Paula stayed in Charlotte, leading the team in hits, doubles, triples and total bases, batting .309 and, if one local newspaper is to be believed, Paula once launched a 559-foot home run.

On Sept. 6, 1954, more than seven years after Jackie Robinson debuted, the Washington Senators became the 12th of 16 teams to integrate its roster.

It was not front page news, nor even worthy of a headline. Instead, the *Post* buried the news in the last paragraph of the game story: "Carlos Paula, Cuban outfielder, became the first Negro player to break into action in a regular game with the Senators."

Even so, Paula played in only 12 of the Senators' first 28 games in 1955, 11 times as a pinch hitter. In his one start, he banged out three hits, then went back to pinch hitting. By the end of May, Paula was hitting .333 and earned regular playing time.

He played in 115 games during the 1955 season, batting .299 with six home runs and 55 runs batted in. The average newspaper reader, however, might not have noticed. Even the weekly *Baltimore Afro-American* gave Paula short notice.

In a regular feature called "Tabbing the Stars," the paper updated statistics on black ballplayers, from stars like Jackie Robinson, Roy Campanella, and "Monte" Irvin, to players like Bob Thurman (who hit .217 in '55), Milton Smith (who hit .196 in 36 games, then never played again), and Paula's fellow countryman Ramon Mejias (who finished 1955 hitting .216). Sadly, Carlos Paula's name and numbers were never listed.

If the *Afro-American* ignored Paula, the *Washington Post* did something else. On July 20, after Paula had gone 3-for-5, the paper found fault with Paula's base running on squeeze plays. The next day, Paula homered, but the headline read "Paula's Lapse Allows Smith to Score from First Base on Single." On Sept. 20th, a syndicated game recap opened with, "Washington's rookie right fielder, Carlos Paula, was the Yankees' best weapon in the night game, playing a foul-line line drive into a double in the three-run third and kicking a bases-loaded single allowing three runs to score, and misjudging a hard wallop into a triple in the six-run seventh."

In 1956, he appeared in only 33 games and batted .183. His last game was on June 23, 1956.

Career totals for 157 games include a .271 batting average (124-for-457), 9 HR, 60 RBI, 44 runs scored and a slugging percentage of .416. In his 111th appearances in the outfield, he handled 211 out of 222 total chances successfully for a fielding percentage of .950, well below the league average during his era.

Paula died in 1983 at the age of 55 in Miami, Florida of unknown causes.

The Senators signed three "dark skinned" Cubans and brought them up in 1955. The first was Vince Gonzales, who appeared on April 13, 1955, and only played in one game.

Wenceslao Gonzales O'Reilly (September 28, 1925–March 11, 1981) was a Cuban-born professional baseball player during the 1950s and 1960s. A left-handed pitcher, Gonzales appeared in one major-league baseball game in 1955 as a member of the Washington Senators.

Gonzales entered pro baseball in 1951 as a member of the Cuidad Juarez Indios and in his first season, leading the Class C Southwest International League with 32 victories. He followed by winning 25 and 22 games for the Indios in 1952 and 1953. In 1954, he won only two games due to an injury.

In 1955, Gonzales was a member of the Senators' early season roster and appeared in the second game of the campaign, a road contest against the New York Yankees. Called into the game in the seventh inning with Washington already losing 13–1, he worked the final two innings, allowing six hits, six earned runs, and three bases on balls in an eventual 19–1 rout. Gonzales spent the rest of the 1955 season in the Arizona-Mexico League and the rest of his career pitching in Mexico, appearing in a game as late as in 1969.

Vince died on May 11, 1981.

The second player to play for the Senators was Juan Delis, who played in 54 games, making his debut on April 15, 1955.

Juan Francisco Delis (February 27, 1928–July 23, 2003) was a third baseman in major-league baseball. He played for the Senators in 1955.

Delis' organized baseball career began in 1952 when he was signed as a free agent by the Washington Senators

Juan played in 1952 in the Washington Minor League organization. where he batted .298.

Delis also played in the Cuban Winter League, winning the "Rookie of the Year" award in 1953–'54.

Delis was 27 years old when he broke into the big leagues on April 16, 1955, with the Washington Senators. In 54 games, he batted .189 with 11 RBI.

After his major league career, Delis played in the high levels of minor league baseball through 1964 mainly with Cincinnati Minor League teams. He led the Mexican League in doubles with 43 in 1960 and 37 in 1962.

Juan Dellis retired after the 1966 season.

He died on July 23, 2003.

The third player to play for the Senators was José Valdivielso who appeared on June 21, 1955, and played through 1961.

José Martinez de Valdivielso (born May 22, 1934) is a Cuban-born former professional baseball player. A shortstop, he appeared in 401 games over all or part of five seasons in major-league baseball, between 1955 and 1961, for the Washington Senators and their later incarnation, the Minnesota Twins.

Jose Valdivielso was 21 years old when he broke into the big leagues on June 21, 1955, with the Washington Senators.

A light-hitting shortstop with a good glove, he appeared in 401 games during his five seasons in the majors. Jose managed to hit major league pitching at just a .219 average while with the Washington Senators in 1955, 1956, 1959 and 1960 and the Minnesota Twins in 1961. He spent the 1957 and 1958 seasons in the minor leagues with the Indianapolis Indians, Minneapolis Millers and Phoenix Giants.

From 1953 to 1961, Valdivielso played in the Cuban Winter League as well. In 1958-59 and 1959-60 Juan led the Cuban Winter League in sacrifice hits.

Jose finished out the last three years of his ten-year minor league career (1962-1964) with the Vancouver Mounties and the Indianapolis Indians, winding up with a .264 career hitting average in 745 games with 2,536 at-bats. Jose had a few fond memories of his time in baseball memorializing them by saying:

"Coming to Yankee Stadium as a player was my biggest thing," said the former shortstop. "To me it was the greatest accomplishment of my life. The first time I was in New York with the Washington Senators, we had a game at two o'clock on a Saturday afternoon. I was so excited I arrived at the Stadium between 8-9 in the morning. It was the greatest game of my life. Whitey Ford was pitching and I went three-for-three."

Jose was also a part of the only all-Cuban triple play in big league history. He recalled: "It was at Kansas City. Whitey Herzog was hitting with runners on first and second and Camilo Pascual was pitching. Herzog hit a line drive to Camilo (one out). Pascual threw to Julio Becquer at first base (two outs). Julio then threw to me at second base (three outs). A 1-3-6 triple play."

In 1960, the team's sixtieth and last season in Washington, Valdivielso was the Senators' most-used shortstop, starting in 92 games and playing a career-high 117 contests. By late September he had lost his starting job to Zoilo Versalles, a 20-year-old fellow countryman.

Valdivielso's professional career extended through the 1964 season. All told, he collected 213 hits in the majors, with 26 doubles and eight triples to go along with his nine home runs.

After baseball, Jose became a New York City Youth Recreation Director before becoming a sports announcer for a Spanish speaking television station. He also did radio in Newark, NJ where he had broadcasted New York Yankees games also on Spanish language radio stations.

Jose is one of the oldest living ex-Major League players at age of 85.

CHAPTER 13

New York Yankees

The Yankees were one of the last four teams to integrate. Some say it was because they were so successful.

In an eighteen year span from 1947 to 1964 other than 1948, 1954, and 1959, the Yankees represented the American League in the World Series.

In the years 1947, 1949, 1951–1953, and 1955–1956, both teams in the World Series were from New York, with the Yankees playing against either the Dodgers or Giants.

The delay by America's most popular and successful team to integrate led to everything from editorials to picket lines, all of which were ignored by New York's top brass.

In his book, *Baseball's Great Experiment*, author Jules Tygiel quotes General Manager George Weiss as saying; "The Yankees are not going to promote a Negro player to the Stadium simply in order to be able to say that they have such a player. We are not going to bow to pressure groups on this issue."

Others would say the Yankees just did not want a black player. In 1947, Effa Manley, business manager for the Eagles, believed her club's close relationship with the New York Yankees might place Larry Doby as the American League's first black player in a Yankees uniform, but the Yankees did not take any interest in him.

General Manager Weiss had previously passed on opportunities to scout and possibly sign Ernie Banks and Willie Mays amongst others and comments from Yankees staffers suggested prejudice had been a factor.

In *Baseball's Great Experiment,* traveling secretary Bill McCorry is quoted as saying of the then 19-year-old Mays, "The kid can't hit a curveball" and after Mays' early success with the Giants, "I got no use for him or any of them. No n----- will ever have a berth on any train I'm running."

As recalled in Roger Kahn's seminal 1972 book, *The Boys of Summer,* Weiss had said in 1952 that having a black ballplayer would draw undesirables to the stadium. "We don't want that sort of crowd," he said. "It would offend box seat holders from Westchester to have to sit with n-----s."

Money was another factor behind the resistance of the Yankees to integrate. In August 1946, the team's then owner and general manager, Larry MacPhail, chaired a special committee that reported to the new commissioner "Happy" Chandler. The report stated, in part, "the relationship of the Negro player, and/or the existing Negro Leagues to Professional Baseball is a real problem," in large part because MLB integration could cause the demise of the Negro leagues. That, MacPhail's committee noted, would cost teams like the Yankees nearly $100,000 it netted annually from renting the stadium to the Black Yankees, a Negro-leagues' team.

In 1953, on the television show *Youth Wants to Know,* Jackie Robinson challenged the general manager of the Yankees, George Weiss, on the racial record of his team, which had yet to sign a black player.

In 1953, the new Negro sports magazine called *Our Sports* published an article titled "Will the Yankees hire a Negro Player?" where they asked why the Yankees had 21 Negroes in their farm system, but none on the major-league roster.

In late July 1953, New York seemed ready to call up Vic Power, a dark-skinned Puerto Rican who was tearing up the Triple-A American Association with his hitting. Instead, Weiss surprised the press and fans by promoting Gus Triandos, a white player from Double A. "It would appear that the only advantage Triandos had was one of circumstance in not being born a Negro," Joe Bostic wrote in *The New York Amsterdam News*.

Power was a strong hitter who was on his way toward winning the American Association batting crown with a .349 average. The Yankees seemed more concerned that he dated light-skinned women, a common convention in his native Puerto Rico, but one that went against American social behaviors at that time. Weiss traded Power to the Philadelphia Athletics that winter. "Maybe he can play, but not for us," Weiss is quoted as saying in Kahn's book, *The Era: 1947–'57*. "He's impudent, and he goes for white women. Power is not the Yankee type."

Elston Howard might have been brought up earlier than 1955, but he served in the military in 1951 and 1952.

New York Yankees

Elston Howard

April 14, 1955

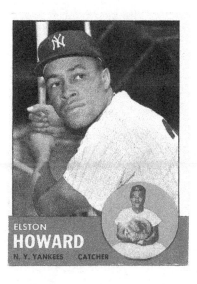

Elston Howard (February 23, 1929–December 14, 1980) was the first African American player on the Yankees roster in 1955, eight years after Jackie Robinson had broken the MLB color barrier in 1947.

Howard was named the American League's Most Valuable Player for the 1963 pennant winners, becoming the first black player in AL history to win the honor.

In the summer of 1945, Howard, then age 16, was playing baseball in a sandlot when Frank "Teannie" Edwards (a former baseball player) approached him. "The biggest kid on the field was hitting the ball so hard and far that it made Teannie mad," wrote Arlene Howard in her book *Elston and Me*. "When he got to the field he found out that the big kid was, in fact, one of the youngest on the lot."

197

Edwards, as a scout wanted Elston for the St. Louis Braves.

On April 21, 1946, Howard debuted in the Tandy League, (a St. Louis semi-pro team) catching in a game. He had two hits and threw out two runners trying to steal second in a 5–4 loss.

The following year, 1947, Jackie Robinson broke the color barrier in the major leagues. Now at the age of 18, Howard was working at Bauer's grocery store and finishing at all black Vashon High School.

He was urged by "Teannie" Edwards to attend an open tryout in 1947 for the St. Louis Cardinals at Sportsman's Park. Elston attended, but the Cardinals showed no interest. The Cardinals would not field a black player until 1954.

Meanwhile, college beckoned with three Big Ten schools (Illinois, Michigan and Michigan State) recruiting him for football, as well as being interested in him for track, basketball, and baseball, Edwards called in scouts from the Kansas City Monarchs to consider signing Elston. The Monarchs were so impressed that they went to his mother to negotiate a professional contract. It was promised that Elston would get $500 a month, mailed directly to his mother.

In 1948 with Kansas City, Howard, like the rest of the Monarchs, was treated like a king. Player-manager Buck O'Neil and Earl "Mickey" Taborn (the Monarchs catcher and Ellie's roommate) showed him the ropes. Because Taborn was the regular catcher, Howard played left field, filling in at first base when O'Neil was out of the lineup. He hit .264 based on the few statistics available.

Then in 1949, Taborn left to play for the Triple-A Newark Bears. By the time he returned in 1950, Howard's new roommate was a young fellow named Ernie Banks. Unfortunately, no statistics are available for this period of time when Elston was playing for the Newark Bears.

Tom Greenwade, the legendary Yankees scout, soon came calling to look at a different player, but Buck O'Neil steered him to Howard. Within days, Elston Howard and Frank Barnes had been sold for $25,000 to the New York Yankees.

Now at the age of 21, Howard debuted on July 26, 1950, in left field for the Class A Muskegon, Michigan Clippers earning $400 a month.

Howard missed the 1951 and 1952 seasons while serving his military service in the U.S. Army.

By 1953, he was playing for the Yankees' top farm team, the Kansas City Blues, where he batted .286.

He spent February 1954 at "Yankee Prospects School" with 28 other ballplayers in Lake Wales, Florida, and March at spring training with the big club, sharing a locker room with "Yogi" Berra, Phil Rizzuto, Mickey Mantle, and Billy Martin.

Bill Dickey, former Yankee great, worked with him to make him a major-league catcher. Some newspapers, like the *Baltimore Afro-American*, criticized the Yankees, claiming the move to catcher was a manufactured setback to keep Howard in the minors. When the Yankees broke camp, they took three catchers north with them: "Yogi" Berra, Charlie Silvera, and Ralph Houk. They didn't want to send Howard back to the Blues, so they arranged for him to play with the Toronto Maple Leafs in the International League. Canada was a bit more welcoming to black players. Howard won the league MVP Award, hitting.330, with 22 homers and 109 RBI's.

Media reports that Howard would be a Yankee by the following spring increased, as did protests pressuring the Yankees to integrate. The Yankees won 103 games in 1954, but not the league pennant. Cleveland, featuring black outfielder Larry Doby, won the flag with 111 wins, a sign that the Yankees might need to integrate their team.

Elston's on-field debut followed on April 14, 1955, at Fenway Park, subbing for Irv Noren, who had been ejected for arguing with an umpire. He got a base hit and knocked in a run. Perhaps the most memorable effect of Howard's presence on the Yankees that year, was that the team changed its hotel policy, staying only in hotels that would accept Howard as a guest.

In 1955 he hit .290 in 97 games his rookie season, with another five hits in the World Series, including an impressive home run in his first World Series at-bat.

Howard's pay jumped in 1956 from $6,000 to $10,000. He appeared in only 98 games, 26 at catcher, and finished the year with a .262 batting average, five homers, and 34 RBI.

In 1957, he was with the Yankees once again hoping for more playing time. After "Moose" Skowron got hurt, Howard got more playing time and in midseason, Stengel named him to the American League All-Star team. He ended the season hitting .253, with eight home runs and 44 RBI, playing in 110 games.

As the 1958 season opened, hope for regular catching duties again flared. Stengel again hinted that Berra could not catch so much. Howard ended the year hitting .314, with 11 homers, and 66 RBI in 103 games, 67 behind the plate.

In 1959, Casey's annual prediction that Berra would catch less was again wrong. In fact, "Yogi" caught 116 games, more than the previous year. Though Elston reached his career high in games played at 125, the platoon system made him feel like a part-time player. One thing that did change was that the Yankees picked up another black player, Panamanian Héctor López, who came from Kansas City in a trade.

Because the club had done poorly, General Manager George Weiss tried to cut salaries in 1960. Howard's offer was $5,000 less than his previous year's wages and he held out, missing the reporting date for spring training. Weiss relented, giving him $25,500, a $3,000 raise. Shelved by a few injuries, he nonetheless did get in 107 games, batting .245 and catching in 91 games and made the All-Star team.

Ralph Houk, the former second-string catcher pushed back to the minors in 1960 by Elston's emergence, became the manager in 1961. Preferring a more stable lineup than Stengel had, Houk plugged Howard in as his catcher 111 times, playing Berra more in left field. Howard responded with a career year, hitting .348 with 21 home runs in 129 games.

The year 1962 brought another improvement. Pressured to stop segregating their black players in spring training housing, the Yankees moved their camp to Fort Lauderdale.

In 1962 Howard's pay raise was significant, to $42,500, and he earned it. He hit another 21 home runs with 138 hits and a .279 average while playing in a career high 136 games. The three catchers, Howard, Berra, and Johnny Blanchard, combined for 44 homers that season. Howard made the All Star team again.

In 1963 Elston switched to a heavier bat, 38 ounces, which he said helped his power to right field. He hit a career high 28 home runs that year. He ended the season with a .287 average and became the first African American to win the American League MVP Award. He also took home the Gold Glove with his .994 fielding percentage.

His salary for 1964 jumped to $60,000, making him one of the best paid players in baseball. (Mantle earned $107,000.) In a career-high 150 games, he tallied a career-high 172 hits for a .313 average, although his homer total dropped to 15. He also walked a career-high 48 times.

In 1965, Howard injured his elbow during spring training and it worsened over the next few weeks. By April 13th, it was so swollen that he couldn't bend his arm enough to eat breakfast. Bone chips were surgically removed from his elbow and the Yankees slipped in the standings. Howard didn't catch again until June 13th catching 95 games after his return despite the sore arm. He ended with the lowest average of his career, .233, while the Yankees went nowhere.

The year 1966 was not much better. The arm still hurt, and the now 37-year-old Howard hit .256, while the Yankees were stuck in the cellar.

In 1967 the Yankees offered a $10,000 pay cut. After a 4-day holdout, Howard accepted only a $6,000 cut and a clause that if he performed well, he could earn the money back.

On August 3, 1967 Houk telephoned to tell him he had been traded to the Red Sox. Boston was in second place at the time and unlike the Yankees, they had a chance to reach the top. He joined the Sox on the road in Minnesota and was greeted by Manager Dick Williams, two years his junior.

How fitting that Elston Howard's tenth and final World Series would be against his old hometown, St. Louis. Unfortunately, the Cardinals beat the Sox as Elston managed only two hits in the series. During the offseason of 1967 he pondered retirement. The Red Sox asked him to play and later coach. The Yankees suggested a minor-league coaching job or scouting position. Bill Veeck said he wanted to make Howard the game's first black manager if he could buy the Washington Senators.

When spring of 1968 came, the Red Sox offered a $1,000 raise to Howard and he decided to play 1 more year.

The Red Sox and Elston were banged up including Howard's elbow that was acting up again. At midseason, he couldn't straighten it, and did not want surgery. Howard played in only 71 games that season, but in his final game at Fenway, he received a standing ovation. He batted .241, with five homers and 18 RBI.

He held a press conference on October 21, 1968, to announce his retirement from baseball.

Then on October 22, 1968 at another press conference in New York, he announced he was taking the first-base coaching job with the New York Yankees.

Elston became the first black coach for an American League team, but never reached his goal of becoming the first black manager. (That honor would be held by Frank Robinson in 1975 with the Indians.)

In mid-February 1979, after nearly collapsing at La Guardia Airport, Elston was diagnosed with myocarditis. A virus was attacking the muscles of his heart and the doctors prescribed total rest.

Sadly, his heart was giving out and on December 4, 1980 he was admitted to Columbia Presbyterian Hospital where he died two weeks later at age 51.

In 1984, the Yankees retired his number, "32".

New York Yankees

Harry Simpson

(See Chapter 2, Cleveland Indians for more details on Harry)

The second black player on the New York Yankees was Harry Simpson. He played in 75 games in 1957 and 24 games in 1958

On June 15, 1957 Simpson was traded by the Kansas City Athletics along with Ryne Duren and Jim Pisoni to the New York Yankees for Woodie Held, Billy Martin, Bob Martyn, and Ralph Terry.

Continuing his career, on June 15, 1958 Simpson was traded by the New York Yankees along with Bob Grim to the Kansas City Athletics for Duke Maas and Virgil Trucks.

New York Yankees
Héctor López
1959–1966

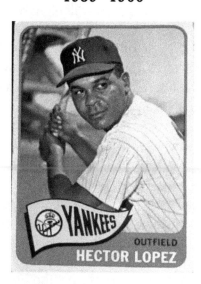

Héctor López Swainson (born July 9, 1929) is a former left fielder and third baseman in major-league baseball who played for the Kansas City Athletics and New York Yankees from 1955 to 1966. He is notable as the first black manager at the AAA baseball level and as the third outfielder on the Maris/Mantle Yankees.

Lenny Pecou, a part-time scout and career minor leaguer who played outfield in 1950 for St. Hyacinthe, Quebec, in the Class C Provincial League, saw López playing winter ball and recommended him to St. Hyacinthe. The independent club signed the 21-year-old Panamanian and he played the 1951 season for the fifth-place Saints, hitting .297.

In 1952, López returned to the Provincial League, down from eight to six teams, and hit .329 with six home runs, 75 RBI, and a league leading 115 runs scored.

In 1953, Philadelphia signed Héctor and sent him to Williamsport of the Class A Eastern League. The A's finished sixth, but he hit a solid .270 with eight homers and 51 RBI.

Assigned to Ottawa of the Triple-A International League in 1954, López continued to play well, batting .316 with eight home runs and 53 RBI.

In 1955, he went to spring training with the Athletics, after the franchise had been shifted to Kansas City, but was sent to Triple-A Columbus, also in the International League, to learn how to play second base. After he batted .321 in the first month of the season, the Athletics called him up on May 12th.

Héctor enjoyed a good year in 1955 with the Kanas City Athletics, averaging .290 with 15 doubles, two triples, 15 homers, and 68 RBI. López played 128 games, 93 at third and 35 at second, but he committed 23 errors at third (for a total of 29 total errors), a figure that topped all American League third basemen.

In 1956, López enjoyed a good season at the plate, hitting .273 with 27 doubles, three triples, 18 homers, and 69 RBI. He played 121 of his 151 games at the "hot corner", where he led American League third basemen with 26 errors.

In 1957, he hit a career high batting average of .294 with 19 doubles, four triples and 11 home runs.

In 1958, López enjoyed his fourth solid season with the Athletics, hitting .261 with 28 doubles, four triples, and 17 home runs, his fourth straight season of double-digit homers. Of his 151 games, Héctor played 96 at second base.

López saw his solid career shift to a better team when the A's traded him to the New York Yankees on May 26, 1959.

After more than four seasons in Kansas City as a regular infielder, mostly at third base, López continued to play well, hitting .283 in 112 games for the third-place Yankees the rest of the '59 season. He slugged a career-best 22 home runs in 1959. In 147 games, he played 76 at third base, 35 in the outfield and 33 at second base, committing 31 errors.

In 1960, Manager Casey Stengel moved light-hitting Clete Boyer to third base and took advantage of López's versatility by using him as a utility player. At one time or another for Kansas City and New York, López handled all four infield and all three outfield positions. For the Yankees, he usually played left or right field. In 1960, he played in 131 games, 106 in the outfield, five at second base, one at third base, and 25 games solely as a pinch hitter (in some games, he appeared in multiple capacities).

In 1960, averaging .284 in 408 at-bats, he contributed 14 doubles, six triples, and nine home runs to help contribute to the Yankees' pennant-winning team.

The Yankees came back in 1961 with another strong ball club, and their pennant-winning season was highlighted by the home-run race between Roger Maris and Mickey Mantle. The "Bronx Bombers," living up to their nickname, capped the season by defeating the Cincinnati Reds in five games in the World Series. López, however, played less during that regular season. In 93 games and 243 at-bats, he hit .222, with three home runs and 22 RBI.

In 1962, López bounced back with a solid season. Playing in 106 games, 84 of those in the outfield, batting .275 with six home runs and 48 RBI.

In 1963, the Yankees won their fourth straight pennant, and López averaged .249 with 14 homers and 52 RBI's in 130 games.

Overall, López played in five World Series. The Yankees won two of the five, and Héctor averaged .286 in the postseason. But in 1964, when the Yankees (now managed by "Yogi" Berra) fell to the St. Louis Cardinals in seven games in the World Series, López played in only three games, subbing once in right field and going 0-for-2 as a pinch hitter.

The once-dominant Yankees won the 1964 pennant by one game over the Chicago White Sox. López, who hit .260 in 127 games, enjoyed his last season of double-digit homers, hitting 10 round-trippers and producing 34 RBI.

This good hitter from Panama produced similar numbers in 1965, averaging .261 in 111 games with seven homers and 39 RBI.

But in 1966, his final major-league season, he played in only 54 games, batted 117 times, and hit .214.

The Yankees released him after the 1966 season.

After being released, López played two seasons in the minors. He batted .295 with 13 homers for Hawaii of the Pacific Coast League in 1967 and he hit .258 with 13 round-trippers for Buffalo of the International League in 1968.

Héctor became the first black manager of a Triple-A club, piloting Buffalo to a seventh-place finish in 1969.

In his 12 big-league seasons for Kansas City and New York, Lopez averaged .269, collecting 1,251 hits, including 193 doubles, 37 triples, and 136 homers.

During the 1960 to 1964 seasons, López played in five straight fall classics, batting .286 in the postseason.

Considering that he grew up in Latin America at a time when black players could not make it to the major leagues, López enjoyed a very successful professional career.

López was one of three black men (along with Sam Bankhead and Gene Baker) to manage in the minor leagues in the twenty-five years after Jackie Robinson broke the color barrier in 1947. In 1994 and 1995, he managed the Gulf Coast League Yankees, the rookie-league team. Lopez was the manager of the Panama national baseball team in the 2009 World Baseball Classic.

López retired following the 1966 season from Major League baseball at the age of 36. That year, he also participated in his first Old-Timers' Day. He has returned to the annual event every year (totaling 52 years as of 2018).

New York Yankees

Jesse Gonder

After his 1955 high school graduation Gonder signed with Cincinnati Redlegs scout Bobby Mattick.

Gonder was assigned to Cincinnati's Ogden, Utah affiliate in the Class C Pioneer League. He carried the bulk of the club's catching responsibilities while placing among the league leaders with eight triples and 15 home runs. This success did not warrant an advance in 1956 as Gonder toiled in Class C Wausau, Wisconsin. He carried a .300 average into August when a slight decline in the later weeks caused Gonder to slip to .296. He still placed among the Northern League leaders in doubles (23) and home runs (14). Continued success followed in 1957 as Gonder raced through three Class B teams. In August of 1957 he was acquired by the Monterrey Sultanes, initiating a two-year love-hate relationship between player and country. Gonder loved Mexico and learned to speak Spanish fluently. Teamed alongside many Negro League players he witnessed no racism, a vast difference from the humiliations and insults he received stateside.

But Gonder also worried about his career. He viewed the Mexican League as a graveyard for ballplayers and was hopeful of returning stateside in 1959.

Jesse was assigned to the Havana Sugar Kings Minor League team in 1959.

Gonder enjoyed his time with the Havana Sugar Kings. Though he slumped offensively, Gonder returned fulltime to his familiar catching responsibilities, and was even behind the plate on those occasions when Fidel Castro took to the mound (who most don't know was a pitcher) before and during his reign as Prime Minister of Cuba.

In 1960 Cincinnati sent Gonder to the New York Yankees and he was assigned to the AAA Richmond Virginians. Gonder was the only African-American on the team based in the Confederacy's capital and his career exploded. Though his .327 average lacked enough at bats to capture the 1960 International League batting crown, Gonder drew notice with his power as well.

Given a September call-up with the Yankees, **Jesse Gonder** made his debut on September 23, 1960, in Boston as a pinch hitter. He appeared in 7 games in 1960.

In another pinch-hit role in Yankee Stadium a week later, Gonder connected against Boston hurler Bill Monbouquette for his first major-league hit, a home run. The next day, he made his catching debut, driving in Roger Maris with a third-inning single in a 3-1 win over the Red Sox. After the season, Gonder barnstormed across the South with Hank Aaron and other African American All-Stars. Journalists anticipated that during the following spring camp Gonder "will be watched closely at St. Petersburg."

In a sportswriters' poll in 1961 Gonder's near-.400 Grapefruit League average and improved defense earned him the label as the Yankees' hottest young prospect. He was runner-up to Roland Sheldon for the James P. Dawson Memorial Award as the top performing rookie in the Yankees' fold. With the prospect of breaking camp with four catchers, Berra, Elston Howard, Johnny Blanchard, rumors emerged of the Yankees dangling Howard to the Los Angeles Dodgers in exchange for Duke Snider and Johnny Podres. Gonder heard years later that the Los Angeles Angels had approached the Yankees about him. Nothing happened and the crowded catching field afforded Gonder little playing time when the season opened.

Used exclusively in pinch-hitting roles, Gonder had a mere 12 at bats through May 28th, 1961 before he went back to Richmond. A pulled ligament in his hand affected his play and his batting average slumped to .225 with 9 homers and 34 RBI's in fewer than 300 plate appearances.

The Yankees appeared to have soured on Gonder as quickly as they had lauded him months earlier. On December 14, 1961, Gonder was traded to the Reds in exchange for lefty hurler Marshall Bridges.

In 1962, he played in four games with the Reds and then through 1969, played with the Reds, Pirates, and Mets in the major leagues and several PCL minor teams.

In 1962 he played for San Diego in the PCL and was voted MVP batting .342.

Gonder reverted to part-time status in 1965, and for the remainder of his big-league career played behind regular catchers Chris Cannizzaro, Joe Torre and Jim Pagliaroni. He was sent to Triple-A in June 1967 and wrapped up his pro career in 1969. In the Majors, Gonder collected 220 hits, including 28 doubles, two triples and 26 home runs. Five of those home runs came as a pinch hitter playing in 395 games

Jesse died on Nov 14, 2004 after a brief illness

New York Yankees

Al Downing

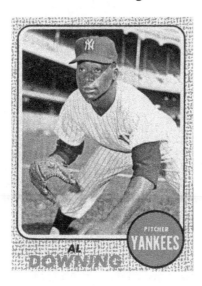

Alphonso Erwin Downing (born June 28, 1941) is an American former professional baseball pitcher. He played in major league baseball for the New York Yankees, Oakland Athletics, Milwaukee Brewers and Los Angeles Dodgers from 1961 through 1977.

Downing signed with the New York Yankees as an amateur free agent in 1961, and was promoted to the major league roster by July of that season.

Al played in the Yankees minor league system going 9 and 1 in 1961, and winning 12 games in parts of 1962 and 1963.

Downing appeared in six games in '61–'62 for the Yankees with one loss and then in 1963 was a starter with a 13–5 record and played through 1969 with the Yankees, winning 72 games.

On August 11, 1967, he struck out three batters (Tony Horton, Don Demeter, and Duke Sims) on nine pitches in the second inning of a 5–3 win over the Cleveland Indians. Downing became the sixth American League pitcher and the thirteenth pitcher in major-league history to accomplish this feat.

Injuries limited Downing to only twelve starts in 1968. Then in 1969, Yankees manager Ralph Houk began using Downing out of the bullpen more frequently as he made fifteen starts and fifteen relief appearances.

He was traded to the Oakland Athletics prior to the 1970 season along with catcher Frank Fernández for Danny Cater and Ossie Chavarria. Downing posted a 3-3 record with Oakland and was traded to the Milwaukee Brewers in 1970 where he went 2 and 10.

Prior to the start of the 1971 season, the Brewers traded Downing to the Los Angeles Dodgers for Andy Kosco. In his first season with the Dodgers in the National League (NL), Downing won 20 games and pitched a league-leading five shutouts. He earned NL Comeback Player of the Year honors, as well as finishing third in NL CY Young Award balloting.

In 1972 thru 1977 Al started 170 games winning 26 games and totaling 3 saves.

On April 8, 1974, Downing allowed a home run to Hank Aaron that was the 715th of Aaron's career, breaking the all-time record set by Babe Ruth. Downing made his third, and final, postseason appearance that season. His Dodgers lost 4 games to 1 to the Oakland A's.

Downing played two more full seasons with the Dodgers and then was released during the 1977 season with a 0–1 record and 6.75 ERA.

In his 17 year career he pitched in 405 games with an ERA of 3.22 and a record of 123 wins and 107 losses.

Downing served as a color analyst on Dodgers cable-TV broadcasts from 1980–87 and on Dodgers radio in 2005. He also broadcast for CBS Radio in the 1990s, and the Atlanta Braves in 2000. As of 2006, he remains on the Dodgers Speaker's Bureau working many events.

CHAPTER 14

Philadelphia Phillies

The Phillies were the last National League team to sign a black player, a full 10 years after Jackie Robinson made his debut for the Dodgers. Many thought that the 1950 Whiz Kids who won the National League pennant, with a young core of talented players, would be a force in the league for years to come. However, it was not to be, as the team finished with a 73–81 record in 1951, and (except for a second-place tie in 1964) he did not finish higher than third place again until 1975. Their lack of success was partly blamed on Carpenter's (the Phillies owner) unwillingness to integrate his team after winning a pennant with an all-white team.

Even economic results (the 1942 team won only 42 games and drew about 234,000 fans) did not seem to sway Philadelphia. The late 40's and early 50's saw the Phillies draw under 1,000,000 fans (except for 1950) each year while most east coast teams were drawing over 1,000,000 fans.

In 1942, they had announced a tryout to include Roy Campanella but never set it up.

The following year in 1943, Bill Veeck attempted to purchase the Phillies. Various articles and a book claimed Veeck planned to field an all-black team. Veeck visited Commissioner Landis to discuss his plans and believed he had a deal. The next day the National League took control of the Phillies and later sold them for half of what Veeck had offered.

Due to fans' and writers' complaints and economic conditions, the Phillies finally integrated in 1957 when John Kennedy joined the team but played in only five games.

The Phillies also purchased Joe Black from the Reds on May 25,1957, but he never played a game with them.

In the early 1960's, they did trade and bring up players such as Tony Taylor, Tony Gonzalez, and Pancho Herrera.

It would be 1964 before Dick Allen, a true black star, joined the team.

Philadelphia Phillies

John Kennedy

April 22, 1957

John Irvin Kennedy (October 12, 1926–April 27, 1998) was an American major-league baseball shortstop.

The Phillies' first African American player came out of spring training in 1957 hyped as "a prize package" and was compared to superstar Ernie Banks. Weeks later, after only five regular season at-bats in 1957, he was gone. John Kennedy would never play in the major leagues again.

That Kennedy would make any major-league roster was a surprise as he didn't even play organized baseball in high school in his hometown of Jacksonville FL, instead, favoring football and basketball. He finally started playing baseball after he graduated from high school.

In the first part of the 1950's, Kennedy played for a Canadian team. Unfortunately, no statistics could be found for this period of his career.

He signed as a free agent with the New York Giants before the 1953 season and batted .262 with the San Francisco minor-league team, but was released before the 1954 season.

In 1954, Kennedy caught on with the Birmingham Black Barons and later, the Kansas City Monarchs, both of the Negro American League, playing with them until 1956. In 1956, with the Monarchs, he hit .385 with 17 home runs.

Near the end of the 1956 season, with Kennedy having led the NAL batting race for most of the year, the Monarchs sold his contract to the Philadelphia Phillies. He was invited to work out for the Phillies after that season. Kennedy performed poorly over a 3-day period. Fortunately for him, scout Bill Yancey told management Kennedy was a better player than he showed and was selected to join the Phillies in spring training of 1957.

By March 1957, he was in a position to be the Phillies' first black player.

His original goal had been to make a top Phillies minor-league team, but he quickly became one of the best players on the entire roster. Kennedy hit above .400 for much of spring training, and by the end of it, was hitting .333, second highest on the team.

Though the club signed him to a contract on April 6, 1957, 10 days before the season opener, they quickly traded for Cuban shortstop Chico Fernandez, who had been in the Dodgers' organization, spending $75,000 to acquire his rights.

The answer for the Phillies' quick turn against Kennedy is complicated, but it is known Kennedy lied about his age. He entered spring training claiming to be 22. He was actually 30.years old. Exactly when the Phillies found out is unclear. Some surmise it was on the eve of the season, and that's why they traded for Fernandez, who was 25.

The opening day lineup was revealed with Fernandez starting at shortstop. As a Cuban, he became the Phillies' first minority player to appear in a game, though Kennedy was still the first African American.

When Kennedy made his major-league debut (April 22, 1957, at Roosevelt Stadium), he became the first black player in Philadelphia Phillies' history.

His next game was 2 days later, playing against the Pittsburgh Pirates at Connie Mack Stadium. He entered the game in the bottom of the 6th as a pinch runner for Harry Anderson, who had singled, and later scored on a bases-loaded triple by Ed Bouchee.

He played in a total of just five games, the last one being on May 3, 1957. At the plate, he was 0-for-2, including one strikeout. In his two appearances at shortstop, he had one assist, one error, and participated in one double play.

On April 16, the day of the first game for the Phillies, the *Tribune* featured a picture of Fernandez and Kennedy joined by two autograph seekers, with the headline "City Hails Phil's' Negro Players." The last line of the first paragraph read, "Thousands of negroes are happy because the Phillies have finally seen the light."

Throughout the years the Phillies have honored several Negro leaguers who played in Philadelphia, but there is no record of any celebration for Kennedy.

John Kennedy died on April 27, 1998.

Philadelphia Phillies

Chico Fernández

April 16, 1957

CHICO FERNANDEZ, Philadelphia Phillies

Although Chico was not considered black he was a Cuban minority and warrants to be included as he helped the Phillies reach a decision to send John Kennedy back to the minors.

Humberto Fernández Pérez (March 2, 1932–June 11, 2016), better known as **Chico Fernández,** was a Cuban professional shortstop. He played eight seasons in major-league baseball from 1956 to 1963 for the Brooklyn Dodgers, Philadelphia Phillies, Detroit Tigers and New York Mets. In 1965, he played one season in the Nippon Professional Baseball (NPB) for the Hanshin Tigers.

Chico was signed as a free agent in April 1951 by the Brooklyn Dodgers. Fernández began his career as a bright prospect for the Brooklyn Dodgers but was not able to break into the lineup with

Pee Wee Reese at the shortstop position. He remained in their Minor League system thru 1956.

On April 5, 1957, Fernández was traded by the Brooklyn Dodgers to the Philadelphia Phillies in exchange for Ron Negray, Tim Harkness, Elmer Valo, Mel Geho, $75,000, and a player to be named later.

Fernández made his first appearance with Philadelphia on April 16, 1957. Fernández was the Phillies' regular shortstop for two seasons. In his first year with the Phillies, Fernández collected 131 hits for a .262 batting average and a .302 on-base percentage. He also stole 18 bases, the fifth best in the National League.

In 1958, Chico played in 148 games and stole 12 bases while batting .230.

He then saw limited time in 1959 playing in 45 games and hitting .211.

In December 1959, the Phillies traded Fernández to the Detroit Tigers, where he became the Tigers' regular shortstop for the next three seasons from 1960 through 1962.

In 1960, Chico led American League shortstops with 34 errors; his fielding percentage was .947 while batting .241 with 35 stolen bases.

In 1961 Chico committed 23 errors and batted .248.

By 1962, he improved his fielding percentage to .960. More surprising, Fernández displayed power as a hitter in 1962. After six seasons in which he never hit more than six home runs, Fernández hit 20 home runs and 59 RBI for the Tigers in 1962. Both were career highs.

Detroit traded Fernández to the New York Mets in May 1963. Fernández played 58 games for the Mets in 1963 and then was traded to the Chicago White Sox in April 1964. Fernández did not play for the Sox. He finished his career playing in Japan in 1965 for the Hanshin Tigers.

Fernández died June 11, 2016, in Florida, aged 84 from complications of a stroke suffered the month before.

Philadelphia Phillies

Chuck Harmon

The second black was Chuck Harmon acquired via trade in 1957.

Chuck Harmon

Charles Byron Harmon (born April 23, 1924) is an American former professional baseball utility player in major-league baseball who played for the Cincinnati Redlegs (1954–1956), St. Louis Cardinals (1956–1957), and Philadelphia Phillies (1957).

(See Chapter 11 for more details on Chuck)

May 10, 1957: Traded by the St. Louis Cardinals to the Philadelphia Phillies for Glen Gorbous.

Philadelphia Phillies

Hank Mason

September 12, 1958

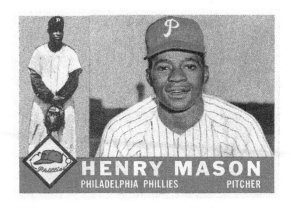

HENRY MASON
PHILADELPHIA PHILLIES   PITCHER

Henry Mason (born June 19, 1931) is an American former professional baseball player. Mason was a right-handed pitcher whose eight-seasons (1955–'62) minor-league career included brief stints as a relief pitcher with the 1958 and 1960 Philadelphia Phillies of major-league baseball. He began his career with the Kansas City Monarchs of the Negro American League in 1952.

Hank "Pistol" Mason made a name for himself while pitching for the Kansas City Monarchs of the Negro Leagues crossing paths with the likes of Buck O'Neil and Satchel Paige. In 1951, after completing high school, Mason left Marshall, Missouri and headed to Kansas City, where he was offered a tryout with the Kansas City Monarchs. Manager Buck O'Neill was so impressed with Mason that he signed him with the team. On opening day in 1952, Mason hurled 16 amazing innings to defeat the Philadelphia Stars 3-2.

Hank was the starting pitcher in the 1954 Negro Leagues East-West All-Star Game.

On October 15, 1954, Hank was purchased by the Philadelphia Phillies from Kansas City (Negro American) Monarchs.

In 1955-1956, Mason broke barriers by becoming the first black to play for the Schenectady Blue Jays, a Philadelphia Phillies farm team. After two phenomenal seasons, with records of 12-4 (1955) and 14- 7 (1956), leading the league with seven shutouts and placing second in the league with 176 strikeouts, Mason joined the Phillies in 1958 for one game and another three in 1960. He played until 1962.

Mason's MLB debut was not promising. On September 12, 1958, he appeared in a one-sided Phillies' loss, a 19–2 defeat at the hands of the San Francisco Giants at Connie Mack Stadium. Mason entered the game in the second inning as the Phillies third pitcher of the day, with the Giants already ahead, 8–0. He went the next five innings, surrendering seven hits and six earned runs, although he only allowed two extra-base hits, both doubles. He made three more appearances at the start of the 1960 Phillies season, and spent the balance of the 1960 campaign with the Triple-A Buffalo Bisons.

All told, Mason allowed 12 earned runs in four games played and $10\frac{2}{3}$ major-league innings, yielding 16 hits and seven bases on balls, striking out six.

In the minors through 1962, he won 60 of 106 decisions for a .556 winning percentage.

As of 2009, Mason was a clergyman living in Richmond, Virginia.

CHAPTER 15

Detroit Tigers

The Tigers were next to the last team in major-league baseball to promote a black player to their roster. They averaged well over 1.2 million in attendance from 1947 through 1959, coming close to 2 million in 3 seasons, so economics did not drive them to integrate.

The examples of Brooklyn and Cleveland in promoting black players and having winning teams gave the other teams something to seriously consider. Teams could continue to ignore black talent, but there would be a cost, fewer wins. The Detroit Tigers learned this lesson the hard way.

In 1948, the Tigers dropped from second to fifth place in the American League, and during the next 10 years, they would finish among the top three teams only once. In 1952, they wound up in last place in the American League, winning only 50 games and losing 104. No batter on the team hit higher than .284.

While other major-league teams were signing "Satchel" Paige, Willie Mays, Hank Aaron, and other black stars, the Detroit Tigers, under owner Walter Briggs, refused to hire any blacks. Wendell Smith, a black athlete and sportswriter, called Briggs "very prejudiced."

With Detroit in a tailspin, Walter Briggs died, and the Briggs family sold the Tigers in 1956 to Fred Knorr, a Michigan man who was very different from Briggs. Knorr believed in integration on principle and soon contributed $75,000 to help bring in and develop 17 black players in Detroit's minor-league system.

They would not win another World Series until 1968.

Detroit Tigers

Ozzie Virgil

June 6, 1958

Osvaldo Virgil Pichardo (born May 17, 1932) is a former professional baseball player and coach was the **first Dominican to play in major-league baseball**. He was a utility man who played in MLB between 1956 and 1969 for the New York Giants (1956–'57), Detroit Tigers (1958; 1960–61), Kansas City Athletics (1961), Baltimore Orioles (1962), Pittsburgh Pirates (1965), and San Francisco Giants (1966; 1969). Basically a third baseman, Virgil played all positions except pitcher and center field.

Ozzie attended DeWitt Clinton High School. "I did not make the baseball team in high school, but did play sandlot ball," he recalled in a 1997 interview with William M. Anderson in *Michigan History* magazine. "I played in a Puerto Rican league, which had eight or nine teams." After graduating from high school in 1950, Virgil joined the U.S. Marine Corps Reserves. "They called me up to active duty. I played baseball with the Marine Corps team at Camp LeJeune, North Carolina.

Ozzie served in the United States Marines from 1950–52 and began his 17-season professional playing career in 1953. He was signed by the New York Giants as a free agent just before the 1953 season.

Virgil made his minor-league debut in 1953 with St. Cloud, Minnesota, in the Northern League, where he hit .259.

In 1954, he upped his average to .291 at Danville, North Carolina, in the Piedmont League.

By 1955, Virgil had developed into a highly touted prospect. Past midseason, he was hitting .309 for Dallas in the Texas League. Virgil led Texas League third basemen with a .975 fielding percentage and was named to the All-Star team.

After spending the 1956 season with Minneapolis, where he hit .278 with 10 home runs and 73 runs batted in, Virgil made his major-league debut with the New York Giants on September 23rd. He appeared in three games, collecting five hits in 12 at-bats. In 1956, he became the first native Dominican to play in the major leagues.

Virgil spent the 1957 season with the Giants batting .235 while playing in 96 games. Before the 1958 season Virgil was traded to the Detroit Tigers along with first baseman Gail Harris for infielder Jim Finigan and $25,000. "I was very disappointed when I was traded to Detroit," Virgil told *Michigan History* magazine in 1997. "I thought the Giants needed a third baseman at that particular time. I knew that the Tigers did not have any black players on their roster or had never invited one to spring training. I wondered what they were going to do with me."

Virgil began the season with the Tigers' Charleston farm club, where he hit .293 and led the American Association with 34 runs batted in. On June 5th, he was promoted back to the big leagues. The following day **June 6, 1958, he made his debut** against the Washington Senators in the nation's capital.

Virgil had earned his opportunity with the Tigers and his Briggs Stadium debut was triumphant. In his first game in the Detroit ballpark, on June 17, he went five-for-five, doubling and singling off Washington Senators' pitcher Pedro Ramos and adding three singles off Al Cicotte. After his final hit, the crowd of 29,794 serenaded him with a standing ovation.

His call-up was of utmost significance to Detroit's black community, some of whose leaders were threatening to organize a boycott of Tigers' games because of the team's reluctance to integrate. The *Detroit News* reported that Virgil's promotion was "received with satisfaction by Negro leaders and fans." Virgil's own version of his promotion is more ambiguous. In 1997, almost 4 decades after integrating the Tigers, Virgil told *Detroit Free Press* reporter Jodie Valade, that, "although warmly received by most Tigers' fans, he was not acknowledged as a "true representative" by the city's black community. "The only thing I didn't like was that the black people in Detroit didn't accept me," he explained. "They thought of me more as a Dominican Republic player instead of a Negro."

In a nine-season, big-league career, Virgil posted a .231 batting average with 174 hits, 14 home runs, and 73 RBI in 324 games played.

After his playing career ended, Virgil spent 19 seasons as a coach for the Giants (1969–'72; 1974–'75); Montréal Expos (1976–'81); San Diego Padres (1982–'85); and Seattle Mariners (1986–'88). From 1977–'88, he served as the third-base coach for the Oakland A's on the staff of Baseball Hall of Fame manager Dick Williams.

His son, catcher Ozzie Jr., played in all or parts of 11 MLB seasons (1980–'90) and was a two-time National League All-Star.

The Monte Cristi Province airport in the Dominican Republic was renamed the Osvaldo Virgil National Airport in his honor in 2006.

Detroit Tigers

Larry Doby

April 10, 1959

First black African American player on the Tigers

Doby was traded to the Tigers from the Indians on March 21, 1959, and appeared in only 18 games for the Tigers before the White Sox purchased him on May 13, 1959.

On March 21, 1959, Larry Doby was traded by the Cleveland Indians to the Detroit Tigers for Tito Francona.

On May 13, 1959, Doby was purchased by the Chicago White Sox from the Detroit Tigers for $30,000.

See chapter 2 (Cleveland Indians) for details on Larry's career

Detroit Tigers

Jim Proctor

September 29, 1959

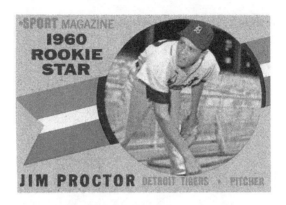

James Proctor (born September 9, 1935 in Brandywine, Maryland) is an American former professional baseball player who played for the Detroit Tigers in 1959.

Jim was the third black player to play for the Tigers but only appeared in two games in 1959.

Proctor went to Maryland State College, starring on a state-championship baseball team. After graduating, he signed with the Negro League Indianapolis Clowns.

Jim was originally signed by the Boston Braves in 1955 and assigned to West Palm Beach team in the Florida league.

He was purchased by the Detroit Tigers in October 1955 and continued in the minors until 1959.

In 1956 with multiple minor league teams, he posted an 11–8 stat with a 2.07 ERA. The following year in 1957, he went 14–8 with an

ERA of 2.64 with 125 strikeouts.

In 1958, he only appeared in two games due to injuries.

In 1959, he went 15–5 with an ERA of 2.19 with 131 strikeouts at Knoxville before being called up by the Tigers.

On Sept. 29, 1959, he debuted at Detroit, but he only got into two games, losing one.

In 1960 in the Minor Leagues he went 15 and 8 for Detroit but received no call up.

He ended his career by playing in the minor leagues for the Cleveland Indians through 1963 before retiring.

Detroit Tigers

"Jake" Wood

April 11, 1961

Jacob "Jake" Wood Jr. (born June 22, 1937) is a former professional baseball player. He played seven seasons in major-league baseball with the Detroit Tigers (1961–1967) and the Cincinnati Reds (1967), primarily as a second baseman.

Many articles defend Detroit's lack of black players by saying they were signing and developing them in the minor leagues. "Jake" is considered by some to be the first true black Tiger.

Wood was signed as an amateur free agent by the Tigers in early 1957. He attended Detroit's minor-league camp in Lakeland, Florida, worked his way up through the Tigers' system, and batted more than .300 with five teams in the minors.

Jake made his major-league debut at age 23 on the Tigers' season-opener on April 11, 1961, starting at second base and batting leadoff in a 9–5 home loss to the Cleveland Indians.

Quiet, agile, and talented, Wood remained the Tigers' starting second baseman from 1961 to 1963. He was fourth in the American League in stolen bases in 1961 with a total of 30. During his rookie season in 1961, Wood was also among the American League leaders in runs (96), hits (171), and games (162).

Wood batted .262 in 1962 while playing in 111 games. Wood injured a finger in late July 1963, and missed the rest of the season, batting .271 in 85 games.

Starting in 1964, after Detroit acquired veteran second baseman Jerry Lumpe, Wood became a utility infielder and backup second baseman. He appeared in 64 games in 1964 batting .232 and 58 games in 1965 batting .288.

In 1966 he appeared in 98 games batting .252.

On June 23, 1967 during his seventh season with the Tigers, his contract was purchased by the Reds. He played 16 games for them, with his final major-league career appearance coming on August 11, 1967.

Jake ended his major-league career with a .250 batting average with 35 home runs, 168 runs batted in, and 70 stolen bases.

Jake played in the minor leagues in 1968 and 1969.

Jake lives in Pensacola, Florida, where, as of 2012, he continued to remain active, playing in over-70 softball leagues and tournaments, as well as playing racquetball.

CHAPTER 16

Boston Red Sox

The Last Team to Integrate

The Red Sox could have been the first team with a black player by signing **Jackie Robinson** and **Sam Jethroe**, (who both went on to be Rookie of the Year) but failed to provide a real tryout.

Clif Keane, a former reporter for the *Boston Globe*, claims in the spring of 1945, pressed by city councilman Isidore Muchnick and sportswriter Dave Egan, the Boston Red Sox staged a trial for three black players, Robinson, Jethroe, and Marvin Williams. Someone yelled, "Get those N-----S off the field!" Keane believed it was Boston's owner Yawkey.

Later in 1945, Jackie Robinson, with all his strength and intelligence, was going around on tryouts. He went to Fenway Park in Boston for the second time, accompanied by the baseball writer Wendell Smith who was trying to help. There was a clubhouse attendant who let them into the park and a batboy operating the pitching machine. Jackie Robinson was ready to show what he could do and nobody was watching. Robinson hit a few pitches and decided to leave.

Boston also scouted a young player by the name of Willie Mays who was playing in Birmingham for the Black Barons in the Negro Leagues, but they did not attempt to sign him.

To most observers, the reasoning behind these decisions was clear. Despite their obvious talent and potential to improve Boston's team, the franchise's decision makers did not want to hire black players. As the rest of the league integrated, Boston remained an all-white club for 12 more years after the Dodgers signed Jackie Robinson in 1947. Along with the Philadelphia Phillies, who waited to integrate until 1957, and the Detroit Tigers, who did not hire a black player until 1958, the Red Sox floundered in the 1950s, while teams like the Dodgers, Giants, Braves, and Indians spent that decade winning with black stars in the lineup.

The Red Sox owner, Tom Yawkey, would spend many years keeping blacks off his team, and ultimately got what he deserved, which was nothing in the way of titles.

The Red Sox had multiple black players in their farm system during the 1950s, with the team failing to promote them despite the successes other teams realized after integrating black players. During this period, the Red Sox went from perennial contender to failing to finish within ten games of first place for 16 years (1951–1966). As owner of the Boston Red Sox, the team's policy on integration ultimately was Yawkey's responsibility.

Boston blamed the "curse" and not their failure to integrate for their lack of success. The curse stated that Boston would not win another pennant after they sold Babe Ruth to the New York Yankees.

Red Sox historians often single out Higgins, (manager in 1955-1959) along with Yawkey, when they discussed the root of the club's reputation for resisting racial integration. Higgins was quoted by one Boston baseball writer, Al Hirshberg, as saying, "There'll be no N-----s on this ball club as long as I have anything to say about it." He also reportedly called sportswriter Cliff Keane "a f------ N----r lover" after hearing Keane praise the talents of White Sox outfielder Minnie Miñoso, a Cuban of African descent.

Higgins had no control over the big league roster until he became

Red Sox manager in 1955, and the club's policy of refusing to break the color line appeared to be in place well before then under Yawkey and his front office bosses, Eddie Collins and Joe Cronin.

Boston's superstar Ted Williams was the greatest hitter in baseball during the 1950's, but without roles for black players, his Red Sox languished during the 1950s.

The team's problems with race persisted long after they signed their first black player, "Pumpsie" Green, in 1959.

Tommy Harper, who played for the Red Sox from 1972 to 1974 and was a coach from 1980 to 1984 and from 2000 to 2002, might have had a longer first coaching stint if he hadn't complained about how the team segregated its players during spring training meals while he was playing in the early '70s. The comments led to Harper's firing, after which he successfully sued for racial discrimination.

Not surprisingly, then, it was big news when the Red Sox called on Green. He later told *The Boston Globe*, "One day in July, I got a phone call, and I was heading to Boston. Then the cameras came on." Green was a switch hitter and a good fielder who had been the Most Valuable Player of the Red Sox Triple-A farm team the year before. He got his first start for the Sox on July 24, 1959.

Boston Red Sox

Elijah "Pumpsie" Green

July 21, 1959

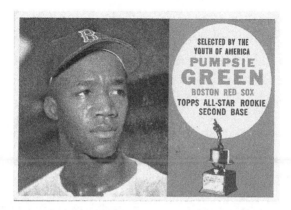

Elijah "Pumpsie" Green (born October 27, 1933) is an American former major league baseball infielder who played with the Boston Red
Sox (1959–'62) and New York Mets (1963). Green had the distinction
of being the first black player to play for the Red Sox, the last pre-ex-
pansion major-league club to integrate. In his Boston tenure, he was
used mostly as a pinch runner or day-off replacement for infielders
Pete Runnels and Don Buddin. He made his debut on July 21, 1959,
pinch running in a 2–1 loss against the White Sox.

Since major-league baseball had not yet expanded to the West Coast,
Green grew up a fan of the Oakland Oaks of the Pacific Coast League.
Green later stated that he might have been even better at basketball,
but chose to play baseball when he was offered a baseball scholarship at Fresno State University.

In 1953 Green's final year of college, he tried out for the Oaks, and
was signed to a contract.

In 1953, with the Wenatchee Chiefs, an affiliate of the Oaks, Green batted .244 in 88 games.

In 1954, Green batted .297 in his second season with the Wenatchee Chiefs, an affiliate of the Oaks.

In 1955, he was promoted to the Stockton Ports, the Oaks' top affili-ate. Green's contract was purchased by the Boston Red Sox during the 1955 season, but he was allowed to finish the season with Stockton. In 1956 he played with the Albany Senators, a Red Sox affiliate, where he batted .273.

Green spent the 1957 season with the Oklahoma City Indians and San Francisco Seals, where he batted .333 and the 1958 season with the Minneapolis Millers where he batted .253.

In 1959, Green was invited to the Red Sox spring training camp and hit .400 during spring training with the parent Sox and was named "Camp Rookie of The Year" by the press. Even with those accomplishments, Green had not secured a solid position with the team. When writers asked owner Tom Yawkey if Green would make the team, he replied, "The Sox will bring up a Negro if he meets our standards." By the time camp broke, General Manager Bucky Harris seemed to indicate that Green had made the team, but this was not the case. Reports were that Manager Pinky Higgins had gone to Yawkey and had Harris overruled. Boston sportswriter, Al Hirshberg, later claimed that Higgins had made the following statement: "There will be no N------ on this team as long as I have anything to do with it."

Discrimination followed Green through the Red Sox's organization including in 1959 when he played magnificently in spring training, but was denied an opening day roster spot. The Red Sox still were not ready to break from their prejudiced practices. At the end of training camp, Green was returned to the minors where he batted .320 in 98 games. "That was the best spring I've had in my life," Green said. "The best ball I ever played in my life. I had the whole package. I was a shoo-in. ... I didn't know I was that good."

The demotion of Green to the minor leagues in Minnesota caused a furor among civil rights groups. The NAACP (National Association for the Advancement of Colored People) called for an investigation into the affair. The Massachusetts Commission Against Discrimination held hearings into the matter. Neither Yawkey nor Harris attended. They put the team's defense into the hands of a young team lawyer by the name of Dick O'Connell. He argued that the Red Sox were employing eight black personnel at the time, one at Fenway Park and eight in the minor leagues. The outcome of the hearing resulted in the Red Sox being absolved of any charges of discrimination for the promise of making every effort to end the apparent segregation that existed on the team.

By July of that year, Green was hitting .325 at Minneapolis and had just been named an American Association All-Star for the second straight year.

On July 21, 1959, Green made his debut for Boston to become the first African American to play for the Red Sox.

Green played his first nine games on the road and made his Fenway Park debut on Aug. 4th against the Kansas City A's in the opener of a doubleheader. Green led off, three spots ahead of Ted Williams, playing second base. The crowd was far bigger than normal and included a large contingent of African American fans.

"There were a lot of blacks there that wanted to get into the park, but the Red Sox had many season-ticket holders, so many of the black fans could not get in," Green said. "So they roped a part of center field off. There were about 500 blacks sitting out there. They wanted to get in to see me, I guess. That's the first time I remember being nervous. I did a lot of talking to myself." I said, 'Well, just do what you've been doing. You know how to play this game so just go play.' I got a standing ovation running out to second base." Then came Green's first at-bat, leading off the bottom of the first inning.

"The place was rocking," he said. "I took a deep breath. I looked at the umpire. He said, 'Pumps, how are you doing?' I said 'fine." I hit a line shot to left-center field, high off the Green Monster. I kept running toward second. I saw the ball still in the outfield. I just kept going, and I slid into third very easily.'

One week after Green's debut, pitcher Earl Wilson was called up, becoming the Red Sox's second black player. Green would play 50 games during the 1959 season, batting .233 and playing second base almost exclusively.

'When I came along, the biggest thing was where will you stay, where are you going to eat, what are you going to do, where are you going to go?" said Green, noting he wasn't initially allowed to stay or eat with his white Red Sox teammates.

"It practically overshadowed a lot of things I might've enjoyed more, but the conditions I was in, it just took a lot away from me, but I never let it get to me. Well, except a couple times", Green shared.

Including the time one of his teams passed through San Antonio, where a heckler sitting alongside the dugout directed constant racial slurs toward Green. "He weighed about 300 or 400 pounds, and he sat and drank beer, and I guess his thing was to give me hell," Green said. "He talked about me like a dog." He said, 'You got sent down because you're not going to play with Ted Williams. Boy, what's wrong with you?' "He was loud and belligerent. People had to move away from him. I guess they got tired of him."

Green enjoyed a much more full-time role in 1960, playing 133 games, 69 at second base and 41 at shortstop while batting .242.

Green may have had his best season in 1961, posting career highs in home runs (6), RBI (27), doubles (12), and stolen bases (4), although he also had the most errors of his career that year, with 16. He batted .260.

After the 1962 season in which he batted .231 in 56 games, Green was traded to the New York Mets along with Tracy Stallard and Al Moran in exchange for Felix Mantilla. Green played the majority of the 1963 season with the Buffalo Bisons where he batted .309 in 130 games, but also played 17 games with the Mets.

He played his final major league game with the Mets on September 26, 1963, although Green would play two more seasons in the minor leagues before retiring after the 1965 season.

In a five season major league career, Green was a .246 hitter with 13 home runs and 74 RBI in 344 games.

After retiring from playing baseball, Green worked at Berkeley High School in Berkeley, California for over 20 years, serving as a truant officer, coaching baseball and teaching math in summer school. Green has lived in El Cerrito, California, since his retirement seven years ago from baseball.

On April 17, 2009, Green was honored by the Red Sox in a first-pitch ceremony, in recognition of 50 years since his breaking of the Red Sox color barrier.

In February 2012, Green was honored by the city of El Cerrito, and presented with a proclamation honoring his "distinguished stature in baseball history."

In April 2012, he threw out the ceremonial first pitch before Jackie Robinson day at Fenway Park, and also attended Fenway's 100th anniversary celebrations later that month.

In May 2018, Green was inducted to the Boston Red Sox Hall of Fame.

Boston Red Sox

Earl Wilson

July 28, 1959

Earl Wilson (October 2, 1934–April 23, 2005) was a professional baseball pitcher. He played all or part of 11 seasons in major-league baseball for the Boston Red Sox (1959–'60, 1962–'66), Detroit Tigers (1966–'70), and San Diego Padres (1970), primarily as a starting pitcher.

Wilson grew up loving sports. He went to Hammond Colored High School where he played varsity basketball. His passion, however, was baseball, and he played whenever and wherever he could get the chance. Wilson began playing as an outfielder, but soon switched to catching. He was always a strong hitter.

It was during the 1953 season that the Boston Red Sox began to notice the young ballplayer. The scouting report sent to the team's head office is indicative of the racial bias that Wilson had to overcome in his early years as a professional ballplayer. It stated, "He is a well mannered colored boy, not too black, pleasant to talk to, well educated, has a very good appearance and conducts himself as a gentleman." When the Red Sox signed Earl in 1953, he was the first black player signed by Boston.

The Boston Red Sox because of his strong arm, changed Earl into a pitcher. He went 4–5 with a 3.81 ERA, with more walks (61) than strikeouts (56) for the Bisbee-Douglas Copper Kings of the Arizona-Texas League.

In 1954 through 1956, Earl pitched in the Boston minor leagues compiling a 32 wins and 17 loss record.

Earl was drafted into the marines in 1957. Although he continued to play military ball, his opportunity to become the first black player to crack the Red Sox lineup was truly a setback.

In 1959, he went 10 and 2 with 129 strikeouts in the minor leagues before being called up to the major leagues by Boston.

Wilson made his debut on July 28, 1959. During the remainder of the 1959 season, Wilson appeared in nine games and compiled a modest 1–1 record with a 6.08 ERA. He recorded his first victory in the majors on August 20th in an 11–10 win over the Kansas City A's. Besides picking up his first big league win, he also showed his bat was a serious weapon as he picked up three RBI's in the game.

During the 1960 season, Wilson appeared in 13 games and had a 3–2 record. He lowered his ERA to 4.71 as well as lessening his walk to strikeout ratio as well. His control at this early stage of his career was always a concern.

In spite of what appeared like good progress, Wilson would not make a major-league start in 1961 as he was demoted to Seattle of the PCL and went 9–12.

The following season, 1962, saw Wilson come back to stay. It did not take long for him to distinguish himself. On June 26th of that year, he took the mound against the Los Angeles Angels and Bo Belinsky in front of 14,002 fans in Fenway Park. **That night, he became the first African American to hurl a no-hitter in the American League,** pitching the Sox to a 2–0 win. He helped his own cause by hitting a home run, which proved to be the game-winning run. Owner Yawkey gave Wilson a $1,000 bonus for his achievement, declaring, "I am more excited now than I was during Mel Parnell's no-hitter as Wilson is just arriving at what could be a brilliant career."

The victory was Wilson's sixth of the 1962 season. He went on to finish the year with a 12–8 win-loss record with a 3.90 ERA. He pitched 191.1 innings. For the first time, his strikeouts out numbered his walks (137–111). It was also in 1962 that Wilson became one of the first professional athletes to have an agent represent him in contract negotiations. It occurred as a result of a minor accident in which Earl was involved. He was referred to a young lawyer by the name of Bob Woolf. The association of Woolf with Wilson marked the start of Woolf's career as a sports agent. It worked out well for both parties, besides being involved in contract discussions for Earl, Woolf also achieved several endorsement deals for the player.

Wilson's next few seasons saw his win-loss record reflect the overall ineptitude of the Red Sox. In 1963, he earned 11 victories and 16 defeats. Still, he lowered his ERA to 3.76. He also threw more than 200 innings for the first time in his career.

The 1964 season saw Wilson compile an 11–12 record with a 4.49 ERA. Once again he had more than 200 innings of work.

In the 1965 season, Earl had 13 wins to lead the Red Sox in victories in addition to 14 losses with an ERA of 3.98 while throwing 230 innings and giving up 77 walks while striking out 164 opposing hitters.

Early 1966 presented an event that had a monumental effect on the rest of Wilson's life. During spring training, while in Lakeland, Florida (the spring home of Wilson's next team, the Detroit Tigers), Wilson and a couple of his teammates, Dennis Bennett and Dave Morehead, decided to go to a local bar named *The Cloud 9* for a drink after a day at the park. In Bennett's words, he describes what happened that night; "The bartender asked Dave and I what we wanted. He then turned to Earl and said, 'We don't serve N------ in here.' So we all got up and left the place. Earl was upset at first as he had never been refused service before."

Author Peter Golenbock, in his book *Red Sox Nation*, wrote that incidents such as this tended to bring negative publicity to the team rather than to the racist attitudes in the South. Wilson understood this was the case, and although he revealed the incident to Boston writer Larry Claflin, he asked that the writer keep it to himself and not write about it. Claflin agreed, but another writer found out about it and instead of exposing the racism of the incident, he focused his story on the Red Sox players going out drinking.

Most observers, including Wilson, felt this incident was the reason the Red Sox decided to trade him. To Earl, the writing was on the wall when on June 13th, the Red Sox acquired two black players, John Wyatt and Jose Tartabull. That night, Earl told his roommate, Lenny Green, who was also an African American, "There are too many black players on the team and someone will have to go!" The next morning, Manager Billy Herman informed Wilson that that he and a black outfielder, Joe Christopher, had been traded to Detroit for veteran outfielder Don Demeter and a player to be named later (a week afterward, Detroit shipped reliever Julio Navarro to the Red Sox). Earl at the time had appeared in 15 games with the Sox that season and had a 5–5 record. His ERA was 3.84.

Although upset at first, Earl quickly rebounded and went on to post a 13–6 record for the Tigers to finish the year with 18 wins overall and a sparkling Tigers' ERA of 2.59. As it turned out, the trade was one-sided in the Tigers' favor with Demeter retiring at the end of the 1967 season.

His most productive season came in 1967 when he won a career high 22 game tying Jim Lonborg for the American League lead. He also racked up 184 strikeouts. Detroit finished the season just one game behind the "Impossible Dream" Red Sox. The 1968 season saw the Tigers capture the American League pennant, dominating their opponents. They finished 12 games ahead of their nearest rival, the Baltimore Orioles. Besides Wilson, who finished with a 13–12 record and a 2.85 ERA, Detroit also had Denny McLain win 31 games, and Mickey Lolich win 17. Wilson tied his career high with seven home runs during the season. Then in the World Series, the Tigers came from behind to take the fall classic over St. Louis in seven games. Earl pitched the third game of the Series, going 4.1 innings with a no decision.

In 1969, Wilson had his last winning season as a pitcher. He finished with a 12–10 record and a 3.31 ERA. He also pitched more than 200 innings for the last time in his career. The Tigers finished the year in second place, 19 games behind the pennant-winning Orioles.

The 1970 season was his final one in the majors. When he was sold to the San Diego Padres July 15th, his record was 4–6 with an ERA of 4.41. The Padres were a terrible club that season and finished the year with 99 losses. Earl's record with the Padres was 1–6 with an ERA of 4.85.

The Padres subsequently released him on January 13, 1971, at which time he promptly retired from baseball.

In 11 seasons in the big leagues, Wilson had a 121–109 (.526) record. His lifetime ERA was 3.69, and he had 1,452 strikeouts, a rate of better than six for every nine innings pitched. He was considered a dangerous hitter as well. He had 35 home runs in 740 at bats, a ratio of one homer for every 21 at bats, a ratio, which many regulars would covet.

In five-plus seasons, Wilson won 45 games for Boston with a high of 13 victories in 1963.

Wilson died from a heart attack at his home in Southfield, Michigan, on April 23, 2005 at the age of 70.

CHAPTER **17**

The Writers

As I looked into the integration of major-league baseball, I came across names of many writers who worked and wrote about integration long before it happened as well as continuing to write about it as it occurred. Names that frequently came up were: Wendell Smith, Sam Lacey, Lester Rodney and Bill Mardo.

Branch Rickey had not acknowledged being pressured by *The Daily Worker*. However, in recounting the campaign to shatter baseball's color bar, Arnold Ampersand wrote in *Jackie Robinson: A Biography* (1997) that "the most vigorous efforts came from the Communist press, including picketing, petitions and unrelenting pressure for about 10 years in *The Daily Worker*, notably from Lester Rodney and Bill Mardo."

Wendell Smith (March 23, 1914–November 26, 1972) was an African American sportswriter who was influential in the choice of Jackie Robinson to become the first African American player in major league baseball in the twentieth century.

A Detroit native, Smith graduated from West Virginia State College where he pitched on the baseball team. Wendell Smith developed into a quality young pitcher on his way to professional ball until a fateful day in 1933. At nineteen years old, Smith pitched a shutout for his integrated American Legion team. After the game, he was approached by Detroit Tigers scout Wish Egan. Egan told Smith that he hoped he could sign him to a Tigers contract, but he did not have the authority to sign a black man.

After that, Smith promised himself that he would do whatever he could to see an African American play major league baseball.

His professional baseball writing career began in 1937 with the *Pittsburgh Courier*, then the most popular paper within the black community in the country. He started as a sports writer and then a sports editor the year after. He covered the Homestead Grays and Pittsburgh Crawfords of baseball's Negro leagues for the *Courier*.

Smith also petitioned the Baseball Writers' Association of America for membership, but was turned down because he was with the *Courier* and not one of the white owned papers.

Some credit Smith with recommending Jackie Robinson to Brooklyn Dodgers' general manager, Branch Rickey, who was searching for the individual with strong character to start the integration of baseball successfully.

"As Jackie Robinson was making history, Wendell Smith wrote it" as recapped in an article written by Bill Plaschke. Sportswriter Wendell Smith, who chronicled Robinson's breaking of baseball's color barrier, is all but forgotten today. Baseball's greatest story will be rewritten every year as the sport celebrates the 66th anniversary of Jackie Robinson's breaking the major leagues' color barrier. In every game, players from every team will wear "42", the number on the back of Robinson's jersey when he debuted for the Brooklyn Dodgers on April 15, 1947. Yet the man who wrote the story will be forgotten.

Nobody will sit in the stands with a manual typewriter atop their knees in memory of the man who, even as he wrote about integration on the field, was barred from the press box because he was black.

Nobody will honor the man who endured the same prejudice as Robinson as he fought that prejudice with his words. Nobody will remember the man whose hidden fight became an inspiration for Robinson's public battle.

Everyone will remember the headline, but few will remember the byline—*Wendell Smith*.

The humble, bespectacled journalist was Robinson's chronicler, his confidant, and sometimes even his conscience. As sports editor and columnist for the African American-owned *Pittsburgh Courier*,

Smith accompanied Robinson throughout his first major-league season, creating his image, reporting his words, and crusading for his rights. As Robinson grew more popular, Smith became more invisible, until he eventually became Robinson's ghostwriter in the literal sense, the memory of him turning ethereal and nearly vanishing altogether. The movie, "42", which depicts Robinson's entry into the major leagues, it is the rare piece of work that illuminates Smith's role in Robinson's life. Smith is the first voice heard in the movie, and his presence as Robinson's guide and companion is visible throughout the movie.

The *Courier* offered to pay for Smith to travel with Robinson, who had to stay in separate hotels from his teammates due to segregation policies prevalent at the time. Smith traveled with Robinson in the minors in 1946 and with the Brooklyn Dodgers in 1947.

In 1948, Smith released his book, *Jackie Robinson: My Own Story*.

Later, Smith moved on to Chicago and joined the white-owned *Chicago Herald-American*. Smith left his baseball beat and covered mostly boxing for the American. In 1948, his application to join the BBWAA (Baseball Writers Association of America) was approved and he became the first African American member of the organization.

Smith moved to television in 1964 when he joined Chicago television station WGN as a sports anchor, though he continued to write a weekly column for the *Chicago Sun-Times*.

Smith died of pancreatic cancer at age 58 in 1972, just a month after Robinson's death. Smith had been too ill to attend Robinson's funeral, but he wrote Robinson's obituary.

In 1993, he was a posthumous recipient of the J. G. Taylor Spink Award for excellence in journalism. In 1994 he was inducted into the Writers wing of the Baseball Hall of Fame.

"Sam" Lacy

Journalist and Advocate

Samuel Harold "Sam" Lacy (October 23, 1903–May 8, 2003) was an African American and Native American sportswriter, reporter, columnist, editor, and television/radio commentator who worked in the sports journalism field for parts of nine decades, and is credited as a persuasive figure in the movement to racially integrate sports.

Sam's family moved to Washington, D.C., when he was a young boy. In his youth, he developed a love for baseball and spent his spare time at Griffith Stadium, home ballpark for the Washington Senators. His house at 13th and U streets was just five blocks from the stadium, and Sam would often run errands for players and chase down balls during batting practice.

In his youth, Sam witnessed racist mistreatment of his family while they watched the annual Senators' team parade through the streets of Washington to the stadium on opening day. Sam later recalled what happened after his elderly father cheered and waved an "I Saw Walter Johnson Pitch" pennant.

"Fans like my father would line up for hours to watch their heroes pass by. And so there he was, age 79, out there cheering with the rest of them, calling all the players by name, just happy to be there. And then it happened. One of the white players—I won't say which one—just gave him this nasty look, and as he passed by, spat right in his face. Right in that nice old man's face."

As a teenager, Sam worked for the Senators as a food vendor, selling popcorn and peanuts in the stadium's segregated Jim Crow section in right field.

He enrolled at Howard University, where, in 1923, he earned a bachelor's degree in physical education, a field he thought might lead him to a coaching career.

He joined the *Tribune* full-time in 1926 and became sports editor shortly after that.

In 1929, Lacy left the paper for the summer to play semi-pro baseball in Connecticut while his family remained in Washington. He returned to the paper in 1930 and once again became sports editor in 1933.

In 1936, Lacy began lobbying Senators' owner Clark Griffith to consider adding star players from the negro leagues; in particular, those playing for the Homestead Grays team that leased Griffith Stadium for its home games. He finally gained a face-to-face meeting with Griffith on the subject in December 1937. Griffith listened but was not keen on the idea, as Lacy later told a Philadelphia reporter:

"I used that old cliché about Washington being first in war, first in peace and last in the American League, and that Griffith could remedy that. But he told me that the climate wasn't right. He pointed out there were a lot of Southern ballplayers in the league that there would be constant confrontations, and, moreover, that it would break up the Negro leagues. He saw the Negro leagues as a source of revenue."

In August 1941, Lacy moved to Chicago to work for another black newspaper, the *Chicago Defender*, where he served as its assistant national editor. While in the Midwest, he made repeated attempts to engage major league baseball commissioner, Kennesaw Mountain Landis on the topic of de-segregating the game, writing numerous letters, but his efforts went unanswered.

In 1943, Lacy returned east, joining the *Afro-American newspaper* in Baltimore as sports editor and columnist. He continued to press his case for integrating baseball through his columns and editorials and many other black newspapers followed suit.

However, Lacy did not make any headway on the issue until Landis died in late 1944. Lacy began a dialogue with Brooklyn Dodgers' owner Branch Rickey, and Landis's successor in the commissioner's office, "Happy" Chandler, who lent his support to the effort. It ultimately led to Jackie Robinson signing with the Dodgers' minor-league team, the Montreal Royals on October 23, 1945, which was Lacy's forty-second birthday.

Like Robinson and the other black athletes he had covered, Lacy encountered racist indignities and hardships. He was barred from press boxes at certain ballparks, dined at the same segregated restaurants with Jackie, and stayed at the same "blacks only" boarding houses, as did Robinson.

Not just content to see black ballplayers reaching the major leagues, Lacy began pushing for equal pay for athletes of color and for an end to segregated team accommodations during road trips. His first success on those fronts was persuading New York Giants' general manager, Chub Feeney, to address team accommodations on road trips.

Over the ensuing decades, Lacy pushed for the Baseball Hall of Fame to induct deserving negro league players. He also pressured national TV networks over the lack of black broadcasters, criticized major league baseball for the absence of black umpires, targeted corporations for their lack of sponsorships of black athletes in certain white-dominated sports and highlighted the National Football League's lack of black head coaches.

"Sam" Lacy wrote his final column for the paper at age 99 in 2003 and filed the piece from his hospital bed.

He died at age 99 of heart and kidney failure on May 8, 2003, at Washington Hospital Center in Washington, D.C.

In 1948 Sam was the first black member of the Baseball Writers association of America.

In 1984 Sam was the first black journalist to be enshrined in the Maryland Media Hall of Fame.

In 1985 Sam was inducted into the Black Athletes Hall of Fame in Las Vegas.

In 1997, he received the J. G. Taylor Spink Award for outstanding baseball writing from the BBWAA, which placed him in the writers' and broadcasters' wing of the Baseball Hall of Fame in 1998.

Bill Mardo

Bill Mardo (October 24, 1923–January 20, 2012) was a writer for *The Daily Worker*, the Communist Party of America newspaper. He is known for helping fight major-league baseball's color barrier as well as sports in general. He was the last living sportswriter deeply involved in the battle against segregation.

Mardo joined *The Daily Worker* in 1942 and remained with them through the early 1950s, when he joined the Soviet news agency Tass.

In the years before the Brooklyn Dodgers signed Jackie Robinson as the first black player in modern organized baseball, Mr. Mardo was a leading voice in a campaign by *The Daily Worker* against racism in the game, a battle it began in 1936 when Lester Rodney became its first sports editor.

The Daily Worker asked fans to write to the New York City baseball teams urging them to sign negro league players at a time when the major leagues had lost much of their talent to military service.

In April 1997, Mr. Mardo and Mr. Rodney spoke at a symposium at Long Island University's Brooklyn campus marking the fiftieth anniversary of Robinson's debut with the Dodgers.

Mr. Mardo noted that Rickey had not signed blacks when he ran the St. Louis Cardinals for more than 2 decades and suggested it was not idealism, but pressure from black sportswriters, trade unions, and the Communist Party that persuaded him to sign Robinson.

Bill Mardo died from Parkinson's disease on January 20, 2012, in Manhattan at the age of 99.

The following tribute was written by Gary Glenneal Toms (known as blogger G-Man) after Mr. Mardo's memorial:

"There were a total of 70 to 80 people that came to pay their respects, including celebrated historian and writer Joseph Dorinson, who co-edited: Paul Robeson: Essays on his Life and Legacy (McFarland & Company, Inc., 2002) and Jackie Robinson: Race, Sports and the American Dream (M.E. Sharpe, 1998). Dorinson eloquently shared his fondest memories of Mardo and noted that the sportswriter often came under vicious attack for publishing his views on inequality, poverty and racism in America, which was something a white man wasn't supposed to do on a sports page. However, Mardo wasn't your average sportswriter and "The Daily Worker" wasn't your average New York City newspaper.

During the tribute, I made efforts to suppress my anger. I was angry because I felt that an entire nation should've also been mourning the loss of Mardo, especially every black man and woman in the country. Moreover, Mardo's tribute served as a powerful reminder of what Blacks and Jews could accomplish if they worked together toward a common goal: unity.

I've repeatedly stated, personally and through this news and information site, that everyone from President Obama to professional athletes should do something to honor Bill Mardo.

Apparently, some very powerful people, in and out of government, have very long memories and refuse to acknowledge the phenomenal achievement of Bill Mardo because they worry about being associated with, or being viewed as supportive of, "communist doctrine". There is no other explanation for this unconscionable treatment, and Black America, as well as Americans of all races, should be as saddened "

Lester Rodney

Lester Rodney (April 17, 1911–December 20, 2009) was an American journalist who helped break down the color barrier in baseball as a sports writer for *The Daily Worker*.

Lester Rodney, who occupied an unlikely niche in journalism as a sports editor of the *American Communist Party* newspaper, The Daily Worker, using that platform to wage an early battle against baseball's color barrier. Rodney's favorite jobs involved sports and in 1936, he parlayed his high school background in sports writing into a job with *The Daily Worker* and its Sunday edition, the *Sunday Worker*, the party organ of the Communist Party USA. There, Rodney was able to combine sports journalism with his developing sense of social justice, to champion social issues, most notably the desegregation of major league baseball. He leveled much of this criticism at Branch Rickey, the general manager of his beloved Dodgers.

Rodney served in the South Pacific in World War II, and it was during his service that Branch Rickey announced the signing of Los Angeles native and war veteran Jackie Robinson to a minor league contract. Rodney's paper had touted Robinson's abilities for years, leading up to this event, and *Daily Worker* editor, Mike Gold, wrote an editorial praising Rodney's efforts as bringing desegregation to fruition.

Rodney was one of the few white sportswriters of his time to devote a great deal of space and praise to black athletes. Rodney stayed with *The Daily Worker* until the mid-1950s, keeping on top of racial issues in sports.

Following Nikita Khrushchev's 1956 speech detailing the crimes of the Joseph Stalin era, Rodney joined *Daily Worker* editor John Gates in an attempt to open the pages of the paper to debate. Soviet leaders suppressed this staff revolt, and suspended publication of the paper as a daily publication.

After 22 years as the *Daily Worker's* sports writer, Rodney resigned from the CPUSA (Communist Party of the USA) and the paper in January 1958 to seek a new life in California. The Rodney's moved from New York to Torrance, California, in 1958, where they lived for 31 years. Rodney continued to work as a journalist, most notably as the Religion editor of the *Long-Beach Press Telegram*.

Rodney died in 2009 in Walnut Creek, California at the age of 98.

CHAPTER **18**

Black Baseball Scouts

Starting in the 1940's major-league baseball started to heavily scout black players. Scouts such as Cylde Sukeforth, George Sisler, and Abe Saperstein, were amongst many who were hired to provide data on black players. These scouts were dependent on black managers, coaches, owners, and players for much of their direction and information. Owners recognized they had a need for black scouts.

In 1949, the Chicago White Sox hired the first black scout, John Wesley Donaldson, to scout for them.

In its June 1967 issue, *Ebony* magazine noted that Sam Hairston (White Sox) was one of eight full time black scouts in the majors in the 1950s. In addition to him and Buck O'Neil (Cubs), the others were Charles Gault (also of the White Sox), Quincy Trouppe and David "Showboat" Thomas (Cardinals), Hiram "Jack" Braithwaite (Senators), Alex P.mpez (Giants), and Bob Thurman (Reds).

We will look at some of the above black scouts who played a significant role in scouting and recruiting black players for major league baseball.

John Donaldson

John Wesley Donaldson (February 20, 1891–April 14, 1970) was an American baseball pitcher in Pre-Negro league and Negro league baseball. In a career that spanned over 30 years, he played in many different Negro leagues and semiprofessional teams, including the All Nations team and the Kansas City Monarchs. Researchers so far have discovered 667 games in which Donaldson is known to have pitched. Out of those games, Donaldson had over 400 wins and 5,002 strike-outs as a baseball pitcher. According to some sources, he was the greatest pitcher of his era.

Although Donaldson never gained full recognition for his pitching skills during his lifetime and was never admitted into major league baseball during his career, he made history by becoming the first full-time black talent scout in the major leagues for the Chicago White Sox in 1949. He is credited with the signing of several prominent Negro players during his time as a scout.

John was the scout who signed Sam Hairston. That summer, Donaldson also signed first baseman Bob "The Rope" Boyd from the Memphis Red Sox. As Boyd recalled in the SABR (Society for American Baseball

Research) biography by Bob Rives, Donaldson rode the Memphis Red Sox bus with the club.

At age 60, Donaldson was voted the first team member of the 1952 *Pittsburgh Courier* player voted poll of the Negro leagues best players ever. He was nominated for a special ballot of pre-negro league candidates for inclusion in baseball's Hall of Fame. A 12-member voting committee, appointed by the Board of Directors and chaired by former Major League Baseball Commissioner Fay Vincent, however, did not choose Donaldson for membership in the Hall of Fame in Cooperstown during a vote in February 2006.

Donaldson died of bronchial pneumonia at age 79 in Chicago, and is buried in Burr Oak Cemetery in Alsip, Illinois.

Jordan "Buck" O'Neil

John Jordan "Buck" O'Neil (November 13, 1911–October 6, 2006) was a first baseman and manager in the Negro American League, mostly with the Kansas City Monarchs. After his playing days, he worked as a scout and became the first African American coach in major league baseball.

Buck O'Neil was the last former Negro league player to appear in a professional game at any level when he made two appearances (drawing two intentional walks with one for each team) in the Northern League All-Star Game in 2006. O'Neil, at 94 years old, started the game as a member of the Fargo-Moorhead Red Hawks and led off the top of the first for the league's West All Stars. He drew an intentional walk, was removed for a pinch runner and was quickly "traded" to the Kansas City T-Bones, which enabled O'Neil to lead off the bottom of the first for the East (drawing a second intentional pass). O'Neil was the second oldest player to appear in a professional baseball game.

On June 19, 1999, another former Negro League star, 96-year-old Ted "Double Duty" Radcliffe, started on the mound for the Northern League's Schaumburg Flyers (against the Fargo-Moorhead Red Hawks) and threw one pitch (a ball).

When Tom Baird sold the Kansas City Monarchs at the end of the 1955 season, O'Neil resigned as manager and became a scout for the Chicago Cubs, and is credited for signing Hall of Fame player Lou Brock to his first professional baseball contract. O'Neil is sometimes incorrectly credited with also having signed Hall of Famer Ernie Banks to his first contract. Banks was originally scouted and signed to the Monarchs by "Cool Papa" Bell, then manager of the Monarchs' barnstorming B team in 1949.

Buck played briefly for the Monarchs in 1950 and 1953, his play interrupted by army duty. O'Neil was Banks' manager during those stints, and Banks was signed to play for the Cubs more than 2 years before O'Neil joined them as a scout.

He was named the first black coach in the major leagues by the Cubs in 1962, although he was not assigned in game base coaching duties, nor was he included in the Cubs' "College of Coaches" system, and consequently was never allowed to manage the team during that time. After many years with the Cubs, O'Neil became a Kansas City Royals scout in 1988 and was named "Midwest Scout of the Year" in 1998.

In his later years, he became a popular and renowned speaker and interview subject, helping to renew widespread interest in the negro leagues, playing a major role in establishing the Negro Leagues Baseball Museum in Kansas City, Missouri.

Buck O'Neil would have been the oldest Hall of Famer at the time of being voted in, if only a special Negro League Committee had inducted him in February 2006. The committee notoriously enshrined 17 Negro League contributors, but not O'Neill as the most famous representative of black baseball.

"We made a big mistake," the chairman of that committee and former MLB commissioner Fay Vincent told Sporting News. "We should have put Buck O'Neil in the Hall of Fame. I was a big supporter, but I didn't have a vote. I think that was an embarrassment. Not that he was the greatest player or a great manager, but he was a great human being and had a major role in keeping the black consciousness, and the black baseball history alive."

Buck had a lifetime batting average of .288 mostly with the Kansas City Monarchs from 1937 thru 1949.

O'Neil died in October 2006 at 94, less than eight months after the Hall of Fame spurned him and barely two months after speaking at induction ceremonies for the 17 Negro League contributors. He embodied black baseball in the 1994 Ken Burns PBS miniseries Baseball and founded the Negro League Baseball Museum in Kansas City.

The Hall of Fame created the Buck O'Neil Lifetime Achievement Award following the debacle with its committee and has a life size statue of O'Neil inside. Unfortunately, a decade later, O'Neil still does not have a plaque in his honor. As of this writing, Buck O'Neil still is not a Hall of Famer. Sadly, there is no guarantee that this will ever change.

Sam Hairston Sr.

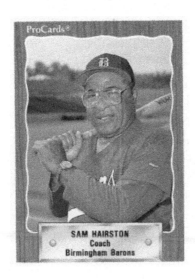

See chapter 6 (White Sox) for more details on his playing career

Samuel Hairston (January 20, 1920–October 31, 1997) was a Negro-league baseball and major league baseball player. He played for the Birmingham Black Barons and the Indianapolis Clowns of the Negro leagues and played part of one season (1951) with the Chicago White Sox as a catcher.

Patriarch of a three generation, big-league family, hard-hitting Negro leaguer Sam Hairston played, coached, and scouted in pro-baseball for over half a century. As a scout, Sam brought in at least five men who played for the Chicago White Sox, for whom he played briefly with in 1951.

In May 1960, Sam retired as an active player to scout the Alabama area for the White Sox. *The Sporting News* noted in its June 1st issue that his first signing was shaping up to be his own son Jerry Hairston.

Sam was scouting unofficially several years before he quit playing. Jerry Hairston Sr. said, "He recommended Lee Maye to the White

Sox, but they didn't sign him." Arthur Lee Maye, a Tuscaloosa native, signed with the Milwaukee Braves in 1954.

In 1961, the White Sox also passed on Lee Andrew May, who signed with Cincinnati and went on to hit 354 big-league homers. The White Sox drafted Carlos May in the first round of the 1966 draft; according to Jerry Sr., Sam said, "You missed his older brother [Lee]; you better not miss this one!"

Other major leaguers Hairston recruited for the White Sox were Lee "Bee Bee" Richard, Lamar Johnson, and Reggie Patterson. Roland Hemond remembered that Sam was also high on pitcher Jimmy Key, who grew up in Huntsville, Alabama. The lefty was another one who got away from the White Sox, although the Toronto Blue Jays drafted him out of Clemson in 1982.

Although SABR's Scouts Committee shows Hairston's scouting career running through 1982, many reports after that showed him as still active in that role. The latest was the August 1992 issue of *Ebony*.

Hairston spent the last 12 seasons as a coach for the Birmingham Barons of the Southern League. The city held a "Sam Hairston Day" in 1996 and named a sports park complex in his honor.

Hairston died from pulmonary cardiac arrest at a Birmingham nursing home on October 31, 1997 at the age of 77.

"Alex" Pompez

Alejandro "Alex" Pompez (May 3, 1890–March 14, 1974) was an American executive in negro league baseball who owned the Cuban Stars (East) and New York Cubans franchises from 1916 to 1950. Outside of baseball and numbers (illegal gambling), he owned and operated a cigar shop in downtown Manhattan.

Alejandro (Alex) Pompez (1890-1974) was the son of Cuban immigrants. He made his money in the Harlem numbers racket.

A colorful and intelligent promoter with underworld ties, Alex Pompez had a long career involvement with Negro League baseball. Not only was he a manager and owner, but also he served as league vice president, scout, and consultant to the Hall of Fame.

His first involvement with baseball was as owner of the Cuban Stars (East), one of two barnstorming mixed race teams in the early 1920s. When the Eastern Colored League was established, Pompez was vital in helping negotiate the first Negro League World Series, in 1924, between the Hilldale Daisies of the ECL and the Kansas City Monarchs of the Negro National League.

The Cubans disbanded because of the Depression in the early 1930s, but Pompez resurrected them as the New York Cubans in 1935. They won the second-half title behind the sensational play of star Martin Dihigo, who not only hit .372, but also fired up a 7-3 record on the mound.

However, trouble was lurking for Pompez who by this time was an important member of Dutch Schultz's mob, and according to biographer Jim Riley, one of the wealthiest men in Harlem. New York County District Attorney Thomas Dewey targeted Pompez and a grand jury indictment came for him in 1936. Pompez, the sly numbers dealer, was tipped off by an elevator operator and escaped to Mexico after shutting down his team. He returned to the U.S. and turned state's evidence to avoid jail time. Two years later, he was back in baseball with his Cubans, who won a championship playoff in 1941 and then won both the Negro National League pennant and World Series in 1947.

However, things were changing during this time in baseball. The signing of Jackie Robinson and other Negro Leaguers were starting to mark the end for the black leagues. Pompez saw that the Negro Leagues would soon end so he started by selling off two of his best players, Ray Dandridge and Earl Barnhill, to give them shots at major league careers. Then he swung a deal with New York Giants owner Horace Stoneham to make his Cubans a Giants farm club and also for Pompez to scout the Caribbean for New York.

Pompez was responsible for scouting and signing, either directly or through his network, quite a few quality ballplayers. The list includes Felipe Alou, Jesus Alou, Matty Alou, Sandy Amoros, Damaso Blanco, Ossie Blanco, Marshall Bridges, Jose Cardenal, Orlando Cepeda, Tito Fuentes, Gil Girrido, Monte Irvin, Sherman Jones, Willie Kirkland,

Coco Laboy, Juan Marichal, Willie McCovey, Minnie Minoso, Manny Mota, Ray Noble, Jimmy Rosario, Jose Santiago, Jose Tartabull and Ozzie Virgil. Many reports also cite Pompez having a hand in the signing of Willie Mays.

In 1950, Pompez submitted a favorable scouting report to the Giants on Fidel Castro. No one signed Fidel.

When the Hall of Fame decided to select players from the Negro Leagues in 1971, Pompez's vast experience proved invaluable. He served on the committee of Negro Leagues for the last four years of his life, helping promote greats such as Satchel Paige, Josh Gibson, Cool Papa Bell, Monte Irvin, and Buck Leonard attain the fame they merited.

He died at age 83 in New York City on March 14, 1974.

Alex was elected to the Hall of Fame in 2006.

Quincy Trouppe

Quincy Thomas Trouppe (December 25, 1912–August 10, 1993) was an American professional baseball player and an amateur boxing champion. He was a catcher in the negro leagues from 1930 to 1949.

In 1942, as World War II intensified, Troupe wanted to enlist in the military. He was rejected for being married with dependents, and therefore decided to work in a defense plant, the Curtiss-Wright Aircraft Company

He also played in the Mexican League and the Canadian Provincial League. His teams included St. Louis Stars, Detroit Wolves, Homestead Grays, Kansas City Monarchs, Chicago American Giants, Indianapolis ABCs, Cleveland Buckeyes (whom he managed to Negro American League titles in 1945 and 1947), New York Cubans, and Bismarcks (aka Bismarck Churchills).

He played in Latin America for 14 winter seasons and barnstormed with black all-star teams playing against white major league players. He managed the Santurce Crabbers in the Puerto Rican Winter League, winning the 1947–'48 season championship.

Trouppe caught six games for the 1952 Cleveland Indians of major league baseball and made 84 appearances with their Triple-A farm club.

When he made his major league debut on April 30, 1952, at Shibe Park, he became one of the oldest rookies in MLB history at the age of 39 years old.

On May 3, 1952 he was behind the plate when relief pitcher "Toothpick" Sam Jones entered the game, forming the first black battery in American League history.

Trouppe got his first start with the Indians the following day. His only other start came on May 10th. He had his first hit and scored his first run in the majors; it turned out to be his final game with the Indians and in major league baseball. In his stint with Cleveland, he had played in six games and had 11 plate appearances, with one hit.

In the spring of 1953, Trouppe chose not to report to the Indianapolis minor league team. Trouppe traveled to the Dominican Republic having received an offer to play "that was too good to refuse."

However, after 3 weeks of spring training, Trouppe received a telegram from the St. Louis Cardinals regarding his application for a scouting position. He returned to St. Louis, met with Cardinals' owner August A. Busch and chief scout Joe Mathes, and was offered the job. **Trouppe accepted the position, becoming the first African American scout in the Cardinals' organization.**

Trouppe enjoyed his scouting responsibilities, but met disagreement and challenge as he recommended players. He had the opportunity to meet and observe talented players, but he was consistently bewildered when some of his recommendations were rejected. They included Ernie Banks (who signed with the Cubs), Roberto Clemente (originally a Brooklyn Dodgers' farmhand), and Vic Power (New York Yankees).

In 1957, however, the Cardinals' management decided that Trouppe's approach to scouting did not fit with the team's philosophy and he learned that his services were no longer needed.

At the age of 45, and now out of baseball, Trouppe took a position with the St. Louis Land Clearance Authority, helping to relocate families to "standard housing quarters."

Around 1967, hoping to return to baseball, Trouppe contacted George Silvey of the Cardinals to discuss a scouting job (Trouppe had worked with Silvey during his earlier stint with the Cardinals) and Quincy signed a contract to scout for the Cardinals. He scouted talent in California for the Cardinals until 1970, when he and his wife Bessie left California for Hattiesburg, Mississippi.

Late in life, Quincy Trouppe suffered from Alzheimer's disease. He died on August 10, 1993 at the age of 80, in Creve Coeur, Missouri. He is buried at the Calvary Cemetery and Mausoleum in St. Louis.

Bob Thurman

Robert Thurman (May 14, 1917 – October 31, 1998) was a professional baseball pitcher, outfielder, and pinch hitter. He played in the Negro leagues, the Puerto Rican Winter League (where he was a star) and for a few years at the end of his career in major league baseball with the Cincinnati Reds.

Thurman started his baseball career playing semi-pro ball with various teams in the Wichita area before entering the U.S. Army at the beginning of World War II. He was stationed in New Guinea and Luzon and saw combat action in the Pacific Theater of Operations. His baseball talent became evident while playing military baseball in the Philippines and when he was discharged in 1945 received an offer to play for the Homestead Grays in the Negro National League.

Thurman, who originally signed with the New York Yankees and then spent several years as property of the Chicago Cubs, was a month shy of his 38th birthday when he made his major league debut with the

Cincinnati Reds on April 14, 1955. His obstacle strewn path to the big leagues was long and winding with many detours along the way. When he finally got an opportunity, the former Negro League star developed into one of the most respected pinch-hitters in baseball.

Thurman's big league debut occurred on the same day (April 14, 1955) that Elston Howard became the first black man to play for the Yankees.

Thurman ended his major-league career with a .246 lifetime batting average in 334 major-league games, spread mainly over four seasons. He belted 35 homers while driving in and scoring 106 runs in 663 at-bats. More than one-half of his appearances were as a pinch hitter and he blasted six homers in that role, including four in 1957. In addition, he played 12 winters in the Puerto Rican Winter League, 11 with the Santurce Crabbers. He is a member of the Puerto Rican League Hall of Fame and the leagues' all time home run leader.

The likeable, hardworking Thurman joined the Minnesota Twins in 1962 as a scout after his playing days were over. His first signee was Rudy May, who would pitch in the majors for 16 years. After about a year and a half, he returned to the Cincinnati organization to scout for the Reds. In 1970, he moved closer to his Wichita roots when he became a special assignment scout for the Kansas Royals. Later, when the Major League Scouting Bureau was established, he signed on with them.

Bob fell victim to Alzheimer's disease and died on October 31, 1998 in Wichita at the age of 81.

Dave ("Showboat") Thomas

Dave "Showboat" Thomas did not play in major league. He played and managed in the Negro leagues and Mexico from 1928 to 1946. He was a member of the 1937 New York Cubans team that won the first half championship in the National Negro League.

Thomas was considered perhaps the finest defensive first baseman to have played in the Negro leagues.

Joe Bostic, a sports editor of Harlem newspaper, the *People's Voice*, arrived at the Brooklyn Dodgers' spring training camp at West Point Academy in Bear Mountain, New York, shortly before noon on April 6, 1945. Two negro league veterans accompanied Bostic; pitcher Terris McDuffie, and outfielder Dave "Showboat" Thomas. Bostic told Harold Parrott, the Dodgers' traveling secretary, he wanted to speak to team president, Branch Rickey about a tryout for the ballplayers.

Bostic's strategy to have a chance of succeeding, required that the talents of McDuffie and Thomas be so obvious that no one could deny them. Neither McDuffie nor Thomas were such ballplayers. Thomas was 40 years old and McDuffie was 35 at the time. Bostic chose them for their availability and not their ability. Far more talented players were either at spring training with their respective negro league teams or playing in Mexico.

When Bostic insisted that sports writers be present for the tryout, Rickey did not object. Even though Rickey had been pressured into giving tryouts to McDuffie and Thomas, he treated the ballplayers like any other prospects. McDuffie and Thomas were assigned Brooklyn uniforms. McDuffie wore #9, while Thomas wore #14. Thomas faced Brooklyn pitchers and Rickey observed McDuffie's pitching.

The tryout lasted about an hour. Upon its conclusion, Rickey shred his personal observations on the ballplayers, something he did with everyone in camp. Rickey was unimpressed with Thomas. He was more charitable toward McDuffie. Rickey McDuffie had good control and a good fastball and curve, but lacked an effective changeup. Neither player heard from the Dodgers again.

After the tryouts concluded, Bostic released a statement that expressed his satisfaction. "Today's extensive tryouts, by Terris McDuffie and Dave Thomas for the Dodgers, represents a constructive and significant step in the effort to have negro players in the major leagues," Bostic said. "I feel it represents the first concrete step toward realization of that goal."

If things went according to plan, Bostic observed, McDuffie and Thomas would become the first black players since Charlie Grant in 1901 to try out for a major league team. John McGraw, the Hall of Fame manager who was managing the Baltimore Orioles at the time, was impressed enough with Grant that he tried to subvert baseball's color line, disguising Grant as a Native American named Charlie Tokohama. McGraw's plan was foiled when Grant's identity was revealed.

After the tryout Dave played in the Negro Leagues in 1945 and 1946 and in the Mexican Leagues in 1947. He then retired from playing at the age of 41.

Dave ("Showboat") Thomas was a major league scout for the Chicago White Sox in the '60s.

He died in 1977 at the age of 72.

Closing Thoughts and Comments

WOW!! What a journey this has been. I have learned much more in this research project than I thought possible. Memberships and visits to the MLB HOF (Baseball Hall of Fame in Cooperstown) and NLBM (Negro League Baseball Museum in Kansas City) were very helpful, and informative in my research for this book.

Going into this project, I had some knowledge and personal opinions on the topic of integration in baseball, but have since learned how lacking I was on many topics.

Why did baseball delay integration? Reasons included racism, economics, politics and financial gains. Depending on the team, some or all of the above reasons were valid.

Many major league teams were making a six figure income from the Negro leagues by renting their ballparks. The owners knew they would lose that money if better black players were to play in the major leagues, and the Negro leagues were to fade away.

Cities with multiple teams whose team had lower attendance in the 1940's, integrated first.

New York: The Dodgers and Giants both averaged over 1.4 million fans, but the Yankees were drawing over 2.2 million.

St. Louis: The Cardinals drew over 1 million fans every year from 1946 to 1951 while the Browns drew over 500,000 fans only once in the same period.

Chicago: The Cubs outdrew the White Sox until 1951 when the Sox brought up "Minnie" Miñoso, Sam Hairston, Bob Boyd and other black players. Beginning in 1951 the White Sox drew over 1 million thru 1959 while the Cubs only topped 1 million in 1952.

Philadelphia: The A's and Phillies both drew poorly with only the Phillies reaching over 1 million at the gates in 1946. The 1950's saw the A's move to Kansas City, and the Phillies averaged only about 900,000 fans. Neither team moved to integrate early.

Boston: The Red Sox and Braves both drew over 1.2 million fans in the late 1940's. The Braves tried to integrate in 1950, while Boston did nothing until the late 1950's.

Washington: Their team had generally poor attendance (795,000 in 1948), but was one of the last teams to bring black players up.

Cleveland, Pittsburgh, and Detroit: These teams had good attendance (over 1 million), but only Cleveland brought up black players in the 1950's.

Cincinnati: They had poor attendance with a low in 1945 of 290,000 and less than a million until 1956 after they integrated in 1954.

Some teams (Yankees and Phillies) thought they had winning teams and saw no need to integrate.

Teams such as Washington, Boston, Phillies, and Cincinnati were owned and/or managed by racists.

While reviewing black populations figures from the 1950 census to obtain a view of how it correlated to segregation, Boston had the lowest percentage of blacks at 2.4%, Pittsburgh at 6.2%, New York at 8.1%, Philadelphia at 13.2%, and Washington was highest at 23.5%. Most other cities were about 10%.

Black players faced not just racial barriers, but also faced the loss of their prime years due to military service as almost all Black/Latino Americans served during WWII or Korea.

Over 40 percent of the players in this book were over 30 years old, and 46 percent between 25 and 30, with "Satchel" Paige being 40 years old when their major-league careers began. Many players lied about their ages to appear younger.

They also faced loss of salary as many players made more money playing in the Negro Leagues than what they were offered to play in major league baseball. Roy Campanella was offered $185 a month compared to $600 a month that he was making in the Negro Leagues.

It does appear that racial quotas were unspoken, but quietly enforced as research shows managers and executives as stating, "three were more than enough" on any team.

The New York Times polled major league players of southern origin and reported that the major league players were almost unanimous in finding no objection to signing Robinson, so long as he played on another team. Several political factors of the time also had a strong influence on the integration of Major League baseball. Civil rights groups were active all over the United States.

Executive Order 8802 (Fair Employment Act) was signed by President Franklin D. Roosevelt on June 25, 1941. This piece of federal legislation promoted equal opportunity and prohibited employment discrimination in the national defense industry. The new law also created the Fair employment Practices Committee and empowered it to investigate complaints and take action against alleged violations.

The New York State Legislature passed the Fair Employment Practices Act in 1945. This law created an investigative committee to look into discriminatory hiring practices. One of the committee's first assignments was to investigate the integration of baseball.

The Ives–Quinn Act, which was also passed in 1945, banned discrimination in hiring practices.

The Mayor of New York City, Fiorello La Guardia, established the Mayor's Commission on Baseball. The purpose of this committee was to study the integration of Major League Baseball.

How good were these baseball pioneers?

Collectively, the players addressed in this book had the following impressive statistics for their careers:

> **Hall of Famers: 7**
> **Most Valuable Players: 9**
> **Rookie of the Year: 3**
> **All-Star Appearances: 90**
> **World Series: 28**
> **World Series Champions: 9**

Twenty-two percent of the black players in Major League Baseball from 1947 thru 1959 earned at least one All Star appearance.

Branch Rickey: Genius, Psychic, or Lucky?

Personally, I believe he had a little of all three traits. His creation and start of a formal farm system was genius. His decision of introducing Jackie Robinson and many other blacks to major league baseball were in many ways both luck and genius. Jackie definitely had the perfect composure for the first black player, but his baseball skills were uncertain and undeveloped.

Did Branch make any mistakes? Perhaps a few.

"Yogi" Berra came for a tryout with the Cardinals along with Joe Garagiola when Rickey was general manager. The scout, after discussing with Mr. Rickey, offered Joe $500 to sign, but only offered "Yogi" $250. "Yogi" turned them down. The rest is history as Yogi's Hall of Fame career with the Yankees shows.

Branch Rickey still owns the major league record for most consecutive steals by a team against a catcher. Branch was catching on June 28, 1907 when Washington stole 13 consecutive bases.

Rickey also headed up the Continental Baseball League in 1959 that was scheduled to compete again Major League Baseball. The league collapsed without playing any games, but did force MLB to expand the number of teams in the 1960's leading to 24 teams while today there are 30 teams.

Roberto Clemente

Branch Rickey signed Roberto Clemente in February of 1954 with the Dodgers. Roberto was sent to Montreal to play ball with the Dodgers minor league team.

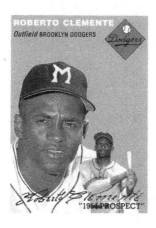

Scouts came to Montreal to mainly look at Joe Black when Clemente was there, but several also looked at Roberto even though he was getting very little playing time.

Roberto was left unprotected in the 1954 rule 5 draft and Pittsburgh made him their first choice in November 22, 1954. The rest is history as Roberto's (called Bob on cards early in his career) Hall of Fame career shows.

Interesting Antidote About Branch Rickey

When Bobby Bragan was young, people used to call him "Nig." He was of a darker complexion than most Negros and surprisingly he liked the nickname. Bobby Bragan grew up in Alabama. The only black people he knew served food and worked for his father's construction company. He did not even consider that his nickname might be offensive to anyone until he reached the major leagues and while playing for the Philadelphia Phillies was told by a teammate.

Bragan began his big-league career as a shortstop. He was not a good hitter, and was an erratic fielder. In 1940 as a rookie, he made 49 errors. A year later, he continued this bad streak by making 45 more errors. That was when he realized that becoming backup catcher was a safer bet for him. He was traded to Brooklyn in 1943, and a couple of years later went to war. When discharged in 1947, he traveled straight to Cuba and the Dodgers spring training. He wanted to reclaim his job as backup catcher.

This was Jackie Robinson's spring and this was Dixie Walkers' Team.

Walker is not at the heart of this particular story, so we are not looking to delve into his motivations. What we do know is that he attempted to start a player revolt that particular spring to force the Dodgers to get rid of Jackie Robinson and refrain from integrating the game. He would express considerable regret about it in later years; he said that he had no personal issues with Robinson or African Americans in baseball, but that he owned a hardware store in Birmingham and worried that playing with a black player would crush his business.

Then there was Bobby Bragan, the backup catcher from Alabama who was just trying to stay in baseball.

Walker probably believed that his popularity along with the support of numerous teammates would force the Dodgers to retreat.

It was a terrible miscalculation, something he probably realized when an angry, red-faced Leo Durocher, the Dodgers manager, addressed the whole team.

"I don't care if a guy is yellow or black, or if he has stripes looks like a (bleeping) zebra," he yelled. "I'm the manager of this team, and I say he plays."

Then Branch Rickey himself summoned each of the potential traitors into his hotel room. He had a different speech for each of them. He screamed at Furillo: "How could you possibly be against a man trying to make something of himself when you have seen the way people treated your father when he came from Italy?"

He told Higbe he would trade him, and he soon dumped him on Pittsburgh.

Rickey wanted to trade Walker also, but that was a lot harder than dealing a 32-year-old journeyman pitcher like Higbe. Walker was the team's star and their most popular player. Thus, the Dodgers would keep Walker all season.

Finally, we learn about Bobby Bragan, who told Rickey that he would give up his career to make a stand. He saw blacks as inferior to whites, plain and simple. He did not know how to tell his family and friends that he was playing baseball with Robinson. He did not see this stance as hateful or even objectionable; it was his view of the world. Bragan asked to be traded. It would have been so easy for Rickey to trade him or release him. The Dodgers didn't need him. He was a backup catcher, only good for a few dozen at bats.

Branch Rickey was many things, some of them admirable, some of them less admirable. Above all, he was shrewd. That day, he saw something in Bobby Bragan that Bragan did not see in himself.

"If Jackie Robinson can play the position better than another player," Rickey said after summoning Bragan, "then regardless of the color of his skin, Jackie Robinson is going to play. You understand that, Bobby? And how do you feel about this?"

"If it's all the same with you, Mr. Rickey, I'd like to be traded to another team," Bragan said.

"If we call Jackie Robinson up," Rickey asked, "will you change the way you play for me?" "No sir," Bragan said. "I'd still play my best." Rickey nodded and dismissed Bragan. He had made his decision. He would not trade Bobby Bragan.

Bragan didn't get it at first. He went into the season bitter, but he began to watch Robinson from a distance. The more he watched Robinson, the more he felt, despite his personal feelings, a grudging respect for Robinson. Bragan thought he was the Dodgers' best player. He marveled at how Jackie ignored the persistent taunts from the crowds and the opposing benches.

Finally he sat next to Jackie Robinson. They didn't talk much. When they did it was mostly just baseball discussions about pitchers or a player. Once in a while Bragan told a little joke and sometimes Robinson smiled.

Eventually, they would sit next to each other on the train. Once Robinson joined a card game Bragan was playing. Bragan would find himself sitting next to Robinson in the dugout, and they would talk, and when Bragan heard his family and friends and others discount Jackie Robinson by calling him "less than a man", Bragan found dissent welling up inside him. "Wait a minute," he would think. "You don't know him." To his surprise, eventually he found himself saying that out loud.

The Dodgers in 1947 were superb and won the pennant. As Bragan would say, players of all racial viewpoints lined up with Jackie Robinson to collect their World Series checks.

Dixie Walker was traded after the season to Pittsburgh. Two players returned in the deal; Billy Cox and "Preacher" Roe, becoming full fledged "Boys of Summer".

This is in reference to Roger Kahn's book **The Boys of Summer** a 1972 non-fiction baseball book. After recounting his childhood in Brooklyn and his life as a young reporter on the *New York Herald Tribune*, the author relates some history of the Brooklyn Dodgers up to their victory in the 1955 World Series. He then tracks the lives of these players (Clem Labine, George Shuba, Carl Erskine, Andy Pafko, Joe Black, Preacher Roe, Pee Wee Reese, Carl Furillo, Gil Hodges, Roy Campanella, Duke Snider, Jackie Robinson and Billy Cox) over the subsequent years as they aged.

What happened to Bragan? He got a big double in Game 6 of the 1947 World Series, and stuck around for a few games the following year. He was then aware that he was done as a player.

Bragan knew that managing was his only way to stay in the game. He went to Fort Worth, where he served as a player-manager, then to Hollywood for a couple of years. In 1955, he was hired to manage the Pittsburgh Pirates. He was hired by the Pirates GM, the one and only, Branch Rickey.

Over the years, Bragan and Robinson became friends, real friends, the sort who would go to each other's houses for dinner, and the sort who would happily embrace whenever they came across each other. Robinson was proud of Bragan and proud of how he changed his outlook on people. In 1958, Bragan was hired midseason to manage a minor-league team in Spokane. There was an angry, young, African American shortstop on that team who had been in the minor leagues for 8 years. He was miserable, both toward himself and everyone around him. The shortstop was Maury Wills.

Bragan talked to Wills every day. He boosted Wills' confidence; spoke of the good things he saw in him as a player. "You have gifts," Bragan told him. "You belong in this game." Bragan noticed something in Maury Wills swing; mainly that he had real trouble swinging from the right side and convinced him to become a switch-hitter. Bragan and Wills worked together every day on this transition. Wills began to become comfortable at switch-hitting.

Perhaps you have heard the story of Maury Wills. He would win the 1962 MVP Award for stealing 104 bases and scoring 130 runs. Many credit him for altering the game. Maury Wills knew in 1958 that Bragan was one of the men who at first refused to play with Jackie Robinson. He knew it, and his instincts would have been not to trust such a man. But he also knew that Bobby Bragan was a different man. His generosity of spirit had been hard earned. His enthusiasm and newfound color blindness were irresistible. Maury Wills has credited much of his success in baseball and life to the friendship and mentorship of Bobby Bragan.

A year later, Branch Rickey died. In the church, in the same pew sat Jackie Robinson and Bobby Bragan. Jackie Robinson talked afterward about how Branch Rickey changed his life. Bobby Bragan talked about the same thing.

Bragan spent a long life in the game of baseball; he died at the age of 92, and to the very end of his life, he continued his passion by teaching baseball to kids.

Key Black Firsts

Baseball's first all-black outfield—Monte Irvin, Willie Mays, and Hank Thompson—appeared in the 1951 World Series for the New York Giants. (*United Press International Photo*)

04/15/47   **Jackie Robinson** is the first black player in modern-day MLB

07/05/47   **Larry Doby** is the first black player in the American League

08/26/47   **Dan Bankhead** is the first black pitcher in MLB

09/30/47   **Jackie Robinson and Dan Bankhead** are the first black players to play in the World Series

07/08/48   **Don Newcombe and Hank Thompson** are the first blacks to face each other in a game

08/13/48   **"Satchel" Paige** is the first black pitcher in the American League

1948   **Larry Doby and Satchel Paige** are first blacks on a World Series Championship team.

1948   **"Sam" Lacy** is the first black sportswriter admitted to Baseball Writers Association of America (BBWAA)

07/12/49   **Jackie Robinson, Don Newcombe, and Roy Campanella** are the first black players to appear in MLB All-Star Game

11/18/51   **Jackie Robinson** is the first black to win the MVP Award

1951   **Emmett Ashford** is the first black umpire in minor leagues

1951   World Series. First all-black outfield. **"Monte" Irvin, Willie Mays, and Hank Thompson.**

10/01/52   **Joe Black** is the first black to win a World Series game

07/17/54   Dodgers are the first team to field a majority black team, **Jim Gilliam, Jackie Robinson, Sandy Amoros, Roy Campanella, and Don Newcombe,** as they all start the game

05/12/55   **Sam Jones** is the first black to throw a no-hitter

1959   **Ernie Banks** is the first black to win two consecutive MVP Awards

1962   **Jackie Robinson** is the first black enshrined in the Baseball Hall of Fame

05/29/62   **Buck O'Neil** is the first black MLB coach

04/11/66   **Emmett Ashford** is the first black MLB umpire

1966   **Frank Robinson** is the first black to win the Triple Crown

09/01/71   Pirates become the first team to field a completely black lineup: **Al Oliver 1B, Rennie Stennett 2B, Jackie Hernandez SS, Dave Cash 3B, Manny Sanguillen C, Dock Ellis P, Gene Clines LF, Roberto Clemente SS, and Willie Stargell RF**

04/08/75   **Frank Robinson** is the first black MLB manager

1992   **Cito Gaston** is the first black manager to win the World Series and won again in 1993

Where are the black players in MLB

- In 1956, 6.7 percent of the players were black.
- In 1980, the highest percent of black players ever in MLB was 18.7.
- In 2018, the Latino players in MLB are at their highest at 29.8 percent.
- In 2019, only 7.7 percent of the players are black, which equates to 68 of 882 players. 11 teams have only one black player while 3 teams have none.

There are sociological and economic reasons for the decline of black ballplayers. The semi-pro, sandlot, and industrial teams that once thrived in black communities, serving as feeders to the Negro Leagues and then the major leagues, have disappeared. Basketball and football have replaced baseball as the most popular sports in black communities, where funding for public school baseball teams and neighborhood playgrounds with baseball fields have declined. Major league teams more actively recruit young players from Latin America.

Many books address these and many other questions on this topic. Three books (amongst many) that I highly recommend are:

The Negro League Baseball by **Neil Lanctot**

Bill Veeck by **Paul Dickson**

Baseball's Great Experiment by **Jules Tygiel**

Another great resource is membership in the SABR (Society for American Baseball Research). Available in this resource are statistics, articles, books, etc., which I found of great value. There are also audio recordings of many of the baseball players mentioned in this book, including Bobby Boyd, "Jake" Wood, Henry Mason, Nino Escalera, Tom Alston, Larry Doby, "Monte" Irvin, writers such as "Sam" Lacy and scout and player Buck O'Neil, plus many others.

I plan on sending out a note to the following:

Ken Burns:

Great subject for one of your documentaries.

Ron Manfred: Commissioner of MLB and selected team owners

This is not my original thought as several articles I ran across suggested this. Wish I had noted their names. Every April, baseball honors Jackie Robinson as the first black player in Modern-Day MLB. This honor is well deserved, but my opinion is each of the first black player for the 16 teams in 1947 should be honored also.

For example, the Cleveland Indians center fielder should wear number "14" for Larry Doby; the White Sox left fielder should wear number "9" for "Minnie" Miñoso; the Detroit Tigers third baseman should wear number "22" for Ozzie Virgil; the Cincinnati Reds shortstop should wear number "21" for Nino Escalara and the third baseman should wear number "10" for Chuck Harmon.

Some of these players are still living and deserve recognition. Why shouldn't we honor all these brave black pioneers?

Food For Thought

My niece, Kelly (see picture below with a great Hall Of Famer, Ozzie Smith) is an avid baseball fan, and while reviewing this writing, asked me to **name my favorite black player** not on my home teams. Several people I asked had to think a while before answering.

Who would you name?

An excerpt from Ted Williams' Baseball Hall of Fame Induction speech on July 25, 1966.

"The other day, Willie Mays hit his five-hundred-and-twenty-second home run. He has gone past me, and he's pushing, and I say to him, "Go get 'em, Willie." Baseball gives every American boy a chance to excel. Not just to be as good as someone else, but to be better. This is the nature of man and the name of the game. I hope that one day Satchel Paige and Josh Gibson will be voted into the Hall of Fame as symbols of the great Negro players who are not here only because they weren't given the chance."

On April 1, 2016, the *Philadelphia News* published an article that the Philadelphia city council had issued the following apology:

"The Philadelphia City Council passed a resolution Thursday naming April 15th in honor of Jackie Robinson, officially apologizing for the racism he experienced when he visited the city in 1947.

The apology will be presented to the baseball icon's widow, the Associated Press reported. Robinson died in 1972."

Robinson became the first black major league baseball player on April 15, 1947. When he visited Philadelphia with the Brooklyn Dodgers that year, he was refused service at a local hotel and targeted with racial slurs by Philadelphia Phillies players and the team's manager Ben Chapman, according to the AP.

"Unfortunately, in Philadelphia, Jackie Robinson experienced some of the most virulent racism and hate of his career," said Councilwoman Helen Gym, who introduced the resolution, ABC News reported. "Our colleagues decided to introduce this resolution to celebrate Jackie Robinson."

This apology only came sixty-nine years late

THE END . . . OR MAYBE JUST THE BEGINNING

In addition to what I have learned while researching information for this book, I look forward to exploring the women, especially Toni Stone, Connie Morgan, Mamie Johnson and others, who played in the Men's Negro Leagues. I also wonder why many players never got a chance.

One example: Of all the Negro League players who never got a shot in organized baseball, the career of Ike Jackson is one of the most baffling. Jackson played for the Kansas City Monarchs in 1951 and 1952 before Baird sold his contract to Major League baseball. In his first season in Minor League ball, Ike hit 18 home runs with 101 runs batted in while hitting for a .388 batting average with Carlsbad of the Longhorn League.

Jackson was a catcher who was extremely versatile on the playing field. Over his four year career in the minor leagues, he also played first base and the outfield. In 1956, his last season in professional baseball with Midland of the Southwest League, Ike hit 31 home runs, had 138 runs batted in and hit for a .347 batting average. Jackson played his minor league ball from 1953 through 1956 in the low minors. Over his four year minor league career, Ike caught, hit for power (averaged over 20 home runs a year with a slugging percentage of .586), was a clutch hitter (averaging over 120 runs batted in a season) and hit for an average of .355. He not only never got a shot at the majors, but also he never moved up in the minor league system.

It is my hope to continue my passion for baseball by researching the many players that I believe should be in the Baseball Hall of Fame based on their statistics. Minnie Minoso would be my first research and then Billy Pierce, as well as many others.

Thank You for Reading My Book!

References for Baseball's Forgotten Black Heroes

Internet:

TheBaseballCube.com

Wikipedia: Free text from Wikipedia under the GFDL and CC-BY-SA licenses. http://creativecommons.org/licenses/by-sa/3.0/

History.com (This Day in History)

Web.archive.org (Negro League Baseball Players Association)

Wikipedia.com

MLB.com (major-league baseball)

CallToThePen.com

NLBM.com (Negro League Baseball Museum)

Baseball-Almanac.com

Baseball-Reference.com

Retrosheet.org

Books:

Crossing the Line (Larry Moffi and Jonathan Kronstadt)

Baseball's Great Experiment (Jules Tygiel)

The Jackie Robinson Reader (Various Authors)

Don't Look Back (Mark Ribowsky)

Negro League Baseball (Neil Lanctot)

Bill Veeck (Paul Dickson)

Branch Rickey (Jimmy Breslin)

Other Resources:

Our Sports **Magazine** (July 1953 Issue)

Henry Ford Foundation Museum

Stacey Weeks, Naperville Librarian

Baseball Hall of Fame (Cooperstown)

Negro League Baseball Museum (Kansas City, Missouri)

Articles

Chapter 1: Ryan Whirty

Chapter 17: Bill Plaschke

Chapter 17: Gary Toms (G-Man)

Acknowledgements

I would like to thank my sons Steve and Brian and my daughters-in-laws Laura and Sara who provided inspiration and support.

My sincere appreciation to my nephew Ryan Blackwell who shared his talent by creating the book cover. Thanks to my long time friend Phil LoPresti and my niece Kelly Meloy who read the original drafts and offered their valuable time and input. Thanks also to my friend Neal Hendrickson, the man who has any computer tool you need.

Appendix

Who Were the Players?

Players by Date of Appearance
(Bold denotes first black on the team)

Last Name	First Name	Team	League	Date
Robinson	**Jackie**	Brooklyn Dodgers	NL	4/15/47
Doby	**Larry**	Cleveland Indians	AL	7/5/47
Thompson	**Hank**	St. Louis Browns	AL	7/17/47
Brown	Willard	St. Louis Browns	AL	7/19/47
Bankhead	Dan	Brooklyn Dodgers	NL	8/26/47
Campanella	Roy	Brooklyn Dodgers	NL	4/20/48
Paige	"Satchel"	Cleveland Indians	AL	7/9/48
Miñoso	"Minnie"	Cleveland Indians	AL	4/19/49
Newcombe	Don	Brooklyn Dodgers	NL	5/20/49
Thompson	**Hank**	NY Giants	NL	7/8/49
Irvin	**"Monte"**	NY Giants	NL	7/8/49
Easter	"Luke"	Cleveland Indians	AL	8/11/49
Jethroe	**Sam**	Boston Braves	NL	4/18/50
Márquez	Luis	Boston Braves	NL	4/18/51
Noble	Ray	NY Giants	NL	4/18/51
Wilson	Artie	NY Giants	NL	4/18/51
Simpson	Harry	Cleveland Indians	AL	4/21/51
Miñoso	**"Minnie"**	Chicago White Sox	AL	5/1/51
Mays	Willie	NY Giants	NL	5/25/51
Paige	"Satchel"	St. Louis Browns	AL	7/18/51

Hairston	Sam	Chicago White Sox	AL	7/21/51
Boyd	Bob	Chicago White Sox	AL	9/8/51
Jones	Sam	Cleveland Indians	AL	9/22/51
Bernier	**Carlos**	Pittsburgh Pirates	NL	4/22/53
Trice	**Bob**	Philadelphia A's	AL	9/13/53
Banks	**Ernie**	Chicago Cubs	NL	9/17/53
Baker	Gene	Chicago Cubs	NL	9/20/53
Roberts	**"Curt"**	Pittsburgh Pirates	NL	4/13/54
Alston	**Tom**	St. Louis Cardinals	NL	4/13/54
Escalera	**Nino**	Cincinnati Reds	NL	4/17/54
Harmon	**Chuck**	Cincinnati Reds	NL	4/17/54
Greason	Bill	St. Louis Cardinals	NL	5/31/54
Lawrence	Brooks	St. Louis Cardinals	NL	6/24/54
Paula	**Carlos**	Washington Senators	AL	9/6/54
Howard	**Elston**	NY Yankees	AL	4/14/55
Kennedy	**John**	Philadelphia Phillies	NL	4/22/57
Virgil Sr.	**Ozzie**	Detroit Tigers	AL	6/6/58
Mason	Hank	Philadelphia Phillies	NL	9/12/58
Doby	Larry	Detroit Tigers	AL	4/5/59
Green	**"Pumpsie"**	Boston Red Sox	AL	7/21/59
Wilson	Earl	Boston Red Sox	AL	7/28/59
Proctor	Jim	Detroit Tigers	AL	9/14/59
Wood	Jake	Detroit Tigers	AL	4/11/61

Note: MLB recognizes "Curt" Roberts as the first black to play for the Pirates, but Carlos Bernier is also included as he preceded Roberts and was a black Latin.

Minnie Minoso is recognized as first black player on the White Sox, but since he is Cuban, some argue Sam Hairston was first. I included both.

Ozzie Virgil Sr is recognized as the first black Tiger player but since he was Domini,can, some argue Larry Doby is the first. I included both.

Player Statistics

Moses Fleetwood Walker

												Minor/Major		
Year	Tm	Lg	G	AB	R	H	2B	3B	HR	RBI	SB	SO	BA	OBP	SLG
1883	TOL	N/A													
1884	TOL	AA	42	152	23	40	2	3	0				0.263	0.325	0.316
1885	Multi	N/A	57	197	37	51	6	2	0				0.259	0.259	0.31
1886	WBY	N/A	44	157	21	33	2	0	0		12		0.21	0.21	0.223
1887	NWK	N/A													
1888	SYR	N/A	77	283	38	48	5	2	3		34		0.17	0.17	0.233
1889	SYR	N/A	50	171	29	37	1	1	0		18		0.216	0.216	0.234
1891	OCO	N/A													
Total 8 years			270	960	148	209	16	8	3	0	64				
1 Year Majors			42	152	23	40	2	3	0				0.263	0.325	0.316

"Johnny" Wright

Minors

Year	Tm	Lg	Lev	W	L	ERA	G	GS	CG	IP	H	R	BB	SO
1937	Newark	NNL	NgM	1	0			1	1	9	6	3	3	6
1938	Newark	NNL	NgM	0	3			4	2	22	15	9	2	0
1939	Toledo	NAL	NgM	1	2			2	0	11.1	16	8	3	4
1940	2 Teams	2 Lgs	NgM-Non	0	2			2	2	17	15	7	3	7
1940	Toledo/Indianapolis	NAL	NgM											
1940	Indianapolis	INDP	Non											
1941	Homestead	NNL	NgM	3	0			3	3	26	15	6	5	12
1942	Homestead	NNL	NgM	3	2			6	3	63.1	64	30	8	22
1943	Homestead	NNL	NgM	14	4			18	12	141.1	122	40	29	72
1944	Homestead	NNL	NgM	2	0			2	1	15	12	9	4	9
1945	Homestead	NNL	NgM	1	2			3	3	28	21	14	4	15
1946	Montreal	IL	AAA/BRO	0	0		2			6	5		5	3
1946	Trois-Rivières	CAML	C/BRO	12	8	4.15	32	22		154	174	88	58	
1947	Homestead	NNL	NgM	3	4			7	4	66	62	30	8	36
All Levels (11 Seasons)				**40**	**27**		**34**	**70**	**31**	**558.3**	**527**	**244**	**132**	**186**

"Johnny" Wright never pitched in the majors.

"Bud" Fowler

Year	Age	Tm	Lg	G	AB	R	H	2B	3B	HR	RBI	SB	BA	SLG
1878	20	Lynn/ Worcester	INTA											
1884	26	Stillwater	NWES	48	189	28	57	10	0	0			0.302	0.354
1885	27	3 Teams	3 Lgs	8	36	5	8	2	0	0				
1885	27	Portland	ENEL											
1885	27	Omaha/ Keokuk	WL	8	36	5	8	2	0	0			0.222	0.278
1885	27	Pueblo	COSL											
1886	28	Topeka	WL											
1887	29	Binghamton	INTA											
1888	30	2 Teams	CISL											
1888	30	Crawfordsville	CISL											
1888	30	Terre Haute	CISL											
1889	31	Greenville	MICH											
1890	32	2 Teams	2 Lgs	27	118	23	38	6	3	2		10		
1890	32	Galesburg/ Indianapolis	CISL	27	118	23	38	6	3	2		10	0.322	0.475
1890	32	Sterling/ Galesburg/ Burlin	ILIA											
1895	37	2 Teams	MICH											
1895	37	Adrian	MICH											
1895	37	Lansing	MICH											
All Levels (9 Seasons)				**83**	**56**	**18**	**3**	**2**		**10**				

Pitching Fowler

Year	Age	Tm	Lg	W	L	ERA	G	GS	CG	SHO	IP	H	R	SO
1884	26	Stillwater	NWES	7	8	2.08	20	13	10	0	130	133	94	57
1885	27	Pueblo	COSL	0	2		2	2	2					
				7	10	2.08	22	15	12	0	130	133	94	57

Roy Partlow

Year	Age	Tm	Lg	Lev	W	L	ERA	G	GS	CG	IP	H	R	SO
1934	23	Cincinnati	INDP	Non	1	0			1	1	9	9	7	0
1937	26	Cincinnati	NAL	NgM	0	1			1	0	2	7	3	3
1938	27	Homestead	NNL	NgM	4	2			6	4	44	38	21	0
1939	28	Homestead	NNL	NgM	2	2			5	4	42	36	14	10
1941	30	Homestead	NNL	NgM	2	1			5	2	38	34	27	11
1942	31	Homestead	NNL	NgM	7	3			12	7	83	61	21	40
1943	32	Homestead	NNL	NgM	1	3			5	2	33.1	37	15	17
1944	33	Homestead	NNL	NgM	1	0			1	1	7	9	5	4
1945	34	Philadelphia	NNL	NgM	7	3			12	9	102.1	89	34	53
1946	35	2 Teams	2 Lgs	C-AAA	12	1	3.77	24	15	1	124	120	60	19
1946	35	Philadelphia	NNL	NgM	0	0			0	0	2.2	3	1	0
1946	**35**	**Montreal**	**IL**	**AAA**	2	0	5.59	10	4	1	29	26	18	19
1946	**35**	**Trois-Rivières**	**CAML**	**C**	10	1	3.22	14	11		95	94	42	
1947	36	Philadelphia	NNL	NgM	2	0			2	1	18.1	19	6	8
1948	37	Philadelphia	NNL	NgM	3	0			3	1	16.1	16	9	4
1950	39	Granby	PROV	C	7	2	1.97	14	10		87	78	42	
1951	40	Granby	PROV	C	8	3	3.41	16	15		116	125	56	
					69	**22**	**3.98**	**78**	**108**	**34**	**847.6**	**801**	**381**	**188**

Roy never pitched in the major leagues.

Jackie Robinson (1)

Year	Team	Games	AB	R	Hits	2B	3B	HR	RBI	SO	AVG	OBP	SLG
1947	Dodgers	151	590	125	175	31	5	12	48	36	0.297	0.383	0.427
1948	Dodgers	147	574	108	170	38	8	12	85	37	0.296	0.367	0.453
1949	Dodgers	156	593	122	203	38	12	16	124	27	0.342	0.432	0.528
1950	Dodgers	144	518	99	170	39	4	14	81	24	0.328	0.423	0.500
1951	Dodgers	153	548	106	185	33	7	19	88	27	0.338	0.429	0.527
1952	Dodgers	149	510	104	157	17	3	19	75	40	0.308	0.440	0.465
1953	Dodgers	136	484	109	159	34	7	12	95	30	0.329	0.425	0.502
1954	Dodgers	124	386	62	120	22	4	15	59	20	0.311	0.413	0.505
1955	Dodgers	105	317	51	81	6	2	8	36	18	0.256	0.378	0.363
1956	Dodgers	117	357	61	98	15	2	10	43	32	0.275	0.382	0.412
10 Years		**1,382**	**4,877**	**947**	**1,518**	**273**	**54**	**137**	**734**	**291**	**0.311**	**0.409**	**0.474**

Larry Doby (2)

YR	Team	Games	AB	R	Hits	2B	3B	HR	RBI	SO	AVG	OBP	SLG
1947	Indians	29	32	3	5	1	0	0	2	11	0.156	0.182	0.188
1948	Indians	121	439	83	132	23	9	14	66	77	0.301	0.384	0.490
1949	Indians	147	547	106	153	25	3	24	85	90	0.280	0.389	0.468
1950	Indians	142	503	110	164	25	5	25	102	71	0.326	0.442	0.545
1951	Indians	134	447	84	132	27	5	20	69	81	0.295	0.428	0.512
1952	Indians	140	519	104	143	26	8	32	104	111	0.276	0.383	0.541
1953	Indians	149	513	92	135	18	5	29	102	121	0.263	0.385	0.487
1954	Indians	153	577	94	157	18	4	32	126	94	0.272	0.364	0.484
1955	Indians	131	491	91	143	17	5	26	75	100	0.291	0.369	0.505
1956	White Sox	140	504	89	135	22	3	24	102	105	0.268	0.392	0.466
1957	White Sox	119	416	57	120	27	2	14	79	79	0.288	0.373	0.464
1958	Indians	89	247	41	70	10	1	13	45	49	0.283	0.348	0.490
1959	Tigers	18	55	5	12	3	1	0	4	9	0.218	0.313	0.309
1959	White Sox	21	58	1	14	1	1	0	9	13	0.241	0.267	0.293
13 Years		**1,533**	**5348**	**960**	**1515**	**243**	**52**	**253**	**970**	**1011**	**0.283**	**0.386**	**0.490**

Hank Thompson (3)

Year	Team	LGE	Lvl	G	AB	R	H	2B	3B	HR	RBI	SB	SO	AVG	OBP	SLG
1947	SL Browns	AL	MLB	27	78	10	20	1	1	0	5	2	7	0.256	0.341	0.295
1949	NY Giants	NL	MLB	75	275	51	77	10	4	9	34	5	30	0.28	0.377	0.444
1950	NY Giants	NL	MLB	148	512	82	148	17	6	20	91	8	60	0.289	0.391	0.463
1951	NY Giants	NL	MLB	87	264	37	62	8	4	8	33	1	23	0.235	0.342	0.386
1952	NY Giants	NL	MLB	128	423	67	110	13	9	17	67	4	38	0.26	0.344	0.454
1953	NY Giants	NL	MLB	114	388	80	117	15	8	24	74	6	39	0.302	0.4	0.567
1954	NY Giants	NL	MLB	136	448	76	118	18	1	26	86	3	58	0.263	0.389	0.482
1955	NY Giants	NL	MLB	135	432	65	106	13	1	17	63	2	56	0.245	0.367	0.398
1956	NY Giants	NL	MLB	83	183	24	43	9	0	8	29	2	26	0.235	0.346	0.415
10 years				**933**	**3003**	**492**	**801**	**104**	**34**	**129**	**482**	**33**	**337**	**0.263**	**0.366**	**0.434**

Willard Brown (4)

Majors

Year	Tm	Lg	G	PA	AB	R	H	2B	3B	HR	RBI	SB	BA	OBP	SLG
1947	SLB	AL	21	67	67	4	12	3	0	1	6	2	0.179	0.179	0.269

Minors

Year	Tm	G	AB	R	H	2B	3B	HR	RBI	SB	BA	OBP	SLG
1935	KCM		25	5	13	3	0	3	3	1	0.520	0.556	1.000
1936	KCM		1	0	0	0	0	0	0	0	0.000	0.000	0.000
1937	KCM		174	36	58	2	7	6	17	6	0.333	0.345	0.529
1938	KCM		78	14	27	5	1	3	7	9	0.346	0.346	0.551
1939	KCM		70	10	22	5	2	1	8	5	0.314	0.333	0.486
1940	KCM		4	0	0	0	0	0	0	0	0.000	0.000	0.000
1941	KCM		87	19	30	3	3	2	19	4	0.345	0.380	0.517
1942	KCM		127	28	47	7	2	5	25	3	0.370	0.398	0.575
1943	KCM		79	15	27	3	0	3	6	2	0.342	0.342	0.494
1944	KCM		4	0	1	0	0	0	0	0	0.250	0.250	0.250
1946	KCM		106	15	27	6	4	2	21	8	0.255	0.275	0.443
1947	KCM		57	12	21	3	5	2	18	0	0.368	0.410	0.702
1947	SLB	21	67	4	12	3	0	1	6	2	0.179	0.179	0.269
1948	KCM		86	18	31	5	1	3	15	4	0.360	0.402	0.547
1949	KCM		3	0	0	0	0	0	0	0	0.000	0.000	0.000
1950	OTT	30	128		45	7	1	1			0.352	0.352	0.445
1953	DAL	138	522	91	162	36	2	23	108	3	0.310	0.357	0.519
1954	STL-min	144	583	92	183	36	4	35	120	2	0.314	0.350	0.569
1955	STL-min	149	544	73	164	34	4	19	104	3	0.301	0.345	0.483
1956	BAL-MLN-CHC-min	127	436	50	130	19	0	17	73	2	0.298	0.351	0.459

		G	PA		R	H	2B	3B	HR	RBI	SB	BA	OBP	SLG
1 Year		21	67		4	12	3	0	1	6	2	0.179	0.179	0.269

Dan Bankhead (5)

Year	Tm	Lg	W	L	ERA	G	GS	CG	IP	H	R	BB	SO
1940	BBB	NgM	1	0			2	1	14	10	5	1	9
1941	BBB	NgM	4	0			2	2	28.1	18	8	7	10
1942	BBB	NgM	2	0			3	1	16.1	15	4	12	5
1944	BBB	NgM	1	0			1	1	7	3	0	3	14
1946	MRS	NgM	5	3			7	4	62.1	39	17	14	61
1947	MRS	NgM	2	1			3	1	18	16	8	3	17
1947	**BRO**	**NL**	0	0	7.200	4	0	0	10	15	8	8	6
1948	BRO-min	B, AAA	24	6	2.530	37			238	154	78	146	22
1949	BRO-min	AAA	20	6	3.760	38	34	18	249	192	118	170	176
1950	**BRO**	**NL**	9	4	5.500	41	12	2	129.1	119	84	88	96
1951	BRO-min	AAA	2	6	3.910	10	8	0	46	50	26	26	16
1951	**BRO**	**NL**	0	1	15.430	7	1	0	14	27	24	14	9
1952	BRO-min	AAA	0	1	6.920	5	1	0	13	14	11	11	7
1953	DRM	C	0	0		47			45	46		26	
1960	PUE	AA	5	2	4.500	16	1	1	48	39	30	27	34
1961	PUE	AA				21							
1962	PUE	AA				47							
1963	PUE	AA				29							
1964	LEO	A				13							
1966	REY	AA				6							
3 Years	**Majors**		**9**	**5**	**6.520**	**52**	**13**	**2**	**153.1**	**161**	**116**	**110**	**111**

Roy Campanella (6)

Year	Tm	G	AB	R	H	2B	3B	HR	RBI	SB	SO	BA	OBP	SLG
1948	BRO	83	279	32	72	11	3	9	45	3	45	0.258	0.345	0.416
1949	BRO	130	436	65	125	22	2	22	82	3	36	0.287	0.385	0.498
1950	BRO	126	437	70	123	19	3	31	89	1	51	0.281	0.364	0.551
1951	BRO	143	505	90	164	33	1	33	108	1	51	0.325	0.393	0.59
1952	BRO	128	468	73	126	18	1	22	97	8	59	0.269	0.352	0.453
1953	BRO	144	519	103	162	26	3	41	**142**	4	58	0.312	0.395	0.611
1954	BRO	111	397	43	82	14	3	19	51	1	49	0.207	0.285	0.401
1955	BRO	123	446	81	142	20	1	32	107	2	41	0.318	0.395	0.583
1956	BRO	124	388	39	85	6	1	20	73	1	61	0.219	0.333	0.394
1957	BRO	103	330	31	80	9	0	13	62	1	50	0.242	0.316	0.388
10 Years		**1,215**	**4,205**	**627**	**1161**	**178**	**18**	**242**	**856**	**25**	**501**	**0.276**	**0.36**	**0.5**

"Satchel" Paige (7)

Year	Team	G	GS	GF	W	L	PCT	ERA	CG	SHO	SV	IP	H	BB	SO
1948	Indians	21	7	5	6	1	0.857	2.48	3	2	1	72.2	61	21	22
1949	Indians	31	5	19	4	7	0.364	3.04	1	0	5	83	70	29	33
1951	Browns	23	3	16	3	4	0.429	4.79	0	0	5	62	67	39	29
1952	Browns	46	6	35	12	10	0.545	3.07	3	2	10	138	116	51	57
1953	Browns	57	4	34	3	9	0.25	3.53	0	0	11	117.1	114	51	39
1965	Athletics	1	1	0	0	0	0	0	0	0	0	3	1	0	0
6 Years		**179**	**26**	**109**	**28**	**31**	**0.475**	**3.29**	**7**	**4**	**32**	**475.3**	**429**	**191**	**180**

"Minnie" Miñoso (8)

Year	Team	Games	AB	R	Hits	2B	3B	HR	RBI	SO	AVG	OBP	SLG
1949	Indians	9	16	2	3	0	0	1	1	2	0.188	0.350	0.375
1951	Indians	8	14	3	6	2	0	0	2	1	0.429	0.529	0.571
1951	White Sox	138	516	109	167	32	14	10	74	41	0.324	0.419	0.498
1952	White Sox	147	569	96	160	24	9	13	61	46	0.281	0.375	0.424
1953	White Sox	151	556	104	174	24	8	15	104	43	0.313	0.410	0.466
1954	White Sox	153	568	119	182	29	18	19	116	46	0.320	0.411	0.535
1955	White Sox	139	517	79	149	26	7	10	70	43	0.288	0.387	0.424
1956	White Sox	151	545	106	172	29	11	21	88	40	0.316	0.425	0.525
1957	White Sox	153	568	96	176	36	5	12	103	54	0.310	0.408	0.454
1958	Indians	149	556	94	168	25	2	24	80	53	0.302	0.383	0.484
1959	Indians	148	570	92	172	32	0	21	92	46	0.302	0.377	0.468
1960	White Sox	154	591	89	184	32	4	20	105	63	0.311	0.374	0.481
1961	White Sox	152	540	91	151	28	3	14	82	46	0.280	0.369	0.420
1962	Cardinals	39	97	14	19	5	0	1	10	17	0.196	0.271	0.278
1963	Senators	109	315	38	72	12	2	4	30	38	0.229	0.315	0.317
1964	White Sox	30	31	4	7	0	0	1	5	3	0.226	0.351	0.323
1976	White Sox	3	8	0	1	0	0	0	0	2	0.125	0.125	0.125
1980	White Sox	2	2	0	0	0	0	0	0	0	0	0	0
17 Years		**1,835**	**6,579**	**1,136**	**1,963**	**336**	**83**	**186**	**1,023**	**584**	**0.298**	**0.389**	**0.459**

Don Newcombe (9)

Year	Tm	Lg	W	L	ERA	G	CG	SHO	SV	IP	H	R	BB	SO
1949	BRO	NL	17	8	3.17	38	19	5	1	244.1	223	89	73	149
1950	BRO	NL	19	11	3.7	40	20	4	3	267.1	258	120	75	130
1951	BRO	NL	20	9	3.28	40	18	3	0	272	235	115	91	164
1952	Did not play in major or minor leagues (military service)													
1953	Did not play in major or minor leagues (military service)													
1954	BRO	NL	9	8	4.55	29	6	0	0	144.1	158	81	49	82
1955	BRO	NL	20	5	3.2	34	17	1	0	233.2	222	103	38	143
1956	BRO	NL	27	7	3.06	38	18	5	0	268	219	101	46	139
1957	BRO	NL	11	12	3.49	28	12	4	0	198.2	199	86	33	90
1958	TOT	NL	7	13	4.67	31	8	0	1	167.2	212	98	36	69
1958	LAD	NL	0	6	7.86	11	1	0	0	34.1	53	37	8	16
1958	CIN	NL	7	7	3.85	20	7	0	1	133.1	159	61	28	53
1959	CIN	NL	13	8	3.16	30	17	2	1	222	216	87	27	100
1960	CIN	NL	4	6	4.57	16	1	0	0	82.2	99	48	14	36
1960	CLE	AL	2	3	4.33	20	0	0	1	54	61	28	8	27
10 Yrs			**149**	**90**	**3.56**	**344**	**136**	**24**	**7**	**2154.2**	**2102**	**956**	**490**	**1129**

"Monte" Irvin (10)

Year	Tm	G	AB	R	H	2B	3B	HR	RBI	SB	SO	BA	OBP	SLG
1949	NYG	36	76	7	17	3	2	0	7	0	11	0.224	0.366	0.316
1950	NYG	110	374	61	112	19	5	15	66	3	41	0.299	0.392	0.497
1951	NYG	151	558	94	174	19	11	24	**121**	12	44	0.312	0.415	0.514
1952	NYG	46	126	10	39	2	1	4	21	0	11	0.310	0.365	0.437
1953	NYG	124	444	72	146	21	5	21	97	2	34	0.329	0.406	0.541
1954	NYG	135	432	62	113	13	3	19	64	7	23	0.262	0.363	0.438
1955	NYG	51	150	16	38	7	1	1	17	3	15	0.253	0.337	0.333
1956	CHC	111	339	44	92	13	3	15	50	1	41	0.271	0.346	0.460
8 Years		**764**	**2499**	**366**	**731**	**97**	**31**	**99**	**443**	**28**	**220**	**0.293**	**0.383**	**0.475**

"Luke" Easter (11)

Year	Tm	Lg	G	AB	R	H	2B	3B	HR	RBI	SB	SO	BA	OBP	SLG
1949	CLE	AL	21	45	6	10	3	0	0	2	0	6	0.222	0.340	0.289
1950	CLE	AL	141	540	96	151	20	4	28	107	0	95	0.280	0.373	0.487
1951	CLE	AL	128	486	65	131	12	5	27	103	0	71	0.270	0.333	0.481
1952	CLE	AL	127	437	63	115	10	3	31	97	1	84	0.263	0.337	0.513
1953	CLE	AL	68	211	26	64	9	0	7	31	0	35	0.303	0.361	0.445
1954	CLE	AL	6	6	0	1	0	0	0	0	0	2	0.167	0.167	0.167
6 Years			491	1725	256	472	54	12	93	340	1	293	0.274	0.350	0.481

Sam Jethroe (12)

Year	Tm	Lg	G	AB	R	H	2B	3B	HR	RBI	SB	SO	BA	OBP	SLG
1950	BSN	NL	141	582	100	159	28	8	18	58	*35*	93	0.273	0.338	0.442
1951	BSN	NL	148	572	101	160	29	10	18	65	*35*	88	0.280	0.356	0.460
1952	BSN	NL	151	608	79	141	23	7	13	58	28	112	0.232	0.318	0.357
1953	BRO	AAA													
1954	PIT	NL	2	1	0	0	0	0	0	0	0	0	0.000	0.000	0.000
4 Yrs			**442**	**1763**	**280**	**460**	**80**	**25**	**49**	**181**	**98**	**293**	**0.261**	**0.337**	**0.418**

Luis Márquez (13)

Year	Tm	Lg	G	AB	R	H	2B	3B	HR	RBI	SB	SO	BA	OBP	SLG
1946	BEG, HG	NgM		87	15	26	3	0	3	17	4		0.299	0.307	0.437
1947	HG	NgM		82	15	28	6	0	2	7	5		0.341	0.386	0.488
1948	HG	NgM		52	11	20	3	0	2	11	3		0.385	0.429	0.558
1949	NYY-min	AAA	150	580	100	167	29	7	5	52	35	81	0.288	0.349	0.388
1950	POR	AAA	194	775	136	241	41	19	9	86	38	98	0.311	0.371	0.448
1951	**BSN**	**NL**	**68**	**122**	**19**	**24**	**5**	**1**	**0**	**11**	**4**	**20**	**0.197**	**0.274**	**0.254**
1952	BSN-min	AAA	136	521	100	180	38	10	14	99	24	91	0.345	0.413	0.537
1953	MLN-min	AAA	130	510	77	149	28	3	13	81	37	76	0.292	0.350	0.435
1954	MLN-min	AAA	58	229	46	76	18	1	8	36	7	22	0.332	0.389	0.524
1954	**CHC**	**NL**	**17**	**12**	**2**	**1**	**0**	**0**	**0**	**0**	**3**	**4**	**0.083**	**0.214**	**0.083**
1954	**PIT**	**NL**	**14**	**9**	**3**	**1**	**0**	**0**	**0**	**0**	**0**	**0**	**0.111**	**0.385**	**0.111**
1955	MLN-min	Opn, AAA	133	456	70	137	30	2	10	65	5	81	0.300	0.348	0.441
1956	BRO-min	Opn	155	602	122	207	27	10	25	110	18	77	0.344	0.385	0.547
1957	CHC-min	Opn	167	610	92	169	31	6	21	85	13	69	0.277	0.326	0.451
1958	CHC-min	AAA	109	335	43	89	13	6	8	42	2	45	0.266	0.331	0.412
1959	DAL	AAA	142	510	80	176	24	4	18	78	14	49	0.345	0.406	0.514
1960	KCA-min	AAA	144	469	57	124	30	3	3	30	6	76	0.264	0.338	0.360
1961	PHI-LAA-	A, AAA	37	97	15	23	4	2	1	10	1	18	0.237	0.321	0.351
2 Yrs	**Majors**		**99**	**143**	**24**	**26**	**5**	**1**	**0**	**11**	**7**	**24**	**0.182**	**0.278**	**0.231**

Ray Noble (14)

Year	Tm	Lg	G	AB	R	H	2B	3B	HR	RBI	SB	SO	BA	OBP	SLG
1945	NYC	NgM		14	2	2	0	1	0	1	0		0.143	0.200	0.286
1946	NYC	NgM		20	1	2	1	0	0	1	0		0.100	0.182	0.150
1947	NYC	NgM		23	2	9	3	0	1	8	1		0.391	0.462	0.652
1948	NYC	NgM		57	2	18	5	1	0	11	2		0.316	0.350	0.439
1949	NYG-min	AAA	67	189	33	49	6	1	7	29	1	39	0.259	0.372	0.413
1950	OLD	AAA	110	345	58	109	23	3	15	76	4	54	0.316	0.382	0.530
1951	**NYG**	**NL**	**55**	**141**	**16**	**33**	**6**	**0**	**5**	**26**	**0**	**26**	**0.234**	**0.265**	**0.383**
1952	OLD	Opn	104	366	54	109	12	3	12	60	2	47	0.298	0.375	0.445
1952	**NYG**	**NL**	**6**	**5**	**0**	**0**	**0**	**0**	**0**	**0**	**0**	**1**	**0.000**	**0.000**	**0.000**
1953	NYG-min	AAA	29	111	21	34	5	0	4	21	2	6	0.306	0.398	0.459
1953	**NYG**	**NL**	**46**	**97**	**15**	**20**	**0**	**1**	**4**	**14**	**1**	**14**	**0.206**	**0.353**	**0.351**
1954	HAV	AAA	125	409	46	117	25	1	7	61	0	47	0.286	0.379	0.403
1955	CIN-min	AAA	123	363	46	92	16	2	10	51	1	40	0.253	0.392	0.391
1956	KCA-min	AAA	132	396	43	91	12	0	13	64	0	56	0.230	0.347	0.359
1957	KCA-min	AAA	118	363	49	91	14	0	21	62	0	58	0.251	0.363	0.463
1958	KCA-min	AAA	127	424	59	114	20	2	20	72	0	71	0.269	0.361	0.467
1959	HSN	AAA	138	415	53	122	21	0	15	68	0	49	0.294	0.400	0.453
1960	CHC-min	AAA	92	208	18	57	6	1	6	21	0	33	0.274	0.353	0.399
1961	CHC-min	AAA	5	4		1	0	0	0				0.250	0.250	0.250
3 Yrs	Majors		**107**	**243**	**31**	**53**	**6**	**1**	**9**	**40**	**1**	**41**	**0.218**	**0.299**	**0.362**

Artie Wilson (15)

Year	Tm	Lg	G	AB	R	H	2B	3B	HR	RBI	SB	SO	BA	OBP	SLG
1944	BBB, NBY	NgM		78	16	32	4	2	0	11	3		0.410	0.452	0.513
1945	BBB	NgM		34	6	7	0	0	0	1	2		0.206	0.229	0.206
1946	BBB	NgM		15	4	4	0	0	0	1	2		0.267	0.267	0.267
1947	BBB	NgM		36	8	11	0	1	0	1	2		0.306	0.359	0.361
1948	BBB	NgM		138	31	59	6	7	0	18	5		0.428	0.484	0.572
1949	CLE-min	AAA	165	607	129	211	19	9	0	37	47	58	0.348	0.410	0.409
1950	OLD	AAA	196	848	168	264	27	17	1	48	31	79	0.311	0.367	0.387
1951	NYG-min	AAA	100	415	51	114	10	2	2	35	6	44	0.275	0.322	0.318
1951	**NYG**	**NL**	**19**	**22**	**2**	**4**	**0**	**0**	**0**	**1**	**2**	**1**	**0.182**	**0.250**	**0.182**
1952	SLE	Opn	160	683	95	216	15	8	1	59	25	20	0.316	0.354	0.366
1953	SLE	Opn	177	638	80	212	23	14	2	76	9	25	0.332	0.380	0.422
1954	SLE	Opn	163	660	92	222	24	16	0	50	20	28	0.336	0.371	0.421
1955	POR	Opn	155	616	88	189	20	2	2	23	12	36	0.307	0.348	0.356
1956	BRO-CIN-min	Opn	101	273	33	80	9	4	0	25	6	19	0.293	0.351	0.355
1957	SAC	Opn	75	315	34	83	10	6	0	17	3	12	0.263	0.292	0.333
1962	KCA-min	AAA,B	39	97	10	18	0	1	0	4	1	24	0.186	0.248	0.206
1 Yr	**Majors**		**19**	**22**	**2**	**4**	**0**	**0**	**0**	**1**	**2**	**1**	**0.182**	**0.250**	**0.182**

Harry Simpson (16)

Year	Tm	Lg	G	AB	R	H	2B	3B	HR	RBI	SB	SO	BA	OBP	SLG
1951	CLE	AL	122	332	51	76	7	0	7	24	6	48	0.229	0.325	0.313
1952	CLE	AL	146	545	66	145	21	10	10	65	5	82	0.266	0.337	0.396
1953	CLE	AL	82	242	25	55	3	1	7	22	0	27	0.227	0.284	0.335
1954	CLE	Minors													
1955	CLE	AL	3	1	1	0	0	0	0	0	0	0	0.000	0.667	0.000
1955	KCA	AL	112	396	42	119	16	7	5	52	3	61	0.301	0.356	0.414
1956	KCA	AL	141	543	76	159	22	11	21	105	2	82	0.293	0.347	0.490
1957	KCA	AL	50	179	24	53	9	6	6	24	0	28	0.296	0.339	0.514
1957	NYY	AL	75	224	27	56	7	3	7	39	1	36	0.250	0.307	0.402
1958	NYY	AL	24	51	1	11	2	1	0	6	0	12	0.216	0.310	0.294
1958	KCA	AL	78	212	21	56	7	1	7	27	0	33	0.264	0.345	0.406
1959	KCA	AL	8	14	1	4	0	0	1	2	0	4	0.286	0.389	0.500
1959	CHW	AL	38	75	5	14	5	1	2	13	0	14	0.187	0.228	0.360
1959	PIT	NL	9	15	3	4	2	0	0	2	0	2	0.267	0.267	0.400
8 Yrs			888	2829	343	752	101	41	73	381	17	429	0.266	0.331	0.408

Willie Mays (17)

Year	Tm	G	AB	R	H	2B	3B	HR	RBI	SB	SO	BA	OBP	SLG
1951	NYG	121	464	59	127	22	5	20	68	7	60	0.274	0.356	0.472
1952	NYG	34	127	17	30	2	4	4	23	4	17	0.236	0.326	0.409
1953	DNP	Military Service												
1954	NYG	151	565	119	195	33	*13*	41	110	8	57	*0.345*	0.411	*0.667*
1955	NYG	152	580	123	185	18	*13*	*51*	127	24	60	0.319	0.4	*0.659*
1956	NYG	152	578	101	171	27	8	36	84	*40*	65	0.296	0.369	0.557
1957	NYG	152	585	112	195	26	*20*	35	97	*38*	62	0.333	0.407	*0.626*
1958	SFG	152	600	*121*	208	33	11	29	96	*31*	56	0.347	0.419	0.583
1959	SFG	151	575	125	180	43	5	34	104	*27*	58	0.313	0.381	0.583
1960	SFG	153	595	107	*190*	29	12	29	103	25	70	0.319	0.381	0.555
1961	SFG	154	572	*129*	176	32	3	40	123	18	77	0.308	0.393	0.584
1962	SFG	162	621	130	189	36	5	*49*	141	18	85	0.304	0.384	0.615
1963	SFG	157	596	115	187	32	7	38	103	8	83	0.314	0.38	0.582
1964	SFG	157	578	121	171	21	9	*47*	111	19	72	0.296	0.383	*0.607*
1965	SFG	157	558	118	177	21	3	*52*	112	9	71	0.317	*0.398*	*0.645*
1966	SFG	152	552	99	159	29	4	37	103	5	81	0.288	0.368	0.556
1967	SFG	141	486	83	128	22	2	22	70	6	92	0.263	0.334	0.453
1968	SFG	148	498	84	144	20	5	23	79	12	81	0.289	0.372	0.488
1969	SFG	117	403	64	114	17	3	13	58	6	71	0.283	0.362	0.437
1970	SFG	139	478	94	139	15	2	28	83	5	90	0.291	0.39	0.506
1971	SFG	136	417	82	113	24	5	18	61	23	123	0.271	*0.425*	0.482
1972	SFG	19	49	8	9	2	0	0	3	3	5	0.184	0.394	0.224
1972	NYM	69	195	27	52	9	1	8	19	1	43	0.267	0.402	0.446
1973	NYM	66	209	24	44	10	0	6	25	1	47	0.211	0.303	0.344
22 Yrs		**2,992**	**10,881**	**2,062**	**3,283**	**523**	**140**	**660**	**1,903**	**338**	**1,526**	**0.302**	**0.384**	**0.557**

Sam Hairston (18)

Year	Tm	Lg	G	AB	R	H	2B	3B	HR	RBI	SB	SO	BA	OBP	SLG
1945	CC	NgM		15	2	1	0	0	0	0	1		0.067	0.176	0.067
1946	IC	NgM		33	5	9	0	0	0	4	0		0.273	0.314	0.273
1947	IC	NgM		23	8	8	2	1	0	5	1		0.348	0.423	0.522
1948	IC	NgM		33	6	11	2	0	0	3	2		0.333	0.421	0.394
1950	CHW-min	A	38	133		38	5	1	1				0.286	0.286	0.361
1951	CHW-min	AAA,A	83	244	15	69	20	2	0	18	3	15	0.283	0.335	0.381
1951	**CHW**	**AL**	**4**	**5**	**1**	**2**	**1**	**0**	**0**	**1**	**0**	**0**	**0.400**	**0.571**	**0.600**
1952	CHW-min	A	134	503		159	29	3	12				0.316	0.316	0.457
1953	CHW-min	A	143	535		166	42	6	8				0.310	0.310	0.456
1954	CHW-min	AAA	139	481	47	129	18	8	1	60	5	31	0.268	0.323	0.345
1955	CHW-min	A	142	546		191	38	4	6				0.350	0.350	0.467
1956	CHW-min	A	123	453		144	38	0	8				0.318	0.318	0.455
1957	CHW-min	AAA	89	264	27	67	15	5	1	35	0	22	0.254	0.314	0.360
1958	BAL-CHW-min	AA, AAA	91	248	19	69	14	4	3	37	0	27	0.278	0.365	0.403
1959	CHW-min	A	120	427	60	141	21	2	10	63	0	23	0.330	0.383	0.459
1960	CHW-min	A	45	160	17	42	8	0	3	21	1	15	0.263	0.320	0.369
1 Yr	**Majors**		**4**	**5**	**1**	**2**	**1**	**0**	**0**	**1**	**0**	**0**	**0.400**	**0.571**	**0.600**

Bob Boyd (19)

Year	Tm	Lg	G	AB	R	H	2B	3B	HR	RBI	SB	SO	BA	OBP	SLG
1951	CHW	AL	12	18	3	3	0	1	0	4	0	3	0.167	0.286	0.278
1952	Minors														
1953	CHW	AL	55	165	20	49	6	2	3	23	1	11	0.297	0.352	0.412
1954	CHW	AL	29	56	10	10	3	0	0	5	2	3	0.179	0.233	0.232
1955	Minors														
1956	BAL	AL	70	225	28	70	8	3	2	11	0	14	0.311	0.395	0.400
1957	BAL	AL	141	485	73	154	16	8	4	34	2	31	0.318	0.388	0.408
1958	BAL	AL	125	401	58	124	21	5	7	36	1	24	0.309	0.350	0.439
1959	BAL	AL	128	415	42	110	20	2	3	41	3	14	0.265	0.312	0.345
1960	BAL	AL	71	82	9	26	5	2	0	9	0	5	0.317	0.364	0.427
1961	KCA	AL	26	48	7	11	2	0	0	9	0	2	0.229	0.240	0.271
1961	MLN	NL	36	41	3	10	0	0	0	3	0	7	0.244	0.256	0.244
9 Yrs			**693**	**1936**	**253**	**567**	**81**	**23**	**19**	**175**	**9**	**114**	**0.293**	**0.349**	**0.388**

Sam Jones (20)

Year	Tm	Lg	W	L	ERA	G	GS	CG	SV	IP	H	R	ER	BB	SO
1951	CLE	AL	0	1	2.08	2	1	0	0	8.2	4	2	2	5	4
1952	CLE	AL	2	3	7.25	14	4	0	1	36	38	30	29	37	28
'53–'54	CLE	Minors													
1955	CHC	NL	14	*20*	4.1	36	34	12	0	241.2	175	118	110	185	198
1956	CHC	NL	9	14	3.91	33	28	8	0	188.2	155	93	82	115	176
1957	STL	NL	12	9	3.6	28	27	10	0	182.2	164	77	73	71	154
1958	STL	NL	14	13	2.88	35	35	14	0	250	204	95	80	107	*225*
1959	SFG	NL	**21**	15	2.83	50	35	16	5	270.2	232	99	85	109	209
1960	SFG	NL	18	14	3.19	39	35	13	0	234	200	112	83	91	190
1961	SFG	NL	8	8	4.49	37	17	2	1	128.1	134	72	64	57	105
1962	DET	AL	2	4	3.65	30	6	1	1	81.1	77	39	33	35	73
1963	STL	NL	2	0	9	11	0	0	2	11	15	12	11	5	8
1964	BAL	AL	0	0	2.61	7	0	0	0	10.1	5	3	3	5	6
12 Yrs			**102**	**101**	**3.59**	**322**	**222**	**76**	**10**	**1643.1**	**1403**	**752**	**655**	**822**	**1376**

Carlos Bernier (21)

Year	Tm	G	PA	AB	R	H	2B	3B	HR	RBI	SB	SO	BA	OBP	SLG
1948	SLB-min	104	270	270		67	7	7	3				0.248	0.248	0.359
1949	PIT--min	122	444	444		149	25	5	15				0.336	0.336	0.516
1950	SJE, BRI	116	434	434		136	19	4	24				0.313	0.313	0.541
1951	TAM	135	501	501		136	11	21	5				0.271	0.271	0.407
1952	PIT-min	171	723	652	105	196	24	9	9	79	65	78	0.301	0.360	0.406
1953	**PIT-NL**	105	366	310	48	66	7	8	3	31	15	53	0.213	0.332	0.316
1954	PIT-min	119	494	431	85	135	24	6	6	41	38	58	0.313	0.392	0.439
1955	PIT-min	168	663	580	93	162	24	8	12	73	29	93	0.279	0.357	0.410
1956	PIT-min	159	701	626	91	177	22	15	3	57	48	77	0.283	0.351	0.380
1957	PIT-min	126	512	445	62	129	17	5	3	49	12	63	0.290	0.371	0.371
1958	PIT-min	151	638	546	121	181	27	11	15	86	34	70	0.332	0.415	0.504
1959	PIT-min	152	618	513	73	144	19	10	9	81	21	85	0.281	0.393	0.409
1960	PHI--min	133	494	401	70	105	15	5	5	41	22	70	0.262	0.386	0.362
1961	KCA--min	146	602	481	96	165	19	6	21	96	23	65	0.343	0.462	0.538
1962	LAA-min	121	488	380	81	119	20	2	17	72	7	73	0.313	0.456	0.511
1963	LAA-min	153	655	544	113	163	16	4	26	84	10	103	0.300	0.405	0.487
1964	LAA-min	124	517	432	92	127	14	5	27	68	22	87	0.294	0.408	0.537
1 Yr	**PIT-NL**	**105**	**366**	**310**	**48**	**66**	**7**	**8**	**3**	**31**	**15**	**53**	**0.213**	**0.332**	**0.316**

Bob Trice (22)

Year	Tm	Lg	W	L	ERA	G	GS	CG	IP	H	R	ER	HR	BB	SO
1948	HG	NgM	0	0			0	0	1.1	1	0			0	0
1951	FHM	C	7	12	5.15	23	18		152.0	172	104	87		67	
1952	PHA-min	C	16	3	3.49	24	19		152.0	162	75	59		29	
1953	PHA-min	AAA	21	10	3.10	38	30	20	229.0	207	90	79	20	84	57
1953	**PHA**	**AL**	2	1	5.48	3	3	1	23.0	25	14	14	4	6	4
1954	PHA-min	AAA	4	8	3.23	13	13	12	117.0	113	58	42	12	35	26
1954	**PHA**	**AL**	7	8	5.60	19	18	8	119.0	146	86	74	14	48	22
1955	KCA-min	A, AAA	5	9	4.83	26	15	1	121.0	129	75	65	14	36	8
1955	**KCA**	**AL**	0	0	9.00	4	0	0	10.0	14	13	10	4	6	2
1956	MXD	AA	3	4		18	9		81.0	79				53	
3 Yrs			**9**	**9**	**5.80**	**26**	**21**	**9**	**152.0**	**185**	**113**	**98**	**22**	**60**	**28**

Ernie Banks (23)

YR	Team	Games	AB	R	Hits	2B	3B	HR	RBI	SO	AVG	OBP	SLG
1953	Cubs	10	35	3	11	1	1	2	6	5	0.314	0.385	0.571
1954	Cubs	154	593	70	163	19	7	19	79	50	0.275	0.326	0.427
1955	Cubs	154	596	98	176	29	9	44	117	72	0.295	0.345	0.596
1956	Cubs	139	538	82	160	25	8	28	85	62	0.297	0.358	0.530
1957	Cubs	156	594	113	169	34	6	43	102	85	0.285	0.360	0.579
1958	Cubs	154	617	119	193	23	11	47	129	87	0.313	0.366	0.614
1959	Cubs	155	589	97	179	25	6	45	143	72	0.304	0.374	0.596
1960	Cubs	156	597	94	162	32	7	41	117	69	0.271	0.350	0.554
1961	Cubs	138	511	75	142	22	4	29	80	75	0.278	0.346	0.507
1962	Cubs	154	610	87	164	20	6	37	104	71	0.269	0.306	0.503
1963	Cubs	130	432	41	98	20	1	18	64	73	0.227	0.292	0.403
1964	Cubs	157	591	67	156	29	6	23	95	84	0.264	0.307	0.450
1965	Cubs	163	612	79	162	25	3	28	106	64	0.265	0.328	0.453
1966	Cubs	141	511	52	139	23	7	15	75	59	0.272	0.315	0.432
1967	Cubs	151	573	68	158	26	4	23	95	93	0.276	0.310	0.455
1968	Cubs	150	552	71	136	27	0	32	83	67	0.246	0.287	0.469
1969	Cubs	155	565	60	143	19	2	23	106	101	0.253	0.309	0.416
1970	Cubs	72	222	25	56	6	2	12	44	33	0.252	0.313	0.459
1971	Cubs	39	83	4	16	2	0	3	6	14	0.193	0.247	0.325
19 Years		**2,528**	**9,421**	**1,305**	**2,583**	**407**	**90**	**512**	**1,636**	**1,236**	**0.274**	**0.330**	**0.500**

Gene Baker (24)

Year	Tm	Lg	G	PA	AB	R	H	2B	3B	HR	RBI	SB	SO	BA	OBP	SLG
1953	CHC	NL	7	24	22	1	5	1	0	0	0	1	4	0.227	0.261	0.273
1954	CHC	NL	135	603	541	68	149	32	5	13	61	4	55	0.275	0.333	0.425
1955	CHC	NL	*154*	681	609	82	163	29	7	11	52	9	57	0.268	0.323	0.392
1956	CHC	NL	140	605	546	65	141	23	3	12	57	4	54	0.258	0.309	0.377
1957	TOT	NL	123	458	409	40	108	22	5	3	46	3	32	0.264	0.322	0.364
1957	CHC	NL	12	51	44	4	11	3	1	1	10	0	3	0.250	0.353	0.432
1957	PIT	NL	111	407	365	36	97	19	4	2	36	3	29	0.266	0.318	0.356
1958	PIT	NL	29	66	56	3	14	2	1	0	7	0	6	0.250	0.338	0.321
1959	Injured															
1960	PIT	NL	33	40	37	5	9	0	0	0	4	0	9	0.243	0.275	0.243
1961	PIT	NL	9	13	10	1	1	0	0	0	0	0	2	0.100	0.308	0.100
8 Yrs			**753**	**2948**	**2639**	**305**	**698**	**131**	**26**	**42**	**273**	**24**	**251**	**0.265**	**0.321**	**0.385**

"Curt" Roberts (25)

Year	Tm	Lg	G	AB	R	H	2B	3B	HR	RBI	SB	SO	BA	OBP	SLG
1947	KCM	NgM		12	1	4	0	1	0	3	0		0.333	0.385	0.500
1948	KCM	NgM		61	9	15	4	0	0	6	1		0.246	0.303	0.311
1951	BSN	A	132	459		129	24	5	5				0.281	0.281	0.388
1952	PIT	A	129	503		141	25	4	3				0.280	0.280	0.364
1953	PIT	A	151	587		171	32	2	12				0.291	0.291	0.414
1954	**PIT**	**NL**	134	496	47	115	18	7	1	36	6	49	0.232	0.309	0.302
1955	PIT	Opn	123	452	79	145	22	3	8	49	17	33	0.321	0.366	0.436
1955	**PIT**	**NL**	6	17	1	2	1	0	0	0	0	1	0.118	0.211	0.176
1956	KCA-PIT	AAA	98	362	50	115	18	1	9	35	0	28	0.318	0.386	0.448
1956	**PIT**	**NL**	31	62	6	11	5	2	0	4	1	12	0.177	0.239	0.323
1957	NYY-min	AAA	147	572	115	174	36	7	10	81	23	56	0.304	0.391	0.444
1958	NYY-min	AAA	138	544	93	162	33	5	11	60	7	48	0.298	0.352	0.438
1959	LAD-NYY	AAA	138	500	84	148	34	1	11	56	11	56	0.296	0.352	0.434
1960	LAD-min	AAA	126	498	76	145	24	2	2	45	9	53	0.291	0.323	0.343
1961	LAD-min	AAA	91	371	55	114	18	3	4	28	1	31	0.307	0.346	0.404
1962	LAD-min	AAA	142	542	62	138	22	6	8	65	3	67	0.255	0.320	0.362
1963	CHW-min	AA	109	334	43	95	10	1	3	43	6	32	0.284	0.361	0.347
3 years	Majors		1,695	6,372	721	1,824	326	50	87	511	85	466	0.223	0.299	0.301

Tom Alston (26)

Year	Tm	Lg	G	AB	R	H	2B	3B	HR	RBI	SB	SO	BA	OBP	SLG
1952	SDG, PTV	Opn, C	132	482	29	142	28	6	14	26	0	41	0.295	0.319	0.465
1953	SDG	Opn	180	697	101	207	25	5	23	101	8	82	0.297	0.353	0.446
1954	STL-min	AAA	79	290	43	86	15	5	7	42	4	40	0.297	0.352	0.455
1954	**STL**	NL	66	244	28	60	14	2	4	34	3	41	0.246	0.317	0.369
1955	STL-min	AAA	117	430	68	118	21	9	6	59	7	44	0.274	0.334	0.407
1955	**STL**	NL	13	8	0	1	0	0	0	0	0	0	0.125	0.125	0.125
1956	STL-min	AAA	122	418	88	128	25	4	21	80	4	61	0.306	0.394	0.536
1956	**STL**	NL	3	2	0	0	0	0	0	0	0	0	0.000	0.000	0.000
1957	**STL**	NL	9	17	2	5	1	0	0	2	0	5	0.294	0.333	0.353
4 Yrs	**Majors**		**721**	**2,588**	**359**	**747**	**129**	**31**	**75**	**344**	**26**	**314**	**0.246**	**0.311**	**0.358**

Nino Escalera (27)

Year	Tm	Lg	G	AB	R	H	2B	3B	HR	RBI	SB	SO	BA	OBP	SLG
1949	BRI	B	62	245		85	19	4	1				0.347	0.347	0.469
1950	NYY-min	B,C	119	444		162	21	10	10				0.365	0.365	0.525
1951	NYY-min	A, AAA	130	502	7	180	27	1	16	3	0	8	0.359	0.37	0.512
1952	CHW-min	AAA	148	530	73	132	22	6	4	39	15	58	0.249	0.329	0.336
1953	CIN-CLE-min	AA, AAA	139	532	95	162	22	19	6	47	17	35	0.305	0.389	0.451
1954	**CIN**	**NL**	73	69	15	11	1	1	0	3	1	11	0.159	0.234	0.203
1955	CIN-min	AAA	151	509	76	151	29	5	9	65	11	54	0.297	0.387	0.426
1956	CIN-min	AAA	150	537	72	151	25	9	6	63	15	28	0.281	0.348	0.395
1957	CIN-min	AAA	63	213	26	54	8	2	5	24	1	23	0.254	0.376	0.38
1958	CIN-min	AAA	151	562	76	148	20	12	9	53	11	68	0.263	0.333	0.39
1959	PIT-min	AAA	148	556	82	160	29	7	11	57	28	52	0.288	0.339	0.424
1960	PIT-min	AAA	126	466	59	125	17	3	4	32	5	55	0.268	0.34	0.343
1961	PIT-min	AAA	86	181	24	51	7	2	3	23	3	21	0.282	0.379	0.392
1962	BAL-min	AAA	83	247	26	59	5	1	4	25	1	24	0.239	0.323	0.316
1 Yr	**Majors**		**73**	**69**	**15**	**11**	**1**	**1**	**0**	**3**	**1**	**11**	**0.159**	**0.234**	**0.203**

Chuck Harmon (28)

Year	Tm	Lg	G	AB	R	H	2B	3B	HR	RBI	SB	SO	BA	OBP	SLG
1947	SLB-min	C	54	200		54	10	1	0				0.270	0.270	0.330
1949	SLB-min	D,C	45	185		58	13	3	1				0.314	0.314	0.432
1950	OLE	D	125	551		206	47	10	22				0.374	0.374	0.615
1951	OLE	D	113	467		175	37	10	15				0.375	0.375	0.593
1952	CIN-min	B	124	479		153	34	6	5				0.319	0.319	0.447
1953	CIN-min	AA	143	566	86	176	24	11	14	83	25	41	0.311	0.353	0.466
1954	**CIN**	NL	94	286	39	68	7	3	2	25	7	27	0.238	0.277	0.304
1955	**CIN**	NL	96	198	31	50	6	3	5	28	9	24	0.253	0.345	0.389
1956	STL-min	AAA	58	242	50	87	17	6	10	49	4	31	0.360	0.385	0.603
1956	**CIN**	NL	13	4	2	0	0	0	0	0	1	0	0.000	0.000	0.000
1956	**STL**	**NL**	20	15	2	0	0	0	0	0	0	2	0.000	0.118	0.000
1957	**STL**	**NL**	9	3	2	1	0	1	0	1	1	0	0.333	0.333	1.000
1957	**PHI**	**NL**	57	86	14	22	2	1	0	5	7	4	0.256	0.264	0.302
1958	LAD-PHI-min	AAA	74	269	30	67	6	4	0	20	5	33	0.249	0.283	0.301
1959	PIT-DET-min	AAA	138	514	73	154	25	10	11	101	9	55	0.300	0.330	0.451
1960	PIT-min	AAA	136	415	57	119	15	7	4	35	10	41	0.287	0.325	0.386
1961	KCA-min	AAA	7	23		4	0	0	0				0.174	0.174	0.174
4 Yrs	**Majors**		**289**	**592**	**90**	**141**	**18**	**8**	**7**	**59**	**25**	**57**	**0.238**	**0.294**	**0.326**

Bill Greason (29)

Year	Tm	Lg	W	L	ERA	G	GS	IP	H	R	ER	HR	BB	SO
1948	BBB	NgM	7	4			10	89.1	86	46			34	54
1949	BBB	NgM	0	0		0		3	2	0			0	1
1952	OKC	AA	9	1	2.14	11	10	80	53	21	19		26	
1953	OKC	AA	16	13	3.61	37	34	249	206	116	100	19	162	193
1954	STL-min	AAA	10	13	4.10	34	26	191	172	101	87	22	99	110
1954	**STL**	**NL**	0	1	13.50	3	2	4	8	8	6	4	4	2
1955	STL-min	AA	17	11	4.16	34	33	240	222	124	111	25	114	160
1956	STL-min	AA, AAA	12	7	4.68	32	20	154	149	86	80	22	87	80
1957	STL-min	AAA	5	6	3.43	36	4	126	105	54	48	13	72	97
1958	STL-min	AAA	7	10	4.00	38	11	162	152	90	72	16	93	125
1959	STL-min	AAA	2	1	5.59	23	4	58	72	37	36	7	30	44
1 Yr	Majors		**0**	**1**	**13.50**	**3**	**2**	**4**	**8**	**8**	**6**	**4**	**4**	**2**

Brooks Lawrence (30)

Year	Tm	Lg	W	L	ERA	G	GS	CG	SHO	SV	IP	H	R	HR	BB	SO
1954	STL	NL	15	6	3.74	35	18	8	0	1	158.2	141	71	17	72	72
1955	STL	NL	3	8	6.56	46	10	2	1	1	96	102	73	11	58	52
1956	CIN	NL	19	10	3.99	49	30	11	1	0	218.2	210	109	26	71	96
1957	CIN	NL	16	13	3.52	49	32	12	1	4	250.1	234	111	26	76	121
1958	CIN	NL	8	13	4.13	46	23	6	2	5	181	194	89	12	55	74
1959	CIN	NL	7	12	4.77	43	14	3	0	10	128.1	144	74	17	45	64
1960	CIN	NL	1	0	10.57	7	0	0	0	1	7.2	9	12	1	8	2
7 Yrs			69	62	4.25	275	127	42	5	22	1040.2	1034	539	110	385	481

Carlos Paula (31)

Year	Tm	Lg	G	AB	R	H	2B	3B	HR	RBI	SB	SO	BA	OBP	SLG
1952	DEC	D	119	455		152	23	16	6				0.334	0.334	0.495
1953	PAR, DEC	B,D	123	464		139	27	12	9				0.300	0.300	0.468
1954	WSH-min	A	132	495		153	24	13	14				0.309	0.309	0.495
1954	**WSH**	**AL**	9	24	2	4	1	0	0	2	0	4	0.167	0.231	0.208
1955	**WSH**	**AL**	115	351	34	105	20	7	6	45	2	43	0.299	0.332	0.447
1956	WSH-min	AAA	88	304	55	97	12	5	16	58	7	28	0.319	0.385	0.549
1956	**WSH**	**AL**	33	82	8	15	2	1	3	13	0	15	0.183	0.250	0.341
1957	NYG-min	AAA	104	312	48	90	18	3	6	45	3	34	0.288	0.353	0.423
1958	SAC	AAA	120	387	49	122	17	6	11	62	2	43	0.315	0.345	0.475
1959	CIN-min	AAA	100	312	37	92	16	3	10	53	0	30	0.295	0.341	0.462
1960	MCT	AA	85	236	44	80	11	5	5	57	1	28	0.339	0.436	0.492
3 Yrs	Majors		**157**	**457**	**44**	**124**	**23**	**8**	**9**	**60**	**2**	**62**	**0.271**	**0.311**	**0.416**

Elston Howard (32)

Year	Tm	Lg	G	AB	R	H	2B	3B	HR	RBI	SB	SO	BA	OBP	SLG
1955	NYY	AL	97	279	33	81	8	7	10	43	0	36	0.290	0.336	0.477
1956	NYY	AL	98	290	35	76	8	3	5	34	0	30	0.262	0.312	0.362
1957	NYY	AL	110	356	33	90	13	4	8	44	2	43	0.253	0.283	0.379
1958	NYY	AL	103	376	45	118	19	5	11	66	1	60	0.314	0.348	0.479
1959	NYY	AL	125	443	59	121	24	6	18	73	0	57	0.273	0.306	0.476
1960	NYY	AL	107	323	29	79	11	3	6	39	3	43	0.245	0.298	0.353
1961	NYY	AL	129	446	64	155	17	5	21	77	0	65	0.348	0.387	0.549
1962	NYY	AL	136	494	63	138	23	5	21	91	1	76	0.279	0.318	0.474
1963	NYY	AL	135	487	75	140	21	6	28	85	0	68	0.287	0.342	0.528
1964	NYY	AL	150	550	63	172	27	3	15	84	1	73	0.313	0.371	0.455
1965	NYY	AL	110	391	38	91	15	1	9	45	0	65	0.233	0.278	0.345
1966	NYY	AL	126	410	38	105	19	2	6	35	0	65	0.256	0.317	0.356
1967	TOT	AL	108	315	22	56	9	0	4	28	0	60	0.178	0.233	0.244
1967	NYY	AL	66	199	13	39	6	0	3	17	0	36	0.196	0.247	0.271
1967	BOS	AL	42	116	9	17	3	0	1	11	0	24	0.147	0.211	0.198
1968	BOS	AL	71	203	22	49	4	0	5	18	1	45	0.241	0.317	0.335
14 Yrs			**1,713**	**5,678**	**641**	**1,527**	**227**	**50**	**171**	**790**	**9**	**846**	**0.274**	**0.322**	**0.427**

John Kennedy (33)

Year	Tm	Lg	G	PA	AB	R	H	2B	3B	HR	RBI	SB	SO	BA	OBP	SLG
1951	ALB	A	10	29	29		5	1	0	0				0.172	0.172	0.207
1953	NYG-min	C	125	496	496		130	30	7	3				0.262	0.262	0.369
1957	PHI-min	B	120	441	441		119	26	2	19				0.270	0.270	0.467
1957	**PHI**	**NL**	5	2	2	1	0	0	0	0	0	0	1	0.000	0.000	0.000
1958	PHI-min	AA	119	421	364	55	82	12	3	6	35	15	83	0.225	0.322	0.324
1959	PHI-min	B	88	346	281	50	64	10	2	3	41	15	48	0.228	0.344	0.310
1960	PHI-min	A	104	357	317	34	78	13	0	8	44	7	44	0.246	0.317	0.363
1961	JCK	A	1	4	4		1	0	0	0				0.250	0.250	0.250
1 Yr	**Majors**		**5**	**2**	**2**	**1**	**0**	**0**	**0**	**0**	**0**	**0**	**1**	**0.000**	**0.000**	**0.000**

Ozzie Virgil Sr. (34)

Year	Tm	Lg	G	PA	AB	R	H	2B	3B	HR	RBI	SB	SO	BA	OBP	SLG
1956	NYG	NL	3	12	12	2	5	1	1	0	2	1	0	0.417	0.417	0.667
1957	NYG	NL	96	240	226	26	53	0	2	4	24	2	27	0.235	0.278	0.305
1958	DET	AL	49	203	193	19	47	10	2	3	19	1	20	0.244	0.272	0.363
1959	Minors															
1960	DET	AL	62	140	132	16	30	4	2	3	13	1	14	0.227	0.248	0.356
1961	TOT	AL	31	52	51	2	7	0	0	1	1	0	8	0.137	0.154	0.196
1961	DET	AL	20	31	30	1	4	0	0	1	1	0	5	0.133	0.161	0.233
1961	KCA	AL	11	21	21	1	3	0	0	0	0	0	3	0.143	0.143	0.143
1962	BAL	AL	1	1	0	0	0	0	0	0	0	0	0		1.000	
'63–'64	Minors															
1965	PIT	NL	39	53	49	3	13	2	0	1	5	0	10	0.265	0.294	0.367
1966	SFG	NL	42	95	89	7	19	2	0	2	9	1	12	0.213	0.245	0.303
'67–'68	Minors															
1969	SFG	NL	1	1	1	0	0	0	0	0	0	0	0	0.000	0.000	0.000
9 Yrs			355	849	804	77	181	19	7	15	74	6	99	**0.231**	**0.263**	**0.331**

Hank Mason (35)

Year	Tm	Lg	W	L	ERA	G	GS	GF	CG	SV	IP	H	ER	SO
1955	PHI-min	A, AAA	14	9	2.93	43	22				175	124	57	
1956	PHI-min	A	15	11	2.28	34	28				205	144	52	
1957	PHI-min	AAA	4	5	4.04	35	2		0		69	60	31	45
1958	PHI-min	AAA	4	2	3.06	42	5		0		100	92	34	60
1958	**PHI**	NL	0	0	10.8	1	0	0	0	0	.5	7	6	3
1959	PHI-min	AAA	12	3	3.24	41	6		4		125	119	45	82
1960	PHI-min	AAA	2	5	5.01	41	12		2		115	125	64	70
1960	**PHI**	NL	0	0	9.53	3	0	1	0	0	5.2	9	6	3
1961	KCA-min	A, AAA	9	10	4.63	27	19		9		142	145	73	67
1962	LAA-min	AAA	0	1	10.5	3	1		0		6	11	7	1
2 Yrs	**Majors**		**0**	**0**	**10.13**	**4**	**0**	**0**	**0**	**0**	**10.2**	**1**	**12**	**6**

Elijah "Pumpsie" Green (36)

Year	Tm	Lg	G	PA	AB	R	H	2B	3B	HR	RBI	SB	SO	BA	OBP	SLG
1959	BOS	AL	50	207	172	30	40	6	3	1	10	4	22	0.233	0.350	0.320
1960	BOS	AL	133	313	260	36	63	10	3	3	21	3	47	0.242	0.350	0.338
1961	BOS	AL	88	264	219	33	57	12	3	6	27	4	32	0.260	0.376	0.425
1962	BOS	AL	56	104	91	12	21	2	1	2	11	1	18	0.231	0.308	0.341
1963	NYM	NL	17	66	54	8	15	1	2	1	5	0	13	0.278	0.409	0.426
5 Yrs			344	954	796	119	196	31	12	13	74	12	132	0.246	0.357	0.364

Earl Wilson (37)

Year	Tm	Lg	W	L	ERA	G	GS	CG	SHO	IP	H	R	BB	SO
1959	BOS	AL	1	1	6.08	9	4	0	0	23.20	21	17	31	17
1960	BOS	AL	3	2	4.71	13	9	2	0	65.00	61	36	48	40
1961	Minors													
1962	BOS	AL	12	8	3.90	31	28	4	1	191.10	163	86	111	137
1963	BOS	AL	11	16	3.76	37	34	6	3	210.20	184	99	105	123
1964	BOS	AL	11	12	4.49	33	31	5	0	202.10	213	121	73	166
1965	BOS	AL	13	14	3.98	36	36	8	1	230.20	221	119	77	164
1966	BOS	AL	5	5	3.84	15	14	5	1	100.20	88	45	36	67
1966	DET	AL	13	6	2.59	23	23	8	2	163.10	126	49	38	133
1967	DET	AL	22	11	3.27	39	38	12	0	264.00	216	103	92	184
1968	DET	AL	13	12	2.85	34	33	10	3	224.10	192	77	65	168
1969	DET	AL	12	10	3.31	35	35	5	1	214.20	209	93	69	150
1970	DET	AL	4	6	4.41	18	16	4	1	96.00	87	53	32	74
1970	SDP	NL	1	6	4.85	15	9	0	0	65.00	82	36	19	29
11 Yrs			**121**	**109**	**3.69**	**338**	**310**	**69**	**13**	**2051.20**	**1863**	**934**	**796**	**1452**

Jim Proctor (38)

Year	Tm	Lg	W	L	ERA	G	GS	IP	H	R	SO
1955	MLN-min	D	0	0		5		7			
1956	DET-min	A, B	11	8	2.07	35	11	165	119	46	
1957	DET-min	AAA, A	14	8	2.64	44	13	174	146	63	125
1958	DET-min	A	0	0		1		0	0	0	
1959	DET-min	A	15	5	2.19	28	20	181	139	52	131
1959	**DET**	AL	0	1	16.88	2	1	2.2	8	5	0
1960	DET-min	AA	15	8	3.91	29	29	191	182	87	98
1961	CLE-CHC-min	AAA	3	11	4.75	40	12	125	136	78	51
1963	DET-min	AA	1	1	4.5	8	1	26	26	15	20
1 Yr	Majors		**0**	**1**	**16.88**	**2**	**1**	**2.2**	**8**	**5**	**0**

"Jake" Wood (39)

Year	Tm	Lg	G	AB	R	H	2B	3B	HR	RBI	SB	SO	BA	OBP	SLG
1961	DET	AL	162	663	96	171	17	*14*	11	69	30	*141*	0.258	0.320	0.376
1962	DET	AL	111	367	68	83	10	5	8	30	24	59	0.226	0.291	0.346
1963	DET	AL	85	351	50	95	11	2	11	27	18	61	0.271	0.330	0.407
1964	DET	AL	64	125	11	29	2	2	1	7	0	24	0.232	0.254	0.304
1965	DET	AL	58	104	12	30	3	0	2	7	3	19	0.288	0.357	0.375
1966	DET	AL	98	230	39	58	9	3	2	27	4	48	0.252	0.336	0.343
1967	DET	AL	14	20	2	1	1	0	0	0	0	7	0.050	0.095	0.100
1967	CIN	NL	16	17	1	2	0	0	0	1	0	3	0.118	0.167	0.118
7 Yrs			**608**	**1,877**	**279**	**469**	**53**	**26**	**35**	**168**	**79**	**362**	**0.250**	**0.312**	**0.362**

CPSIA information can be obtained
at www.ICGtesting.com
Printed in the USA
FSHW011953030819
60686FS